Message in a

The POW who buried his

Front Cover (clockwise from top)

1. The first image depicts the Nilgiri Railway that runs from near Coimbatore up to Ootacamund (referred to throughout the book as 'Ooty'). Both towns play a prominent part in this book. The section between Mettupalayam and Coonor was built by a Swiss engineer named M. Riggenbach, best known for his invention of the Riggi system of mountain railways. It was conceived in 1882 and built in 1899, and subsequently extended from Coonor to Ooty in 1908. The engine and all of the special equipment came from Switzerland, and used the Swiss rack system. Between the rails there is a comb-like rack, into which the engine digs its sprocket-like teeth, and crawls up the track. In 30 miles it climbs an astonishing 7500 feet through some 16 tunnels. The journey takes a full three and a half hours.

   This railway is the only one of its kind in the world and has featured on television as one or the 'Great Railways of the World'. As it climbs through steep forests, it is similar to the Thai-Burma railway on which Quintus Browne worked when interned as a Japanese Prisoner of War. Alan Elliott, a fellow army officer and POW, refers to this in his preface to this edition.

2. The elephant dragging logs is a scene typical of the Madras Forests, and one to which Quintus refers several times.

3. The scroll in the bottle shows a page of Quintus' original text, written when he was a POW. This manuscript is now held in the archives of the British Empire & Commonwealth Museum in Bristol, England.

4. The Prisoner of War scene comes courtesy of the Prisoner of War Museum near the Bridge over the River Kwai, and is referred to further in the Foreword.

Cover design by Toby Borthen.

Robert 'Quintus' Browne, 1922

Message in a Bottle

The POW who buried his life story in a jar.

Robert 'Quintus' Browne

BECM *Press*

Published in England, 2004 by the
British Empire & Commonwealth Museum Press
Clock Tower Yard, Temple Meads, Bristol, BS1 6QH

Design, page make-up and printing by S P Press, Cheddar, Somerset.

Contents

List of Illustrations

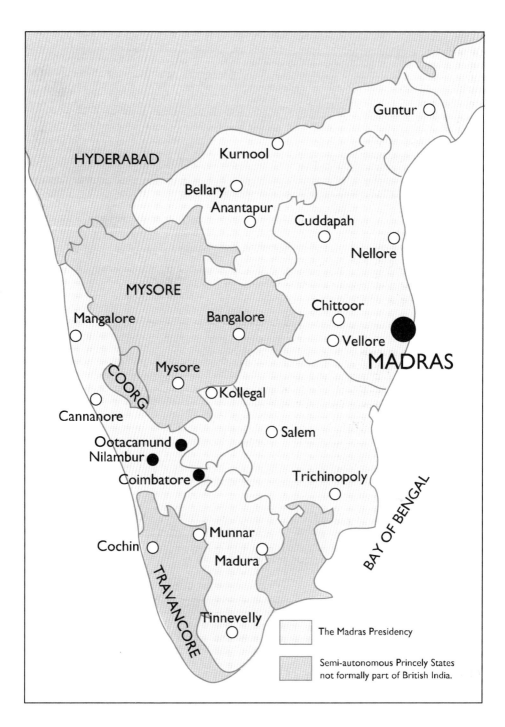

Guntur ○

Kurnool ○

HYDERABAD

Bellary ○

Anantapur
○

Cuddapah
○

Nellore

MYSORE

Mangalore
○

Bangalore
○

Chittoor
○

Vellore
○

MADRAS ●

COORG

Mysore
○

Kollegal ○

Salem ○

Cannanore
○

Ootacamund ●
Nilambur ●

Coimbatore ●

Trichinopoly
○

Cochin ○

Munnar
○

Madura
○

BAY OF BENGAL

TRAVANCORE

Tinnevelly
○

□ The Madras Presidency

▨ Semi-autonomous Princely States
   not formally part of British India.

Author's Biography
By Chloë Willing, daughter of Robert 'Quintus' Browne

My father, Robert Steele Browne, known as Quintus, was born in 1899, the son of the administrator of Sligo Mental Hospital. After graduating in classics at Trinity College, Dublin, he spent two years at Edinburgh University where he met his wife, Elsie. From there he joined the Indian Forest Service.

When the Second World War broke out, he enlisted immediately, leaving his work as a Forest Officer in Madras to become Major Browne in the Second Battalion of the 16th Punjab regiment. After training, the company was sent to the north of Malaya.

The Japanese offensive began in December 1941 and swept south, driving the Allied troops back. I was at school in Bournemouth where the family lived, and we received regular army postcards saying 'I am well'.

In early 1942, the postcards stopped. Like most of the Allied troops fighting on the Malay Peninsula, my father's regiment had retreated to Singapore island, arriving just before the causeway linking it to the mainland was blown up. On the 9th February, Japanese troops were ashore in the Northwest and, by Sunday the 15th, Singapore had fallen.

Father became a prisoner of war. He was packed into a railway goods wagon and transported to Thailand, ending up at a large jungle camp called Chungkai that was full of British, Australian, and Dutch prisoners. There they were put to work on what became known as the Death Railway, forging an overland route to India across the Siam-Burma mountains.

With only rice to eat, the prisoners were forced to clear thick jungle, often with their bare hands. Soon their clothes were in rags and their bodies skeletal. In the letters he wrote on being released, father described himself as having 'a fine, slim, schoolgirl figure'. Many of his comrades died of malaria, cholera or diphtheria. One life was said to be lost for every sleeper laid.

Having worked for several years in the humid teak forests of Madras, he was accustomed to intense heat and difficult conditions. But as he was forty and one of the oldest prisoners, he was eventually taken off coolie work and put in charge of the cemetery, digging graves for his dead colleagues, and keeping records of these deaths.

Father had plenty of time to think, and became increasingly fearful that he might never see his family again. He began to steal scraps of paper and stubs of pencil, and started to write his life story.

He also kept a list of the dead. It was a dangerous venture. In the early years many POWs had taken to writing down atrocities and deaths for evidence against the Japanese after the war. But when the tide of war began to move in the Allies' favour, and the Japanese realised that prisoners had been keeping records, they cracked down, confiscating paper and writing materials. My father had seen people executed for far less, or beaten senseless and left all day under the burning sun.

In the hottest, sleepiest part of every afternoon, he would hide away, often in the latrine, and scribble on the scraps of paper in the tiniest writing. He used stolen paperclips to wire the pages together.

Every so often, when he was burying a body, he would hide one of these handmade notebooks in the grave, keeping a note of its position on a page which he hid under his blanket. Occasionally he stole medicine jars and bottles from the dispensary in which he stored the pages when burying them, as a protection from the monsoon rains.

He knew he was taking an astonishing risk, but he wanted to write about his experiences as a Forest Officer. The buried chapters comprise a manual of forestry with details of how he grew sandalwood, teak, cashew and mahogany, and even a chapter on how to catch a wild elephant, but only in the last chapters did he express his personal feelings. Despite dreadful treatment of the prisoners of war in his camp, he wrote very little about his personal situation as a POW.

Roughly 15,000 out of some 40,000 British and Australian prisoners in Thailand and the Burma borders (officers and men) died. Overcrowding and filthy conditions helped the spread of disease.

My father became more hopeful when the radio news indicated that the tide had turned in favour of the Allies. He allowed himself to wonder about the family. I did not see him for seven years and was almost grown up when he returned.

On August 10th, 1945, the prisoners were herded into open trucks and driven out of Kanchanaburi, the camp where my father had ended up. As they stopped at a bridge, the local Thais jeered at the Japanese, prompting rumours that the war was over. The prisoners were transferred into a stifling river barge and then forced to march through muddy swamps with almost no food or water. Somehow my father managed to keep a diary of these final days. On August 15th he left by rail for Bangkok and this last awful journey out of Thailand is vividly described in his diary.

Two days after the Japanese had surrendered, my father was given a bundle of letters, in which he discovered that his mother had died two and a half years earlier. He was also given a pair of pants and socks, which were the first items of clothing he had received in captivity. But there was still no food other than rice and sweet potato.

Finally, on September 3rd, they were flown to Rangoon, and my father could hardly believe that he was free at last. He returned to Madras for his official discharge that would allow him to go home to his family in England. He also visited Ootacamund where it was Hunt Week and everyone was at the hunt ball. Confused by all the lights, music and gaiety, he appeared at the entrance, looking incredibly thin, pale and puzzled. The dancers froze and silence fell over the place as if they had seen a ghost.

I was sixteen when my father returned home. After everything he had gone through we were terribly lucky to have him back. But he had changed. From being an extrovert, jovial and fun-loving chap he had gone into his shell and never came out. Back home in England he was haunted by his experiences and had nightmares from which he would wake up in alarm.

In 1946 he returned to India as Conservator of Forests for the South Nilgiris, and then as Working Plans Officer in Salem. In 1947 he read in the Madras Mail that his services were no longer required together with all of the other European Forest Officers.

On returning home he could not settle, moving to Northern Ireland and then to Suffolk, back in England. He refused to talk about his time in the camps or to watch films about it, such as The Bridge Over the River Kwai. In 1973, when he was dying in Taunton hospital my father became convinced that he was back in the camp, and all that the nurses were prison guards.

He had told my mother about the buried autobiography but showed no interest in retrieving it, as if that too was a part of a past to be forgotten. After his death, I discovered among his possessions a bundle of scrap paper and homemade notebooks that had been dug up and passed to him by someone from the War Graves Commission.

I forgot about it whilst my husband, Roger, was alive. He died in 1981 after suffering for over a year from a painful degenerative bone disease. It was an awful experience for me and as a therapy I found the forestry notes and started to sort out the folded scraps of paper. It was an enormous task because the pages were stained and the handwriting was small and faint. However, the story was complete except for one chapter and a few pages.

Ben Longrigg, the son of another Forest Officer, put me in touch with the British Empire & Commonwealth Museum in Bristol, who agreed to publish the book.

At forty years old Father had no need to join up at the outbreak of war but felt it his duty to do so. So, when he went back to forestry for just two years before leaving India, I am sure he felt that he had wasted the best years of his life and had failed in what he had really enjoyed. However, his innovative work in growing teak at Nilambur, and the Working Plans he had prepared, were of great long-term value. Perhaps this book is a fitting memorial to his achievements.

Preface

On the 14th of May 1999, five families met all together for the first time in Cambridge to celebrate the recognition that they all shared a common past: namely, that their respective fathers had all been colleagues in the Indian Forest Service - Sweet, Currie, Longrigg, Davis and Browne. One consequence of this synergism was the "unearthing" of Browne's biography, which, like the original sheets of paper, had lain unread for many years. They recognised that it provided a vivid and fascinating historical record of life as a forester in south India between the two World Wars, and thought it should reach a wider public.

This was a period of great strides in forest management. It was also a period of active Indianisation throughout the public services, which proceeded especially smoothly in the forestry service; recruitment of British officers ceased about 1925. Browne's account says little about the organisation and administration of forestry but rather gives a vivid insight into the responsibilities of forest officers, with sideways glances into recreational activities and social life. From his initial selection board in England, through forestry training at Edinburgh and arrival in India in December 1922 at the age of twenty-three, he goes on to describe each of his postings and experiences, from the Western Ghats to the most north-easterly districts of the Presidency.

Learning to speak Tamil and mastering forestry law, walking twenty miles a day up and down steep hillsides to prepare a Working Plan, growing teak from seed and from cuttings, harvesting valuable sandalwood, working through recurrent bouts of malaria, seeing a tiger run across the compound where his young daughter often played, capturing wild elephants in pits, and examining students at the Forest College at Coimbatore – the whole account is written with clarity and wit that makes one forget completely the circumstances in which it was written.

His last few years before the outbreak of war were especially enjoyable and productive as he was in charge of co-ordinating all the Working Plans for Madras forests in his capacity as Personal Assistant to the Chief Conservator. For this work he was awarded the OBE in 1942, although by that time he was already a prisoner-of-war, and his dedication to forestry was aptly summed up in a testimonial he later received from the Chief Conservator. In 1946 he returned to India after home leave but everything was now in a state of flux with the transition to Indian self-rule. An Indian Chief Conservator for the Madras

Presidency was already in post, a Parsee, Lal Masters. In quick succession Browne held the posts of Conservator for South Nilgiris, for Salem and for Working Plans but, along with almost all the other British foresters, he left India for good in 1947. After trying his hand at farming, he returned to forestry, joining ex-Madras friends who had set up the Economic Forestry Group in England but he could not bring himself to do anything further with his writings.

At the time, they might have had a narrow and ephemeral interest among ex-colonials. Today, they recall a period of great historical interest as one of the roots of the modern conservation movement. Forestry now, as then, is concerned with much more than just sustainable timber production. In the final pages of this book, Browne's optimism for the future of Indian forestry shines like a beacon from the past. A postscript to this narrative shows how the baton has been carried forward by succeeding generations of foresters in south west India.

Brian Davis

Major R. S. Browne OBE, 2/16 Punjab Regiment

At the start of World War Two I joined the army instead of going back for my third year at Cambridge. At the end of 1940 I arrived as a newly commissioned Second Lieutenant at the Regimental Centre of the 16th Punjab Regiment at Sialkot in the Punjab. At that time there were six separate Punjab Regiments and each of them had four regular battalions, each engaged on different wartime assignments. The 4th Battalion, for instance, was in action in the Middle East, and the 2nd was on the northern frontier of Malaya, waiting for the probable war with Japan to begin. That was where I was assigned, arriving at our camp among the rubber trees in the Malayan state of Perlis in May 1941. One of the first officers I met was Captain "Quintus" Browne.

At that time the Indian Army was being very rapidly expanded, and the regular battalions were being badly 'milked' in order to provide a nucleus of experienced officers and NCOs for new battalions. They were being replaced by Reserve Officers, of whom Quintus was an example, and Emergency Commissioned Officers from Britain, like myself. According to the Indian Army list of 1945, Quintus had been a Reserve Officer since 1924, and therefore had a great deal of experience; he was also older than most of the officers of his rank. I was the first Emergency Commissioned Officer to arrive from Britain, and was accordingly viewed with great misgiving by the regulars. There were four of these, and three other Reserve Officers as well as Quintus, led by an excellent CO, Lt. Col. Jimmy Larkin who had seen service in World War One. Indian 'other ranks' were being promoted in order to bring up the number of NCOs, and at the lower end of the battalion, numbers were being made up by very raw recruits such as those I had been trying to train at the Regimental Centre. As a regular battalion we were therefore greatly diminished in strength and experience.

Each of our battalions had four rifle companies, of which two were Punjabi Muslims, one was Sikh and one was Dogra (Hindus from the foothills of the Himalayas). Quintus commanded the Sikh Company. As he was a senior officer and considerably older than me (in fact he was over 40, although he didn't look it) I was not among his closer friends, but he had a warm and forthright character and was liked and respected by everyone. I cannot now remember whether I knew at the time that he had been a forestry officer in India, but he was certainly a very able man in getting around in Malayan plantations and the jungle.

The war was soon to come our way. The Japanese bombed Pearl Harbour on 8th December 1941, and attacked the coast of Malaya at the same time. We were originally supposed to go into Thailand and seize the southern ports. That did not happen and we had to fall back on half prepared positions, with many barely trained troops, no tanks and very few aircraft. In terms of experience, I was probably one of very few in the division who had been in even a bombing raid.

The rest barely bears re-telling. We held out for two months before surrendering Singapore. We had quite a number killed and wounded, but by far the greatest losses were of men who had been cut off and surrounded by the Japanese as they advanced more quickly than we could withdraw. We had few casualties among the officers, but the Commander of the Carrier Platoon was badly wounded in winning the military cross.

Our Regiment also had its 3rd Battalion in Malaya, with battle experience as bad as ours, but with the CO killed. We therefore joined up with them to make a single battalion. Quintus was promoted to Major and made second-in-command. Similarly, the two brigades to which we had belonged were united to form a single brigade. At that point I became a temporary Staff Captain at Brigade Headquarters and more or less lost touch with the Regiment.

From the moment the Japanese landed on Singapore Island it was clear that we had lost; but even so, the surrender on 15th February came sooner than expected. More officers were killed in the last days and the new battalion commander was ordered to join one of the official escape parties. So, Quintus was left in charge for the surrender. The first surprise came when the Japanese separated the 'white' officers and other ranks from the Asians, and pushed the whole lot of Europeans, etc. out to an improvised POW camp on the Changi Peninsula.

Towards the end of 1942 the Japanese started sending us up to Thailand, officers and all, to work on the notorious Thai-Burma railway, where we lost 13,000 men. Much has been written about that too. After the fall of Singapore I discovered that I had a cousin with me – a regular Indian Army major who had been unfortunate enough to come in with the late reinforcements. So I joined up with him, instead of remaining with the 16th Punjab officers. From there on we were in different camps until the closing months of the war when they separated the officers from the British other ranks, and moved us off to camps in which they probably had an unpleasant fate in store for us. We never knew because the atom bombs were dropped and Japan surrendered. In the days before that I met Quintus again, but cannot remember much about it, but before then Jimmy Larkin had died a miserable death in the same camp as Quintus. He never really should have been on active service, suffering as he did from severe asthma that he had managed to conceal from the medical authorities. After the war we all went separate ways.

I shall never regret knowing such a fine man as Quintus Browne, and am glad that knowledge of him and his forestry work have come to the public attention so lately and unexpectedly. His family and the families of his Indian forestry colleagues have done an excellent thing in making this come about.

Alan Elliott, November 2000

Foreword to the First Edition

When publishing any manuscript, but especially one with an historiography as rich as Quintus Browne's, it is crucial that the first edition be as true to the original as possible. Any subsequent reprints, research or reference to Quintus' life and achievements will be taken from this version of the text, and knowing this every effort has been made to reproduce Quintus' hand-written original as faithfully as possible.

Sadly, through its turbulent early-life, the manuscript received some inevitable harm from the elements. Several pages were damaged to such a degree that some words were obscured, and unfortunately some pages were lost entirely. Rather than best guessing the obliterated text (surely a cardinal sin for a museum publishing-house), we have inserted spaces […] where words were illegible, and comments [in squared brackets] to show where pages or chapters once were. Text in conventional brackets (like these) represent Quintus' own queries and notes, which presumably he intended to address later.

To compensate for the missing pages, we are indeed fortunate that where chapter 13 should have been, we have been able to at least insert Quintus' original 'Working Draft' that *was* recovered. We have also inserted these original notes for chapters 11 and 14, where there are several pages that were not recovered. Whether these pages will ever be retrieved remains to be seen, but we can be certain that as time passes the chance of the missing pages being found, let alone being legible, decreases with every monsoon.

Credit for the accuracy of this edition is owed almost entirely to the dedication of Chloë Willing (née Browne) whose painstaking transcription produced the version of the text that you now hold. Were it not for the time that Chloë devoted to this remarkable piece of history, the story - with or without missing words and in spite of the work of the Commonwealth War Graves Commission - would have remained buried for evermore.

Simon Boice, British Empire & Commonwealth Museum Press.

Chapter I

TRAINING IN EUROPE

The Indian Forest Service, which administers the Government forests of India, Burma and the Andaman Islands, consists of some 300 officers. In view of its small numbers it is not surprising that the service is little known to the general public outside the sphere of its activities. Less still is usually known of how this small service spends its time, although the idea prevails that its officers do little except shoot tigers - unless it be to photograph the latter. But there must be something more to it than this, since during some 17 years in the Indian Forest Service I cannot claim to have either shot or photographed a tiger. In this book an attempt will be made to describe the conditions of forest life, as I have found it, in South India where my service has been spent.

I shared the common ignorance concerning this service until about two months before I found myself in it. I was pursuing a very leisurely course in arts in Trinity College, Dublin, in the summer of 1920, after demobilisation from the army, when some literature about recruitment to the Indian Forest Service came into my hands. Amongst the qualifications expected in candidates, considerable emphasis was placed on scientific ability, of which I had none that I was aware of, having concentrated on Greek and Latin at school, and having done nothing in the least scientific in the army. However, on the principle of trying anything once, I filled up the necessary application forms, despatched them, and forgot about them. A few weeks later, much to my surprise, I was summoned to appear before a selection board in London, so science was not, apparently, the "sine qua non" that I had expected.

Such hopes as I had entertained on passing this initial obstacle were speedily dashed when I got to the place of interview and found a mob of other applicants already assembled, and heard that this sort of thing had been going on for days, in morning and afternoon sessions, for the selection of some 30 recruits for the vacant posts. Those in the crowd to whom I spoke were all highly qualified in science - or so they said - and full of confidence in their suitability. But I am not sure that it pays to be too self-assured, for despite my own diffidence I turned out to be one of the lucky ones, and I never again saw any of the confident chaps whose scientific ability had depressed me while we waited to appear before the selectors. Presumably they had been rejected.

The successful candidates were required to undergo two years training in forestry before proceeding to India, and were allowed to choose their university,

Oxford, Cambridge or Edinburgh. I elected to go to Edinburgh, chiefly for the greater freedom to be found in a non-residential university. Had I known how much harder I would have to work at Edinburgh as compared with either Oxford or Cambridge, I would probably have chosen differently.

In my day the main object of the average parent who sent his son to Oxford or Cambridge was to have the awkward corners of adolescence rubbed off, to enable the youth to acquire poise and breadth of vision, and to assimilate culture. Learning was, of course, expected as well, but it was more of a secondary consideration. The average son's idea was usually to play games and to have a jolly good time for three or four years before taking up the serious business of life. The university provided the means of satisfying the ambitions of both the parent and child, and threw in a good advanced education in any subjects the young man cared to take up, and the usual result was fairly satisfactory to all concerned.

In Scotland, however, the university has quite a different meaning assuming that Edinburgh is typical, as I believe it is. The average Scottish parent wishes the university to prepare his son for a profession, and the average Scottish son shares the parental idea, and goes all out to attain his object, considering the acquisition of culture and such-like to be a waste of his money and his time. The university provides what the public demands, and provides it in generous measure. But in doing so it inevitably denies the serene atmosphere of humanity which is valued elsewhere. It gives learning but little more.

The hours at Edinburgh were long and the work hard. I made heavier weather of it than most, being a complete stranger to anything in the way of science.

Botany I acquired with the greatest difficulty. In entomology, subjects such as the love-life of a wood-louse left me cold, although I enjoyed much of the nomenclature. "Ovipositor", for example, is a brave-sounding word which speaks for itself. And for a harmless term of abuse as applied to the appropriate sex, what could be better than "wingless, viviparous female"? This expression was constantly cropping up in the study of the insect world, and always reminded me of the story current in Dublin in my time, of a battle of words between a Trinity undergraduate and an old Dublin fishwife. The argument took place outside a pub at closing time. Both "had drink taken" - to use the kindly Irish idiom to describe a state of intoxication short of actual incapability. When both had exhausted the normal vocabulary of abuse within the knowledge of undergraduates and fishwives, the young man sought to use his superior education to finish the argument. "Go home now", said he, "you old scalene triangle". This reduced the fishwife to alcoholic tears. "Skayleen thriangle is

Quintus (left) with a Frenchman.

'ut?" she sobbed. "Glory be to God, what a name to call a dacent woman".

Notes taken at lectures were subject to scrutiny, and one got certain marks for notebooks, which were supposed to be illustrated, wherever possible. Freehand drawing has never been in my line, and I fear I can have got few marks for my notes. I was equally ham-handed at cutting botanical sections for microscopic examination. Engineering drawing came fairly easily, thanks to the use of instruments of precision.

Engineering and surveying were interesting, and the practical work undertaken in the precincts of Holyrood Palace was quite good fun.

Geology, also, I liked, though here again, as with botany, zoology, etc., illustrated notes were required. But luckily all rocks are not crystalline; I found the amorphous type suited my style of drawing fairly well.

I liked most of the forestry subjects, but I found "forest valuation" very tricky, since it is so dependent on compound interest, logarithms and other mathematical contortions, in the use of which I was inept. This abstruse subject was, however, quite popular, since the lecturer, in addition to being a mathematical wizard, had the welcome faculty of keeping his class in a state of almost continuous merriment, the laughter being sometimes with him and sometimes at him. Thus the time passed pleasantly, and though the majority of his class cannot have imbibed more knowledge of valuation than the barest minimum required to satisfy the eventual examiners, the trees grew just the same.

On ordinary week-days lectures finished at 5 P.M., usually at the Botanical Gardens, some three miles away from the university, and from the locality where most of us lived in "digs". On Saturdays there were no lectures, but we were usually expected to go out on organised excursions of one kind and another, such as knocking chunks off Arthur's Seat with a geological hammer, picking wild flowers on the Pentland Hills, measuring standing woods and timber in the woodlands within reach, and so on. One of these Saturday exercises became deadly monotonous through frequent repetition. The university school of forestry maintained a forest nursery on an estate at Dreghorn, a few miles out of Edinburgh. It was very public-spirited of the landowner to allow us this facility, but I fear we did not greatly appreciate the privilege. It was interesting enough to play with baby trees the first few times, but it palled into endless repetition of the same jobs. We played pitch-and-toss for pennies whenever we could evade supervision, and there was a passable pub hard by, which some of us got to know quite well; but still it was a poor way to spend a Saturday morning, when our colleagues in other branches of study were free to enjoy themselves.

My acquaintance with Edinburgh was mostly in the winter, and how I disliked the bitter east wind. I only had one summer term there, since the second summer term was spent on the Continent. To this day my most vivid memory of Edinburgh is of a wintry nature - the sniff of the Scottish student between October and April. Most of us suffered from frequent colds in the head during the long winter. But whereas handkerchiefs were used by the foreigners from warmer climes - such as the English, the Irish, the Indian, the Chinese - the hardy Scot just sniffed, male and female alike. There were, of course, exceptions, but on the whole the sniff was a pretty reliable guide to nationality.

The Christmas vacations were our own, but most of the Easter and summer holidays were spent at practical forestry work, or on tours of instruction in European forests. This outdoor training was usually most enjoyable.

My first Easter vacation was spent in Perthshire with my class of 40 or so, planting larch and pines, felling trees, measuring timber, etc. The bracing spring days in the wooded highlands were a magnificent tonic after two wintry terms of lectures. The work was splendid exercise for young bodies. One acquired an enormous appetite, and I feel that the good landladies of the village in which we lodged cannot have had much profit from us. One was still expected to take notes, but there was nothing much to write about. The beer in the local hostelry was good, and it was pleasant to relax there in the evening, after a tremendous day.

My only summer term spent in Edinburgh was shortened by at least a week, owing to the coal strike of Easter 1921. The strike commenced just as we got back from the Perthshire forests, with a few days of the Easter vacation still in hand. Five of us offered our services at the offices of a mining company in Edinburgh, and they despatched us in a lorry, by night, and with a great air of secrecy to one of their mines in West Lothian. Two other volunteers accompanied us. One was a youth who was studying to be a mine manager, and considered he knew all about everything to do with coal-mines. The other was an unemployed stoker off a North Sea boiler. His was the more useful knowledge, for stoking was the job which fell to all of us. For a week or so we worked at the pit-head, carrying coal and stoking the furnaces to keep the pumps in action and prevent the flooding of the underground workings. We were black as pitch all the time, except where sweat cut runnels through the coal-dust on our faces. We slept, during brief respites from coal-heaving, in a shed adjoining the boiler-house. The management fed us like fighting-cocks, and gave us a liberal ration of beer. Armed naval reservists, recalled for the emergency, guarded us from possible attack by angry, unemployed miners. Actually the sailors seemed to us to be quite as dangerous as the miners; rifles appeared to be a new toy to them, judging by the light-hearted way in which unintentional shots were loosed off.

A compromise was effected between the owners and the miners, and the coal strike was quickly over, without spreading to other trades as had been feared.

Having volunteered for emergency work in the mines, we had not expected more than our rations, but our grateful employers insisted on giving us each a pound a day for our work.

It was while we were spending this windfall back in Edinburgh, that I made my first and last appearance on the stage of a theatre. There were three of us, just out of the coal-mines, having a party with two or three other men. We ended up in a small music-hall, rather late in the course of a variety show. Before our party had had time to evaporate, a strong man act was put on. After toying for a bit with an enormous dumb-bell, the weight-lifter challenged anyone in the audience to lift it. My pals urged me to try it, but I had sense enough to realise my limitations. After a short argument, however, they seized me, and hurled me on to the stage over the heads of the orchestra, from our seats in the front row. The gallery hooted with joy. I quickly collected my wits and decided that to slink back to my seat would look at least as foolish as to fail at the weight-lifting, so I had a crack at it. The dumb-bell seemed to weigh a ton, but to my surprise I succeeded, after a bit of a struggle, to lift it level with my shoulder. Honour was satisfied. I let it drop with a tremendous clatter, being too exhausted to lower it gently, and jumped back to my seat. The strong man gave me such a look, but the gods made a most appreciative noise. The theatre was destroyed by fire late that night - accidentally so far as I know, though we like to think that the strong man had burnt it down in a fit of pique.

Examinations were held at Edinburgh, in every subject, at the end of every term. Each course of lectures lasted one, two or three terms, and if it happened to be the last term in any subject, the examination was a final, and therefore a serious matter. I found I had to burn much midnight oil to qualify in science subjects. And I did not help myself to concentrate by falling in love, during my first summer, with the only young lady who was taking the forestry course, and whom I subsequently married.

My first summer vacation started with a fortnight or so in the country near Harwick, where the Edinburgh class studied the art of fencing a forest property. The work consisted in digging countless holes with picks and crow-bars and what-not, pointing the ends of wooden posts, dipping them in creosote, and planting them in the holes. I don't remember putting up any wire; I think this part of the work must have been reserved for intelligent labour. The work was extremely dull, but it was a wonderful, hot summer, and the Scottish border country in good weather is delightful.

This tour was followed by about two weeks in Perthshire, where the Easter vacation had been spent. The weather continued glorious. The main work this time was the survey of an area of forest, the description of the flora, and the enumeration and measurement of the standing timber. For this exercise we were divided into squads of half a dozen or so, and we did the work in our own time. I was fortunate (or guileful) enough to get into the same party as Elsie, so I had no cause for complaint. Incidentally, I saw less of the local hostelry in the evenings than in the Easter vacation.

At the end of this period of practical work, the Indian Forest probationers, of whom there were eight in this Edinburgh class, had to do a tour in France, along with our fellows from Oxford and Cambridge. We were given Rouen as a rendezvous, and spent the next two weeks or so in a small village in the neighbourhood, from which we made tours of instruction in the oak and beech forests of the locality. There was little hotel accommodation, so most of us used the hotel only for meals and other refreshment, while we lived in the local asylum for the indigent and mentally defective, whose inmates accepted us without question. It was a quiet country life, and I don't remember having learnt very much. It was, however, interesting to become acquainted with our future brother-officers from the other universities.

The second half of this continental tour was spent in the Vosges, where we lived in a hotel at a French summer resort on the borders of an attractive lake. We studied the coniferous forests of the surrounding hills by day. There were boating and bathing in the lake in the evening, the magnificent summer weather still continuing. At nights there was a casino in which one could lose one's money, and there was always dancing to be had, with unlimited opportunity for practising French conversation, for we were about the only British visitors. There were a number of French families from Algeria staying in our hotel. Several of the daughters were of Moorish type and colouring. (It is odd how readily the French seem to pick up a touch of local colour from the countries they colonise.) These French families on holiday did not seem to go in much for sons; or perhaps they had left their young men at home to look after the family business. Whatever the cause, the result was satisfying from the point of view of the Indian Forest probationers, who found no lack of dancing partners.

In the second year of our probation we spent about six months on the continent, starting late in March and returning to England in September. This time the rendezvous was Paris, where many collected some days in advance, presumably to make sure of being punctual. From Paris we went to Normandy, where we spent about two weeks in studying the oak coppice forests. The weather was bitterly cold, with much snow. We used to lunch in the forest, but our hotel's idea of a pic-nic lunch was never adequate for healthy appetites. Returning about four in the afternoon we would repair to *estaminates* in the town, and start off with a large bowl of café au lait, an omelette containing anything up to 15 eggs according to the capacity of the individual, and a long French loaf made into a sandwich by cutting it longitudinally and inserting a small Camembert cheese. This snack was followed by a session on hot rum and water, with sugar and lemon, to keep out the cold, and to pass the time until dinner, after which there was little to do except go to bed.

Our next move was down south, spending a night in Paris on the way - always an acceptable interlude in these forestry tours. From Bordeaux we took a small coasting steamer to an island in the Bay of Biscay, where we studied the work of fixation of shifting sand, the cultivation of the Maritime Pine in the sand dunes, and the process of resin-tapping in the resultant forests. This was extremely interesting. It was not the time of year to be at the sea-side, but the cold and blustery weather was invigorating. The island specialised in delicious small oysters, which were served in restaurants at so low a price that one wondered how they could cover the cost of labour in opening the shells. Excellent Bordeaux wines were also very cheap, and life generally was rosy.

Following this tour in the sand dune country we separated, the Oxford and Cambridge men returning for their final summer term, while the probationers from Edinburgh joined the rest of the Edinburgh final-year class at a small village in the *department* of Allier, right in the heart of France. Here we spent some three months in what must be about the finest oak forests in the world. They have been under scientific management for centuries, and even the first

Great War was not allowed to interfere to any extent in their normal exploitation. It is over twenty years since I saw them, and my memory fails me as to the size these giants of the forest were required to reach before they were considered ripe for the axe. But I do remember that the age at the time of final felling was close on 200 years. The oldest woods were a truly majestic sight, and after felling, the best of the timber was put to a noble purpose. Axe-hewn into staves it was made into casks for the long-term storage of the finest brandy France produces. Thus the weed which had matured under the summer suns and winter snows of a couple of centuries was laid down for yet another hundred years, to mellow, of its own maturity, a spirit which will, one day, compare with the 'Napoleon' brandy of our generation.

For about two weeks we were conducted round the oak forests by the local forest officials, and instructed in their history and management. Though oak is the species of first importance, there is an understorey, usually of beech, occasionally of hornbeam, both of which are commercially valuable, especially the beech, which is much used for furniture making and other purposes. Birch, and a few other deciduous hardwoods are also found, under the oak. The shade, owing to the prevalence of the heavy-foliaged beech, is usually dense, and was a welcome protection from the sun as the season advanced, for the summer heat in this inland part of France is almost tropical.

Our main work was to prepare a working plan for the future management of one of the blocks of oak forest. This was a practical exercise, and the finished plan of each individual was treated as an examination paper, and formed part of the final examination in forestry. We were divided into syndicates of six or seven, for purposes of field-work and collection of statistics. I was considerably annoyed at being separated from my usual cronies and put in charge of one of these field parties. But it was all for the best. My lot were younger and more earnest than the ex-service men with whom I usually consorted, and they made an excellent team.

The field-work consisted of such items as survey and mapping, examination of soil and flora, description and measurement of woods of different ages, and so forth. I appointed the various jobs to pairs or individuals, and so skilfully did I decentralise that I found myself with little to do except co-ordinate results. I spent many a pleasant hour sitting under a shady tree, co-ordinating, with the help of a bottle of red wine, while my industrious companions sweated through the forest on their allotted tasks. They liked work and they did not care for wine, so everybody was happy. The wine in question was nothing to write home about. It was the 'vin compris', or table wine, supplied free by the hotel, and was immature and somewhat watery. But the bottles were of generous size, and taken in sufficient quantity the stuff had a passable kick.

We drew our fair maps, graphs and what-not, and drafted our working-plans in the hotel in the evenings, as the field-work progressed. The work took about two months to complete.

There was a lake near the village, in which we used to bathe, after the burden and heat of the day. This was about our only relaxation. We had one break of about ten days, when we did a motor tour in the coniferous forests of the Auvergnes, which provided a welcome change of scene and occupation. On one occasion we mustered a scratch Rugger team to accept a challenge from the French Rugby Football club in the nearest big town, some thirty miles away. They had over-estimated our ability, and had imported bruisers from distant places such as Bordeaux and Lyons to reinforce the local talent. They beat us, but not by much, as far as I remember. It was, in all respects, the hottest game in which I have ever taken part. Our opponents made an international affair of it, and excitement ran high, both on the field and amongst the spectators. Played under a midsummer sun, the fun was furious even if not very fast. It was hardly what one would call a "friendly" match, but directly it was over the 'entente cordiale' was re-established. We were the guests of the local club for the evening, and they entertained us royally. The Professor, who had come with us to watch the match, was tactful enough to return early. When and in what condition the team got home is nobody's business.

We finished our working plans about the middle of July, when the bulk of the Edinburgh class went home, leaving the Indian Forest probationers to join up with Oxford and Cambridge again, for our final continental tour. I seem to remember a couple of days in Paris while we awaited their arrival.

This final tour was mostly spent in the mountain forests, first in the French Alps, then in the Swiss Alps, and lastly in the Austrian Tyrol. I have never been in the Alps in the popular winter season, and no doubt I have missed much. But even in the summer we found the country perfectly delightful. We did a great deal of walking, often sending our baggage by train while we moved on foot from place to place, studying the forests on the way. We even entered St Moritz in this humble fashion.

I remember eating prodigiously in the keen mountain air. Everywhere we went in Switzerland there seemed to be an inexhaustible supply of large, cream-filled meringues, which were very useful to fill up odd corners after a meal, or to lessen time between meals. During our time in Switzerland we spent about ten days at Zurich University, studying a sideline of forestry known as "yield tables". This is a rather technical subject, and the instruction was in German, which few of us knew sufficiently well to follow the lectures intelligently. I, personally, learnt little. But Zurich, with its boating and its bathing, was a pleasant spot.

We completed our tour with a week in Vienna, spending the days in excursions to the neighbouring forests, and the nights in such entertainment as Vienna had left to offer. This was the summer of 1922. Vienna had ceased to be Europe's gayest capital. The streets were dirty. The lights were dim. The Austrians were in dire poverty. A pound note was worth vast quantities of Kroner. Excellent champagne cocktails cost considerably less than a penny of our money, and the choicest foods could be had for next to nothing, as far as we were concerned. But I cannot say I enjoyed such cheap luxuries when the inhabitants were so down-and-out, and I was glad to leave Vienna to other foreigners who liked making merry on a favourable rate of exchange.

Thus ended our training in Europe. The continental tours, on the whole, had been the greatest fun. We learnt a great deal, without undue effort of the brain. It was learning that came pleasurably, through the eye, in the most attractive surroundings, and usually under enjoyable conditions. Normal young men in their twenties, moving around a peaceful Europe in a band of thirty or so, can be trusted to get the most out of everything, under any conditions. But we were not quite normal. Most of us had fairly recently been released from the shackles of military service, and in our new-found freedom youthful exuberance ran exceptionally high. None of us was overburdened with worldly wealth, but exchange was favourable to England in those early post-War years, and a little money went a long way, especially since we had a subsistence allowance from the India Office, who also paid our travelling expenses. Amongst ourselves we were a very happy company, and we were always treated with the greatest courtesy and kindness by the local staff in the European forests which we visited.

From Vienna we went home in our time. We were due in Oxford towards the end of September for the final examination of Indian Forest probationers. Failure in this examination was unlikely, since all of us had already qualified in the forestry course at our respective universities. In these circumstances few had done any serious study for this particular examination, although it would have paid to do so, for the results fixed our seniority in the Indian list for ever and ever. But since seniority would not affect us for some twenty years, when we might reasonably begin to expect the high administrative posts, the examination was generally considered to be nothing but a bore, and an encroachment on the little spare time still left to us in England. Its immediate effect concerned our posting to provinces in India. One was allowed to name three provinces in order of preference. Those who did best in the examination got their first choice. The last on the list realised that he must go to Bihar and Orissa, a province which everybody shunned, rightly or wrongly. There was much diversity of individual preference, and in the end most people were fairly well satisfied with the allotment of provinces. I made the Presidency of Madras my first choice, and was fortunate enough to get it.

Chapter II

FURTHER TRAINING IN INDIA

About ten probationers of my year were posted to Burma, and left England late in October, 1922. Three Indians left England after the final examination, to spend some time in their homes before starting work. One Englishman also started at the same time. He was said to be walking out to India, via Russia, as he was fond of walking, and had a weakness for Russian princesses. I never heard whether he walked all the way. Another Englishman - or, to be strictly accurate, a Scot - also got away with a flying start. He took an early ship, and reported for duty in India about a month before he was due. This showed commendable keenness on his part, though if there were any idea of acquiring merit, I am sure it cut no ice with his superiors. The remainder of us, to the number of about fourteen, bound for different provinces of India, sailed together from Birkenhead in the second week of November.

We were provided with free passage, so naturally the India Office did not send us by the fastest or most fashionable line. Our ship was ancient, but reasonably comfortable. It was extremely slow, taking exactly a month from Birkenhead to Bombay, with one stop, for coaling, at Port Said.

Although such a voyage was a new experience for most of us, it became somewhat monotonous after the first fortnight. It was the usual, lazy shipboard life. I took part in organised deck games for my first and last time; in fact I think I won a prize for "bull-board" or some such nonsense. (On voyages I have always avoided the eye of the life and soul of the party who arranges competitions, and organises his fellow-passengers to distraction.)

After a day or two in Bombay we went our several ways. There seemed no need for anything in the nature of haste. In the East, tomorrow is at least as good as to-day, if not better, and a few of our number, with acquaintances in Bombay, settled down there for a spell.

A. [This was H.A.H.G. Hicks (known as 'Hicko', see p72).He was a Working Plans Officer in Ootacamund in 1925, a Chief Forest Officer in Coorg in 1930 (see p207) and a District Forest Officer at several stations including Coimbatore, Nilambur and Nilgiris] and I left for Madras two days after landing. As far as I remember we spent three nights and two days in the train. Much of the journey lay across the hot and arid Deccan plateau, and we did not think a lot of India as we first saw it. On the train I made my first acquaintance with Indian cheroots. I bought a box of a hundred nice fat ones for about five shillings, and felt very opulent. I still think that the cheapness of quite good cigars is one of the best things about India in the way of creature comforts.

In Madras we were expected, but not so soon, and we spent a week in a hotel before being sent up-country. We knew nobody, and I, at any rate, had very little money, so we had a pretty dull time. We called on the Governor of the province, and paid a lot of other duty calls on high officials, as advised by the Chief Conservator of Forests. The call at Government House bore fruit, for there was a state ball during our stay in Madras, and we were duly invited. Being strangers we did not get much dancing, but it was a splendid spectacle, and the champagne supper was a banquet to remember.

Our posting up-country depended on the availability of accommodation which was, at that time, very limited. There were five of us newcomers to be considered. One had recently taken to himself a wife, so he was sent to Ootacamund, in the Nilgiri Hills, where there were several hotels and boarding houses. There was a small bungalow, capable of taking two bachelors, at Chittoor, about a hundred miles north-west of Madras, and another shortly to become available at Salem, two hundred miles away, on the main line to the west coast. A. and I decided to go together, and in the draw for stations we picked Salem. We were invited to stay with the Conservator of Forests [This was Anthony Wimbush who came to India in 1907. He became Conservator in 1925 and Chief Conservator in 1937] who had his headquarters there, until our own bungalow should be ready.

We reached Salem just as the Christmas holidays broke out. All things considered, we might just as well have spent almost another month at home in England, for we did not start work until the 3rd or 4th of January, although we had landed in India on the 10th December.

On arrival in Salem, A. stopped just long enough to have breakfast. He then approached the Conservator for permission to spend the holidays in Ceylon, which he immediately proceeded to do. It struck me as being just the least bit tactless to ask for leave as soon as one had reported for duty. But I was soon to find that to the Government servant in India the Christmas holidays are sacrosanct. Nobody works then, unless in extreme emergency. The holidays last at least ten days, giving time to go almost anywhere within reason, even before the days of flying.

Salem is a large town, having several cotton mills, and a biggish trade in cotton and silk fabrics. There are magnesite mines in the vicinity. In my time there were about a dozen European officials in Salem. Increasing Indianization has greatly reduced the number since then.

The so-called "cold-weather" is pleasantly warm. The hot weather is unpleasantly hot. But it is a dry heat, which is much more bearable than the humid warmth of the coastal plains. The annual rainfall is about 20 inches, and sometimes nearly half the total falls in a few hours, which does not leave a great many rainy days in the rest of the year. The country in general bears a parched appearance, except during and for a short time after the scanty North-east monsoon, which centres round November.

We stayed with the Conservator and his wife for a few weeks, and were very hospitably entertained, and put wise to the ways of the country. Thereafter we shared a house with the Superintendent of Police, whose family was in England. Thanks to this arrangement, which suited all concerned, we were able to postpone the cares of housekeeping under Indian conditions.

The young forest officer normally does about two years training in India before he is given an independent charge. In our case, owing to lack of recruitment during the War, this period of inauguration had to be curtailed. We started off, however, in the approved fashion, to learn the language, to study the history and organisation of the forest department and the system of office procedure, and to prepare for the departmental examinations in forest law, revenue, and accounting methods.

This was mostly dull work. We used to start the day with two hours Tamil, with a "munshi", before breakfast. Tamil is not an attractive noise at the best of times. On an empty stomach it was scarcely tolerable, and it was difficult to maintain interest. We beguiled the time by chaffing the old munshi a good deal. He took it in very good part - as well he might, seeing that A. and I each paid him thirty rupees a month, which was rather more than he was earning at his legitimate job as a clerk in the Collector's office. I still remember his reply when A. once asked him whether he kissed his wife good-bye when he left for the office in the mornings. "No," he said, "we only kiss young children. We are not so familiar with the females". Like many good Brahmins, he was the father of a large family, but he was shocked by the suggestion that he might be so familiar with his wife as to kiss her. In our youthful ignorance of Eastern customs this struck us as a very amusing answer.

Salem at this time was the headquarters of no less than three forest districts, in addition to the establishment of the Conservator. A. and I each had the run of one of the district forest offices, whither we used to push-bike every morning, a matter of 2½ miles. There we used to study office routine from 11 a.m. to 1 p.m., returning home very hot and dusty, for lunch. Our respective District Forest Officers seemed to spend almost their whole time out on tour. They were both Indians, in the provincial forest service, so we, being imperial service, were theoretically senior to them; a curious position, but not one that was ever embarrassing. They were both officers of ripe experience, and we accepted our temporary subordination without question.

The office work was quite interesting, as compared with mugging up law etc. for examination purposes. After some brief instruction, the District Forest Officers left us to do the routine part of the work, and to deal, on their behalf, with all except the most important correspondence.

I usually put in some private study of Tamil between lunch and tea-time. After tea there was tennis at the club. Another diversion was riding the Police superintendent's horse, a fat slug which he never rode himself, but had to maintain in order to comply with one of the Travelling Allowance rules. He called it the T.A. horse. We put up some hurdles in the compound, but the nag was not keen on them, and the exercise became too strenuous for the one who had to run behind, with a stick, to hearten the beast over the jumps. So we dropped the jumping and took to leisurely hacking in the country.

Dinner was a moveable feast, depending on how early or late one got home from the club. 9.30 p.m. was a fairly average time, though 11 p.m. or later was not uncommon. Bachelors in the East are usually careless about meal times, especially dinner, and are apt to ruin their digestions by going straight to bed after a late and heavy meal. In passing, it would not be out of place to pay a tribute to Indian cooks, and servants generally. The dinner that is ready to be served at 8 p.m. tastes every bit as good at midnight, and the speed with which the bearer gets hot soup on the table is truly amazing, when one considers that he was fast asleep until a shout from the doorstep announced his returning master. One is well served in India.

The people in Salem were very hospitable, and we frequently found ourselves dining out. This was enjoyable, but not very diverting for it was always the same small circle of acquaintances, and in the days before refrigerators and cold storage delicacies it was also practically the same party menu. One could, however, infallibly count on tinned asparagus, which is excellent.

Mangoes were a great solace during our first hot weather. We ate them in quantity and suffered no ill effects, although it is commonly thought that an excess of mangoes brings one out in boils. A good mango is one of the finest fruits in the world, and a particularly choice variety grown in Salem is known throughout South India.

The hot weather was quite good fun. There was the usual exodus of wives to the hills, so one saw much more of the married men than usual. Life became less formal, and the dinner-hour grew later than ever. We even had a matrimonial sensation. A certain deserted husband in Salem became friendly with a grass widow in the little hill station about 20 miles away. Both were present at a dance given in the club by the real and imaginary bachelors of Salem. The lady's husband was considered to be at a safe distance, since he lived at least 200 miles away. But he must have been of a suspicious nature for he turned up unexpectedly in the middle of the festivities, and socked the first man he saw, in the eye. It was the wrong man, naturally, and it gave the right man time to disappear. I don't know whether they ever met, but I heard it said, later, that when the aggrieved husband went into the matter of divorce proceedings with his lawyers, he found that he himself had no legal status, since his lady had another husband living, about whom he had never heard. Whether this was the case, I cannot say, but at any rate the whole affair simmered down, and the only apparent result of the incident was that one or two other Salem wives curtailed their stay in the hills that year. But this may have been mere coincidence.

Most of the country around Salem is either cultivated land or else barren, rocky hills from which the forest has long since disappeared, owing to the inroads of man and goat in the days before forest conservation. About three miles, however, from the civil residential locality, there are the Shevaroy Hills, on top of which is a steeply undulating plateau of about 4000 feet elevation, largely given over to the cultivation of coffee. The steep outer slopes of the hills, and a belt of level country at their base, are forest reserves. The jungle is of the scrub type but contains tree growth of sufficient size to supply firewood to Salem. The steep, upper slopes are worked for bamboo, and also contain some sandalwood. We were never taken to this forest for instruction. It looked as if the local authorities were rather ashamed of it, and it certainly was a poor example.

Our Conservator and his wife went to England on leave at the beginning of the hot weather. His successor sent his family to the hills very shortly after his arrival, while he himself went out on a protracted tour of his new circle. A. and I joined him, for two short periods, which made a very welcome break in the monotony of office work and home study.

Our first camp was in the Yelagiri hills, about 80 miles away. The word "camp" conjures up a vision of tents, nights round the old camp fire, and all the rest of it. But it very seldom has this meaning in Madras, when an official is said to be "in camp" whenever he is absent on duty from his headquarters. Forest officers use tents more than any other officials, but most districts are so well supplied with forest rest-houses that we seldom require the tents with which we are provided.

On this occasion we started off by rail, going some 70 miles eastwards from Salem. There was only a morning train, and the Conservator had advised us to wait at our arrival station until the cool of the late afternoon, before walking up hill to his camp. We had a beer or two in the railway refreshment room, and then had lunch, and sat around till about 3 p.m. By this time we were so bored that we decided to set off. The forest guard, who had been sent down in the early morning to guide us, did not think much of the idea. But of course we knew better.

From the railway we walked across about a mile of plain. Then the hill-side rose at what seemed almost a right angle. There was a foot-path of sorts, mostly loose boulders and dust, or else bedded granite rocks with smooth surfaces which gave a precarious foot-hold. There was not a vestige of shade, the only vegetation being occasional patches of stunted thorns. The heat of the mid-afternoon sun was terrific, blazing down on and radiating up from the barren hill-side. Once committed to the ascent there was nothing for it but to continue, though we were soon wishing we had heeded the forest guard and waited till 5 p.m. when the sun would have lost its ferocity.

The actual ascent was about three miles in length, with a rise of nearly 3,000 feet. It took us a good two hours, and reduced us almost to grease-spots. Needless to say our baggage coolies did not start till the sun was low.

On the top we found a very pleasant tree-clad plateau, with occasional small patches of grain cultivation. The climate is cool, but has the drawback common to almost all low hills of being malarial. The jungle is deciduous forest of no great height, with bamboo and sandalwood as the most important species.

We spent a very pleasant week in this cool retreat, living in a comfortable two-roomed forest rest-house. There was no forest work going on at the time, so our daily inspections with the Conservator were in the nature of botanical excursions. In the late afternoons we used to look for game, though there was little on this small plateau, owing to the skill of the native hillmen in the surreptitious use of traps and snares. There were a few small herds of chital (spotted deer) on the hills, and A. went tracking every evening, but never came up with a shootable stag. I went after feather, as my only weapon at that time was a shot-gun, and I was very pleased one evening when I returned home with my first jungle fowl. The grey jungle fowl of South India is somewhat bigger than a bantam. The cock is a handsome bird, predominantly grey in colour, with dark wings, a long flowing tail, and the beautiful golden ruff whose small component feathers are known to fly fishermen in the British Isles as jungle-cock hackle. Driven jungle fowl provide very good shooting when they are found in quantity. But one more often comes across them singly, or in pairs, when they either run away in the undergrowth, or else get up unexpectedly, when it takes a quick, snap shot to get them before they disappear amongst the trees.

Some weeks after this short tour we again joined the Conservator at a camp in the foothills, some 20 miles from Salem. I do not remember much about this trip except that it was very hot, and the jungle, of the scrub type, was very thorny, with a lot of prickly pear. The latter was at that time an awful curse in our drier types of forest, but it has now practically disappeared as a result of the introduction of the cochineal insect, which eats this plant without, apparently, going for other vegetation when it has consumed the diet of its choice.

In July we spent nearly a week in Madras at examinations. Both A. and I failed in lower standard Tamil, but we passed the departmental tests in forest law, forest revenue, and office procedure and accounts. Our failure in Tamil was a disappointment to our munshi, since he was looking forward to the reward which custom decrees as payable to the teacher by the successful pupil. But we had not at any time shared his optimism, since we knew our limitations, and also knew that the examining board did not altogether approve of young officers passing at their first attempt, since it was apt to make them conceited and think they knew the language, which of course they could not do in a period of six months. The only European forest officer known to pass both the lower and higher standards within a year was C.[This was Donald MacDonald Currie MC. He was born in Islay in the Hebrides and did, indeed, speak fluent Gaelic. However, he had an aptitude for languages and learnt Spanish, Italian and Arabic at various times in his career so he would surely have mastered Kanarese also. He was a year senior to Browne. After serving as D.F.O. at Nilgiris, Wynaad, Manantoddy, Palghat and Coimbatore, he became Conservator for Ootacamund Circle in 1944] - who was taking Kanarese. A Highlander by birth and inclination, the story goes that instead of Kanarese he broke into Gallic of such speed and fluency that the examiner, fearing that here was one who knew more Kanarese than himself, allowed him to pass without question. In my own case I was actually much better prepared for this examination than for the next one, six months later, in which I was successful.

The Tamil examinations had their amusing side, to compensate in some measure for our lack of success. The unseen paper for translation into English contained one word which our munshi had failed to include in our rather limited vocabulary, but which held the clue to the whole story. There were many other words which we did not know, but either these could be guessed from the context, or else they made little difference to the meaning, if misconstrued. The piece which we had to translate was a complaint from a cultivator to the

Superintendent of Police. It started off with the usual preamble in which was stated the petitioner's name, parentage, full address, occupation and so on. It went on to extol his own merits, as a hard-working, law-abiding, rent-paying peasant, and then burst into a torrent of invective against his neighbour Ramaswamy, who was the subject of the complaint. After this, and in comparatively few words as is usual in such petitions, came the whole substance of the document, which then concluded, as is customary, with prayers for the long life, and prosperity of the Superintendent, and for the happiness and fecundity of his wife, with particular reference to male issue. On tackling the meaty part of the petition, I found it was alleged that Ramaswamy bore enmity towards the complainant, and that he had set fire to something or other (the unknown word) while the complainant and his dog were taking the cattle to the river for water. The quality of the unknown was described as "the only food for the cattle, in the hot weather as your Honour well knows". From this description, and from its inflammability, I correctly placed the unknown as a stack of straw, and the rest was easy.

A. however, did not guess so successfully. He realised that the petitioner was very angry. He knew also that there was some talk about a fire, about cattle, about a dog, and about what "your Honour well knows". But failing to realise the connection, he concluded that since the complainant was in such a rage it could only be a case of "*chercher la femme*". He knew the Tamil for a wife, but this word was nowhere mentioned. So he concluded that the key word to the puzzle must mean a concubine. Starting with this false premise, he made what one might call a free translation so as to conceal apparent irrelevancies. The result was a plausible and human story to the general effect that on the 20th August, while the petitioner was out having a drink, Ramaswamy, the dirty dog, came along and stole his concubine from his own fire-side, women, "as Your Honour well knows", being queer cattle, otherwise she would not have left an honourable man like the complainant to go with a blighter like Ramaswamy.

In the oral part of the language examination I got a hearty laugh out of the predicament of B., [John Mitchell known as 'Bill'. He was Senior Instructor at the Coimbatore Forest College in 1924 and Chief Forest Officer on secondment to Coorg in 1933-1939. He died in an accident in 1947 at Coimbatore, by falling from an upstairs veranda in the dark, just before he was due to return to England] the one of our year who had been sent for training amongst the fleshpots of Ootacamund on account of his married state. I had just been put through my conversation test, and given three manuscript documents to study in a corner of the room for a few minutes, before being called back to read and translate them. While so engaged I overheard the examiner demanding of B. a brief description, in Tamil, of the ethnology of his district. This may seem a tricky question for a beginner, in a strange language, but it was really very simple. There are two very distinct races in the district in question, and the examiner would have been quite satisfied with a few points of contrast between the two types of hillmen. But B. had been in the Royal Navy almost since infancy, and the word "ethnology" - if used at all in the gun-room or ward-room - had just passed him by. He decided that the examiner meant "entomology", of which he knew a good deal, for had not we all dissected centipedes and other loathsome insects at the university. So he proceeded to give the examiner a halting though hair-raising account of the great tarantula spider that lives in the dark corner of the bath-room, and attacks the unwary bather in his vulnerable nudity. Then there were the red ants that lived on human flesh, and the small black ants that ate all the sugar when one was in camp, and out of reach of fresh supplies. I could have told the examiner how they had come to be at such cross-purposes, but it was not my place to intervene. He did not seem to tumble to it, himself. In fact he looked not only puzzled, but somewhat alarmed, as if he thought B. was either mental or in 'delirium tremens', and when there was a pause in the discourse on insect life, he quickly changed the subject, and asked B. to talk in Tamil for five minutes on any other topic he liked. This looked like money for jam, and B. was off at once, on the Warspite, in the Battle of Jutland. But this was not so easy, in an alien tongue, and he soon found himself at a loss for Tamil equivalents of naval terms, and got tied up in knots from which there was no escape. He failed - like the rest of us.

The half-yearly examinations in Madras at this time saw a great gathering of young Europeans from all over the Presidency. There was a spate of junior officers in all the services owing to the absence of recruitment during the recent War, and they all had to pass the language tests. The Indian Civil Service and the Indian Police had to take both the lower and higher standards in one language, and the lower in a second language. The Indian Forest Service had, luckily, to pass the tests in one vernacular only. There were then five different languages in the Presidency - Tamil, Telegu, Kanarese, Malayalam, and Oriya. (For some years now we have had only four, owing to the transfer of the Oriya-speaking territory to the new province of Orissa.) One started on the language of the district in which one first served, so it was a toss-up whether one acquired a widely-spoken language such as Tamil or Telegu, or one of very restricted scope like Oriya or Malayalam, neither of which was of much use outside a single district.

Whether one passed or failed, the examinations were welcomed as giving one a week of the excitements of city life after many months in a small up-country station. Repeated failure, however, was not so funny. The Government paid railway fares for but two attempts at each standard. Thereafter one attended at one's own expense. Worse still, unless one passed both the lower and the higher standard within four years, annual increments of pay were disallowed until one did pass. But for most people the period of four years was more than enough, and the number penalised by loss of pay was small.

We had one officer, however, who found Tamil almost an impossibility. He acquired sufficient knowledge after several years of really hard work to qualify in the written papers, but he simply could not manage the conversation. He had been badly wounded in the War, and his right arm was useless. The Chief Conservator [probably Stephen Cox. He was D.F.O. Nilgiris from August 1908 to January 1915, the longest recorded tenure. During that time he prepared Working Plans for the District. He was Conservator 1st Circle in 1919 and Chief Conservator in 1923] made much of this disability, and finally persuaded the powers that be that it was impossible to talk Tamil with only one arm, and that this officer was being unfairly penalised for his war service. The necessary relaxation was allowed, as a special case. Actually, the officer in question had learnt to write legibly with his left hand. In fact, his left arm did the work of two sufficiently well to allow him to play a good game of both tennis and billiards, to shoot an elephant and a tiger, as well as less dangerous game, and to become a skilled angler for mahseer. Everybody was pleased when his Tamil trials came to an end, for he had worked at the language like a galley slave, and his failure was certainly not for want of trying.

While in Madras for the examinations in July 1923, I bought a big American motor cycle and side-car, and on my return to Salem I sold my humble push-bike for a song, so pleased was I to see the last of it.

Chapter III

MOVING WEST

A. and I returned to Salem after the examinations only to pack up. We were both under orders of transfer, as part of a general post. A new Chief Conservator of Forests reigned in Madras, and he had big plans for the rapid development of the big timber forests of the Western Ghats. With this in view he sent practically all the young officers who were then in training in the dry inferior forests of east and central Madras, to learn their job amongst the big timber of the west. A. was sent to Nilambur, famous for its teak plantations. I went to South Coimbatore, a forest district in the Anamalai hills which produces big timber, and where teak planting was due to be greatly expanded. Others went to different places in the western forests, either to complete their training or to take charge of districts.

Though we scarcely realised it at the time, we were on the threshold of a new era in the history of the Madras forests, and a most interesting era it has proved to be. In order to understand the development which was just commencing at this time, it is necessary to hark back, briefly, to the early history of the forests.

The bulk of the land in the Madras Presidency is the property of the Government. The common form of tenure for cultivation is a permanent lease, which is subject to the annual payment of assessment. Land which has not been assigned, for cultivation or other purposes, remains at the disposal of Government, by whom it may be either used for special objects or kept as waste land available for future assignment, chiefly to agriculturists.

In the latter part of the nineteenth century it was realised that large areas must be set aside as permanent forest, both for the supply of timber and other forest products, and for water catchment and control. In 1882 the Madras Forest Act was passed, and the reservation of forests commenced on a big scale. For many years prior to the passing of this Act, the forests had been ruthlessly exploited and misused. The Government itself had stripped the best areas of teak for the naval dockyards at Bombay, and later for railway construction and public buildings.

The local population had looted the jungle wholesale, except in the remoter parts, and vast areas had been ruined by goat-browsing, and by the pernicious practice of shifting cultivation, that is by cutting and burning a block of forest,

An elephant ride at Kargoodie.

raising one or two crops of grain, and moving on to ruin the next likely spot in the same way.

Certain rules had been in force, before the passing of the Act, for the management of certain forest areas, and the old Jungle Conservancy Board had done its best, with the small staff at its disposal, to stay the process of destruction. But nothing much could be achieved until a complete and comprehensive policy was adopted, with the full force of the law behind it.

From the date of the passing of the Forest Act an increasing number of officers, trained in forestry in Europe, were employed. (The earlier forest officers were mostly without technical training, many of them being soldiers by profession.)

The new Act detailed the procedure to be followed in reserving the areas required as permanent forest. It prescribed rules for the exercise of various rights and privileges in the new "Reserved Forests", and in those notified as awaiting the procedure of reservation. It defined the powers of various types of Government official in enforcing the new forest laws, and prescribed the maximum punishments, by way of fine or imprisonment, for infringement of each individual regulation contained in the Act.

For the next twenty years or so, forest settlement, including the clearing and demarcation of boundaries, was the main work of the forest staff. Arduous work it must have been, often in remote and difficult country, with none of the modern facilities in the way of roads and camp buildings.

In addition to their settlement work the pioneers had to protect the forest against the depredations of the people who, in the course of centuries, had come to regard the forest as property common to all. It was no easy task to reconcile them to the new regime, and to instil respect for the forest laws. There was tremendous friction between the people and the forest officials, and murder of the latter was by no means uncommon. Even to this day the forest department is viewed with distaste by a considerable section of the population.

After settlement, the next phase was the development of the forest estate by the construction of roads and buildings. This phase continued up to the end of the first Great War.

In all this time only the most cautious exploitation of forest resources was possible. What the forests required was rest, coupled with protection from man and beast, and from fire. This essential period of rest and rehabilitation was ensured for us by the vigilance of our predecessors, with the result that by the end of the War, recovery from past abuses had proceeded sufficiently to permit exploitation of accumulated forest wealth on a considerable scale.

Coimbatore, when I first knew it in 1923, was a big civil station. It has grown and developed greatly since then. It is the centre of a cotton-growing district, and has a large number of cotton mills. There is also considerable business in connection with the extensive tea gardens of the Aravalai and Nilgiri hills. Cement manufacture, of more recent date, is a growing and prosperous industry.

I spent August and September in Coimbatore, where I shared a bungalow with C., the District Forest Officer to whom I was attached for training. During this period I went out on tour with him twice.

The first trip was to Mount Stuart, which is the main centre of timber extraction and teak planting in this district. We went on our motor cycles for some 40 miles to a forest rest-house, at the foot of the hills, and walked the remaining 8 miles, up the hill and over the plateau, to Mt. Stuart. Our baggage was sent out by rail and bullock-cart to the same rest-house, whence it was carried to our camp by elephants.

The Anamalai (Elephant Hills) in this locality rise steeply out of the plain to a height of about 3,000 feet above sea-level. From the outer rim they slope inwards and downwards to a plateau of about 2,000 feet average elevation, with undulations of a few hundred feet above the general level, and occasional peaks rising to a total height of 4,500 feet or more.

At that time the only outlet to the plains in this region was a very steep cart-road. Timber was carted down by this route, but carts could only be taken up unladen, and the ascent was too steep for motor vehicles. A new road, of easy gradient, was then in course of construction, and has since proved a great addition to the convenience of travel and of transport of timber, and to the comfort of the forest colony on the Mt. Stuart plateau.

The old road ended at the top of the hill, and from its terminus there was a tramway running inwards, to a distance of about seven miles, to tap the main timber areas then in working. Teams of buffaloes provided the traction power. The tramway has since been superseded by a system of roads on the plateau, in continuation of the new road up from the plains.

The particular hill known as Mt. Stuart is a small feature rising a few hundred feet higher than its surroundings. At that time it was a range headquarters, with houses for the forest Ranger, and for the veterinary inspector who attended to the health of the elephants and other Government livestock. There was also the Ranger's office, and, on the summit of the hill a three-roomed rest-house. The latter is of unusual design in that it faces two ways. There are identical verandahs along both the east and the west sides of the row of rooms. The west verandah having the better view, is the most used, but when the rain is blown up the valley by the south-west monsoon, the other side is dry, and available for occupation.

The view from the west verandah is magnificent. In those days one looked down on a sea of forest stretching away to the horizon, unbroken except for one small clearing occupied by the earliest of the teak plantations. Nowadays, although the view is still beautiful, it is more the beauty of human achievement than of Nature's handiwork, for much of the panorama is filled by the plantations of young teak, thousands of acres of them already, and extending by about 150 acres every year.

As this visit was in August, the south-west monsoon was still active, and showers were frequent and heavy. Most of our time was spent in supervising work in the clearing of the year. The main planting had been completed in July, but gangs of coolies, mostly local women and children, were going round the area, re-planting blanks where the original plants had failed. There were also a lot of coolies engaged in weeding.

This plantation of 1923 was the largest that had been attempted at Mt. Stuart up to that date. As far as I remember it was 100 acres in extent, and it was extremely successful.

Very good natural teak is found growing in these forests, but there is not nearly enough of it, partly due to over-exploitation for the Bombay dockyards in the nineteenth century, and partly because it is not the natural habit of the teak to grow gregariously.

A few small experimental plantations had been tried at various times, but it was not until about 1913 that serious planting was started, under the auspices of the late H.F.A.Wood.

This pioneer had always been a planting enthusiast, but he had the misfortune to spend the first 20 years of his service in the dry districts of north and east Madras, where trees grow with great difficulty. When at last the vagaries of transfer brought him to South Coimbatore, he found, in Mt. Stuart, the chance he had been waiting for. The rainfall was sufficient, the soil was good, and was suited to the growth of teak. He began to plant teak, and was signally successful, right from the start.

There was, however, little if any luck about his success. He set out to succeed and left nothing to chance. He practically lived on the spot during the time of all the important work. He collected enormous quantities of seed, and used it lavishly, in addition to holding big reserves in case of accidents. At Nilambur (South Malabar) where teak has been successfully planted since 1843, the planting distance is 6 feet between plants and 6 feet between rows. At Mt. Stuart, where the rainfall is lighter and less reliable, Hugo Wood expected a high percentage of failure. He therefore started his plantations at the very close spacing of 3 feet by 3 feet. Every other plant might die, but he would still have vastly more teak to the acre than in the Nilambur plantations. Actually every other plant did not die. He did not let them. Under his constant supervision during the planting season, unthrifty plants were immediately replaced by strong ones, and so relentlessly did he drive his subordinates and their coolies that he got practically complete success from the start, and after a few years of these very congested plantations he increased the espacement for future work to 4½ feet.

His system was direct sowing, followed by planting at those stakes where germination of seed was absent or tardy. Two handfuls of seed were sown at each stake, before the commencement of the monsoon. During the succeeding rains the surplus seedlings found at many of the stakes were removed, and planted in blank spaces. The method got results, but was wasteful of seed, and involved much labour. Nevertheless it was followed for a good many years, until a cheaper and equally successful procedure was evolved.

Wood became a Conservator of Forests about 1917, but as he was given the Coimbatore Circle, he still spent a great deal of his time at Mt. Stuart. In fact it was a common joke that he spent more time there than did the District Forest Officer, although he had four or five other districts in his charge.

He retired in 1924, to Ootacamund. By that time the success of the Mt. Stuart undertaking had been established beyond doubt, and the plantations were being extended by more than 200 acres each year. Even in his retirement his interest in the work continued, and he kept in touch with its progress until his death, in 1933, when he was buried, at his own request, in the middle of his earliest plantation.

Had these teak plantations been Hugo Wood's only monument, they would have sufficed to keep his memory green. But his work and his example bore much more than local fruit. As District Forest Officer, and later as Conservator, he trained a large number of forest officers and subordinates in the technique of successful planting. He insisted on 100 per cent success. Anything less, in his opinion, meant failure, and he made no secret of his displeasure at anything inferior to the very best. By his own work, and by the work he expected and extracted from others, he set a standard of excellence, and established the tradition of successful planting which has since spread to every part of the Madras Presidency where conditions are suitable for artificial regeneration.

I fell in love with Mt. Stuart at my first visit, and was very loath to leave it after a camp of about a week. But I was to see much more of it before very long, though I was not then aware of the fact.

My next trip with the District Forest Officer was a week's inspection of an unimportant forest range, by name Udamalpet, in the east of the district.

This range is practically all in the plains, at the foot of the Anamalais. The climate is dry and hot, and the forest poor and parched-looking - a great contrast to the cool greenness we had recently left at Mt. Stuart.

We inspected areas where the scanty tree-growth was being cut for firewood. We inspected miles and miles of boundary to see that the local staff were keeping it clear. We chased forest offenders stealing wood or bamboos, or grazing their cattle without permits. In fact we did all the dull things that make up the routine of a forest officer's job in such forests where no work of any great interest is possible.

We shot a few jungle fowl and green pigeon for the pot, and tried for peafowl, but without success. The peafowl is a wily bird and seldom lets a gun come within a hundred yards of him.

Before leaving the subject of touring with a superior officer, I might mention the time-honoured custom in Madras with regard to joint camps. When two or more forest officers camp together, the senior provides all food and drink for the party, whatever the number involved. During my early service I frequently protested at continually being the guest, but to no purpose. The answer was always the same, that it works out all square in the long run. It is a friendly custom.

Chapter IV
FOREST RANGER

About the end of September 1923, I was put in charge of a range, which is the final stage in the young officer's training. It is usual to leave the Forest Ranger (an Indian in the subordinate service) with him, for a short time, to show him the ropes. But in my case the Ranger had been granted sick leave, and was off the moment I had relieved him of the Government cash, and signed the transfer papers. So I was left to my own devices.

My isolation gave me an excellent opportunity to practise my Tamil, since the only other person in the range who knew English was my clerk. It was not, however, the best preparation for the lower standard examination, which I had still to pass, for a great deal of the Tamil spoken in the course of one's duties is a departmental jargon in which English words, curiously corrupted and contorted, are freely used. Thus, "rijarw parest Bawundarikku" means "to the boundary of the reserved forest", and incidentally, it does not look nearly so silly in the Tamil script as in the Roman. This diglot is easy to understand when one is prepared for it. But when a single twisted English word crops up in what is otherwise pure Tamil, one is apt to be completely at a loss for its meaning - and often has to appeal to an Indian to translate it!

I set up housekeeping on my own, for the first time. I had brought a bearer (called "boy" in South India) and a cook with me from Coimbatore, and I acquired a water-man and a sweeper locally. This completed my establishment, which was small by Indian standards, but it seemed to me to be a lot to look after one solitary male.

My new headquarters was in a small village some 32 miles south-west of Coimbatore. The range office and the Ranger's quarters were in a crowded, dirty and smelly bazaar. The quarters were in a dilapidated state and due for extensive repairs, so I got permission to occupy a bungalow about a mile away, in an agricultural research station which had recently been abandoned. The building was new and clean, but there was no shade near by, so it was rather hot. It consisted of one enormous living room, with a small bedroom and bathroom adjoining. There was a spacious verandah in front. Such was the home to which I transferred the few sticks of furniture which I had collected in the previous eight or nine months. I was very happy. I felt free and independent. And I was going to be married early in the new year.

The range of which I had taken charge was an unusually small one. It consisted of a strip of plains forest and the steep outer slopes of part of the

Anamalai hills. The total length was about twenty miles as the crow flies, but a great deal more as the boundary measures. The average width was about four miles.

Except at the time of sending in the accounts to the District Forest Officer twice a month, there was little to do at the headquarters, and I spent a great deal of time in camp. Near the western end of the range was the forest rest-house already mentioned, from which one sets off up the hills to Mt. Stuart. In the eastern half there was a Public Works Department rest-house which was fairly convenient for inspection of a good deal of that part of the range, though it involved very long walks. These two were my usual camping places. To inspect more remote parts I used tents.

There were, I think, six fuel series in the range and two bamboo series. A block of forest which is being worked for a particular purpose such as extraction of timber, firewood, bamboo or sandalwood, is usually divided, for convenience of management and distribution of supply, into several felling series. Each series is further divided into annual coupes, whose number depends on the number of years in the rotation, or cycle of felling. In the case of these fuel forests the rotation was 20 years. There were therefore twenty coupes in each series. The bamboos were cut on a three year cycle, so each bamboo series consisted of three coupes. Both fuel and bamboo coupes are leased to purchasers, who undertake the felling, removal and disposal of the produce. The leases are sold by auction, every year, the bids being at so much per acre in the case of fuel coupes, and by lump sums for bamboo coupes.

Supervision of the work of the lessees or contractors in the fuel coupes occupied a good deal of my time. The re-stocking of these fuel forests was obtained by the natural growth of coppice from the felled stumps. In those days we were very insistent that the stools should be left with a smooth, convex surface, to prevent accumulation of moisture which might rot the stump, and thus injure the coppice shoots. Nowadays, as a result of experiment, we know that such treatment is unnecessary, so long as the trees are felled almost flush with the ground. All growth in a coupe had to be cut, whether the contractor could use it or not. This entailed a lot of unremunerative work, and unless watched, the contractor would leave the useless, thorny shrubs and creepers, which were of frequent occurrence, and often in almost impenetrable masses. One also had to watch for fellings outside the coupe boundaries, where a contractor might be tempted to rob the coupe of the next year. Each of the six fuel coupes was, as far as I remember, about 20 acres in area.

The bamboo coupes went right up to the tops of the hills, and were of large extent. The distribution of the bamboos was, however, scattered. They grew profusely in the vicinity of moist nullahs and valleys, and were sparse or absent elsewhere. In the rules for working a bamboo lease it is stipulated that not less than a certain number of culms (usually about five) must be left in each clump, in addition to the new shoots of the year. The latter are soft and useless, but coolies are apt to cut them to gain elbow-room. As in the fuel coupes, one has to look out for the cutting of bamboos outside the coupe boundaries. This malpractice is very common amongst bamboo lessees, and it is easy to avoid detection in view of the large areas of bamboos and the difficult terrain. I lost considerable weight sweating up and down the steep hill-sides.

The rest of the work in this range consisted of inspecting the reserved forest boundaries, checking cattle found grazing in the forest, and general patrolling for the prevention or detection of forest offences such as theft of forest produce, grazing cattle without permits, goat-browsing, setting fire to the forest, etc.

A range is divided, for purposes of forest protection, into a number of beats, each beat being the responsibility of a Forest Guard, who sometimes has a second man, a Watcher, to assist him. The beat Guards work directly under the Ranger, who, when he is in charge of a range, is usually known as the Range Officer.

Between the Forest Guard and the Ranger there is the intermediate rank of Forester. The latter class used to be filled mostly by promotion of Forest Guards, but for some years now we have required Foresters with a higher standard of education, and have therefore recruited them direct to this rank from amongst young men with the necessary qualifications. The Foresters, of whom there may be any number, from two to a dozen or more, in a range, are supposed to be employed on specific work as allotted to them from time to time. But many Rangers still try to adhere to an old system, abolished some 15 years ago, of dividing their range into sections, each in charge of a Forester, and making the latter responsible for the beats contained in the section. This decentralisation reduces the Ranger's acquaintance with the work of his range, but increases the number of possible scapegoats between him and his superior officer. In Pollachi range in my time the old section system still obtained. I had two sections under Foresters, about 15 beats with a Forest Guard in charge of each, and three or four Watchers.

Each Forest Guard is required to maintain such portion of reserved forest boundary as falls within his beat. This entails a good deal of work with a bill-hook, cutting tall grass and re-growth of shrubs along the line, of which he may have anything from about 5 to about 15 miles in his charge. The width of the line is usually about 15 feet. At every bend there is a cairn of loose stones, about four feet high, with a number. These cairns have to be kept in repair by the Guard. In some districts the cairns are whitewashed periodically. The proper maintenance of the boundary is important. If neglected the line soon becomes overgrown by jungle, and forest offenders can then pretend, and even prove in court, that they did not know they were on the forbidden side of the boundary.

Most of the forests are open to grazing of cattle and sheep, on permits. Certain areas are closed to grazing for the protection of concentrated areas of young forest growth. Young plantations, and fuel coupes for a few years after felling come in this category. No permits are sold for goats. These animals are anathema to the forest officer. They do not eat grass to any extent, but browse on all tree growth which comes within their reach, and have been responsible, more than any other single agency, for the destruction of Indian forests in the past. One of my first lessons from my first Conservator was a demonstration of the difference between a goat dropping and a sheep dropping, so that one can check, during an inspection, whether the Guards have been doing their duty in keeping goats out of the reserves.

Heavy fines are imposed when goats are caught in reserved forest, and such offences are gradually decreasing as the years go by, and the people realise that we are very much in earnest in this matter. But it is still worth taking a risk, or bribing a Forest Guard to wink the other eye, for the goat is a highly profitable beast. It will eat almost anything, from roadside trees to cigarette ends. Clothes hung out to dry are a very favourite food. The owner's sole expense is the pay of a small boy, who will herd 100 or more. But the small boy is usually the son of the owner, so that even this small expense is eliminated. The nanny goat produces twins twice a year, and gives a small amount of milk if required. The skins of her progeny fetch about a rupee each, and their meat is also saleable. So goats are very good business indeed to the Indian villager.

Counting cattle for check against permits is no easy matter, for the herds are often large, and merge into each other, and the cattle are frequently half-wild. It is easy to miss counting those which stray about singly in the undergrowth, and it is also easy to count animals twice over. I had many an argument with graziers, and many a re-count. But a day of general patrolling rarely ended without the seizure of some cattle in excess of permits, or of small herds with no permits at all. The procedure in such cases is to drive them to the nearest Government cattle-pound, which may be anything up to 10 miles from the scene of the offence. The owner has then to pay the pound fees for their release, and he is also charged under the Forest Act, when he is usually given the option of paying such compounding fees as the District Forest Officer may impose, or of going to court where he may be punished by fine, or imprisonment, or both.

Petty theft of small pieces of timber or of headloads of brushwood is very common. When the offenders are caught they are taken to the nearest village, where the stolen produce, with any property used in connection with the offence, is handed over to the village headman, or some other responsible person, for custody. The properties most commonly seized are knives and axes. But in theft on a bigger scale one may have to seize carts and draught bullocks. Even elephants are occasionally among the properties to be seized in a forest offence. If the offence is compounded out of court, the forest produce involved and the properties seized are returned to the offender, on payment of the compounding fees. If the case is taken to court, and the offender convicted, the seizures are sold and the proceeds credited to Government.

Forest offences, often of a trivial nature, take up a great deal of time of the range subordinates, time which could otherwise be spent in constructive work. Fortunately the offenders usually agree to compound, and accept the District Forest Officer's assessment of compensation. But even so our subordinates have to spend a good deal of time away from their jurisdiction, attending court as prosecution witnesses. Vigilance cannot, however, be relaxed. Each offence may be trivial in itself, but the cumulative effect of disregarded trivialities would ruin the forest. Practically all the forests confer an indirect benefit on the country by conserving and regulating water supply, and preventing erosion and devastation by flood. Their protection is therefore imperative.

As a ranger I became very unpopular locally. I was young, energetic and full of zeal, in my first independent charge. The local population disliked my energy in nosing out forest crime. The subordinate staff were caught out in delinquencies too often for their peace of mind. The lessees of the bamboo and fuel coupes thought me unnaturally fussy about the observance of the regulations governing their contracts.

Every man's hand was against me, and I have no doubt that it was a conspiracy which led to my shot-gun being stolen one night from my tent. I daresay the miscreants - or their employers - thought that I would avoid remoter parts of the range if I were without a gun.

I was camping at the time in the eastern end of the range, far from human habitation. My gun was in its locked case, under my camp-bed. A hurricane lamp, turned very low, was burning in a corner of the tent. I woke suddenly in the middle of the night, with the feeling that something was amiss; presumably a slight noise had been made by the intruders. I immediately felt for the Government cash chest, and found it safe. I then got out of bed, turned up the lamp, and looked around, to find that my gun case was missing. I dashed out, with the lamp, into the night, but could neither see nor hear anything unusual.

The next day the gun case was found, broken open and empty, about a mile away. Enquiries by my own subordinates and by the police failed to throw any light on the matter.

Some six months later, after I had left the district, I got the gun back. It was found by the Ranger who succeeded me, on anonymous information guiding him to the ditch where it was concealed. It was very rusty, and the bore has never quite lost its pitted appearance, but the gun is still quite serviceable.

I have mentioned concern about the Government cash chest as my first reaction to suspicion of loss. The cash chest is, in my opinion, the chief fly in a Ranger's ointment. Wherever he goes it must go with him. It is a strong wooden box reinforced with steel bands, about 20 inches long, 14 inches wide and 10 inches deep, locked with a hasp and a heavy lock, and provided with a thick chain about 6 feet in length. In his house the chest is chained to the Ranger's bed, or to something immovable in his near vicinity. In camp he is supposed to chain it to his camp cot. Thus, to steal the chest at night, the thieves must steal bed, Ranger and all.

Custody of cash is always a nuisance, and I was relieved, some months later, on rising to the status of District Forest Officer, to find that nearly all my monetary transactions were by cheque. The Ranger, however, cannot get away from hard cash. He is constantly collecting Government revenue, in the shape of instalments of lease amounts from lessees, sale proceeds of permits for grazing and other purposes, compounding fees in forest offences, and one thing and another. The revenue is paid into a Government treasury as often as convenient. But as the Ranger is out on tour a great deal, he is frequently out of reasonable reach of the treasury. In addition to revenue, he also has to hold a big sum in cash, especially in the first half of the month, for disbursement of pay to his staff as he moves round their areas, and for payment to coolies and contractors for any works which may be going on in the range.

I found comparatively little use for my motor cycle, while in range charge. I used it to get to the rest-house in the west. But to get to the eastern half of the range one has to cross a wide, unbridged river. It is fordable by bullock-carts, but is too deep for motor vehicles. So for all tours in this direction I used to walk all the way. In both cases, bullock-carts were used for my baggage.

Once in camp, walking was the only means of getting about, for there were no roads of sufficient length to be of any use to me. Except for brief periods spent in my headquarters, I seldom walked less than 20 miles a day all the time

I was in the range, and I often walked considerably more. It made me very hard and fit.

Up to the time my gun was stolen I was often able to shoot jungle fowl for the pot, and they were very welcome as a change from the tough, ornithological freak that goes by the name of a chicken, in an Indian village.

In January, 1924, I went to Madras for my second attempt at the lower standard Tamil, and this time I was successful. I stayed an extra day or two in Madras, buying household furnishings and a wedding ring, as I was about to embark on matrimony.

The Chief Conservator warned me, during this visit, that I would be given charge of a district very shortly. This was unexpected but very welcome news. I had only done a year's training in India, and had not hoped for such early advancement. A district meant a good bungalow, and a more comfortable life generally for my wife than she would have if required to rough it in the range. I feel sure it was the latter consideration which influenced the Chief Conservator, and not any precocious merit on my part.

I went to Madras again early in February, met my fiancee's ship, and escorted her to Coimbatore, where we were married a few days later.

After a fortnight's leave, which we spent in the Nilgiris (the "Blue Mountains", which lie some 30 miles north of Coimbatore), we went back to the new Range Officer, and we proceeded to Coimbatore, since the district to which I had just been posted was the northern of the two forest districts having Coimbatore as headquarters.

Chapter V

A SANDALWOOD DISTRICT

I assumed charge of my first district at the end of February 1924, and had to go out on tour almost at once.

The official year in Government service ends on the 31st March, so the month of March is quite the worst time to take over a new post. There are always certain jobs which have to be completed within the year, and it is only human nature to leave the most distasteful and arduous till the latest possible date. One might be transferred or die in the month of March, and thus avoid them altogether.

In the present case I did not fare too badly. But I had to defer setting up house until I had done a tour in the district. Of obligatory jobs I had to verify a section of the frontier boundary between Madras territory and the Mysore State. I had also to inspect two Range offices and the sandalwood sale depot. But I had the whole of March at my disposal.

In a way it was fortunate that I had these specific jobs to begin with, for my new district was mainly concerned with sandalwood, and at first I had not the least idea what a District Forest Officer did for a living in a charge of this type.

The nearest forests to my headquarters were some 25 miles away, and consisted of the Nilgiris (up to about 3,000 feet elevation), and a belt on the flat, at the foot of the hills, of varying width. These were, however, the least important forests of the district, and I saw little of this range during my year of office.

There were three other ranges in addition to that just mentioned. Two of them had their headquarters at Satyamangalam, 42 miles from Coimbatore, and the forests were still further away. The fourth range, at the eastern end of the district, was over 60 miles from Coimbatore.

There are a few isolated reserves in the plains, but the bulk of my new charge formed an almost continuous block, mainly of hill forest, starting with the Nilgiri foothills at the western end, and continuing in an easterly direction for about 60 miles, as the crow flies, to the river Cauvery. This frontage, facing south to the cultivated plains of Coimbatore, consists of the steep outer slopes of the hills, with the Nilgiris in the west, and what is known as the "Mysore plateau" in the east, the two being separated by the valley of the Moyar river.

All along the southern edge of the hills there is a belt of plains forest from two to about ten miles wide, which continues on the eastern side, up the valley of the Cauvery, to the Kollegal forest district.

From the southern crest-line of the Mysore plateau, the forests in my charge stretched northwards over plateau country for a distance of between 10 and 15 miles, to the southern boundary of the Mysore State, and further west of the Kollegal District.

In the plateau area there were a few hill villages, with enclosures of cultivation and village waste land, but the greater part of the area was under forest. The total area of reserved forest in the district was roughly 800 sq miles. As my first district I thought this was quite enough to be going on with.

We stayed a few days in the bungalow at the Forest College, and then set out on my first tour as a District Forest Officer. I proposed to be away for about a month. This gave my young wife her first problem. All I could tell her was what limited local supplies we could expect to get while away. All other provisions had to be taken out with us. She must have dealt skilfully with the victualling question for I cannot remember any shortage in consequence.

Our first stage was the 42 miles to the Headquarters of the two central ranges at Satyamangalam. Our camp baggage and servants in two double bullock-carts took two nights and a day for this journey, travelling mostly by night and halting all the hotter part of the day. We followed in the morning of the day the kit was due to arrive. The road in those days although metalled was truly awful. It was subject to extremely heavy traffic of bullock-carts laden with cotton and other produce for Coimbatore and was a mass of ruts and pot-holes up to a foot deep with several inches of white dust overall. The journey used to take us 3 hours by motor cycle, zig-zagging at a snail's pace from side to side of the broad roadway in an endeavour to avoid major obstacles. Nowadays the bullock-cart has largely been superseded by motor transport, the road is kept in excellent order and the District Forest Officer performs this journey in about an hour, and can replenish his camp supplies at any time by having his requirements sent out by a regular and reliable motor bus service.

We spent two nights and a day at Satyamangalam and I made a rough tour programme in consultation with the ranger in whose range I proposed to spend the month. The travellers' bungalow in this village is pleasantly situated above the wide Bhavani River, but it is too close to the bazaar and is therefore noisy. The bazaar noises by day and evening were bad enough, but what used to infuriate us was the noise made by the local dhobies, as they battered the village clothes on the rocks of the river-bed starting work about 3 hours before day-light. This bungalow was maintained by the District Board, and was open to all travellers, preference being given to Government Servants. As it was much used, we frequently had to share it with others, but on this first visit we had the two rooms and big verandah to ourselves.

Our next move was to Hassanur, some 24 miles away to the north. The first few miles the road ran through cultivated land, then through the plains portion of the forest reserve to the foot of the hills about 10 miles distant from Satyamangalam. There followed 10 miles of hill-climbing, up a narrow and steep "ghaut" road, with the same deplorable surface and deep dust that we had experienced coming out of Coimbatore. The only difference was the colour of the dust (and of my poor little wife who was smothered by it in the sidecar) from white, through grey to a dirty brown as we proceeded uphill through varying geological strata. We stopped at least twice on the way up to let the engine cool, for grinding up the endless steep slope in a low gear made the cylinders almost red-hot. It was a relief to reach the top and find we had not blown up or seized. The summit of the ghaut (all roads up the mountain-sides of South India are called "ghauts") is about 3,000 feet above sea level. From the summit we proceeded over the plateau, more of less on the level, for about 4 miles, to the forest rest house at Hassanur.

We were now in the natural home of the sandalwood, the most valuable wood in the world - too valuable, I often thought, for the forest officer's peace of mind. Towards the time of the annual auction, later in the year, sandal was worth about £35,000 in the sale depot, while the wood growing in the forest, and of sufficient size to make it worth taking considerable risks to steal, must have been worth at least half a million sterling. The main habitat of the sandalwood is in the drier parts of the "Mysore plateau" both in the Mysore State and in the small province of Coorg and the few districts of Madras which adjoin Mysore; it is also found in quantity in the low hills lying to the south of the Mysore plateau in the district of Salem and North Arcot.

Sandalwood is a luxury product. It has been used in India and the East for centuries both for burning as incense in Hindu temples and for small carved woodwork which is valued on account of the scent contained in the wood. It is the "joss-stick" of China. The greater part of the annual output however is distilled to obtain the sandalwood oil which is used in some of the most costly soaps and perfumes. Some of this distillation is done in India; the Mysore Government runs its own distilleries. I have not been in touch with the sandalwood trade recently but at the period here under reference, much of the wood was exported to Europe, especially to Germany and some of it went as far as America.

Tree-forming, 'Sandalwood'.

The sandal tree itself is a small one and is practically evergreen. The most interesting thing about it, as a tree, is that it is a root parasite and lives by attaching itself to the roots of other trees and shrubs, drawing its nourishment from its hosts by means of 'haustoria' in the roots of the sandal. The seedling, after germination, can live in the soil as an independent plant only for a short time. But this limitation presents no serious obstacle in the way of survival, since even grass and other herbage can be used until the sandal finds more vigorous hosts.

Shortly before the first Great War, I think it was, that sandal trees in Mysore were found to be dying mysteriously. The first indication of trouble was that the leaves instead of being a ......[The missing words were probably 'instead of being [an evergreen and oval shape in] resemblance to the privet], appeared as yellowish [.......]. This phenomenon occurred in trees of all ages and was followed by death within a matter of a few months to a year or so.

This was the beginning of the dreaded 'spike' disease which has since spread outwards from Mysore year by year until very few localities within the natural sandal zone are immune. Large sums of money have been spent both by Madras and by Mysore in research into the disease, but so far no preventative measures have been evolved which would be practicable on a field scale. Before the outbreak of spike disease, our exploitation of sandalwood was limited to trees of 3 foot girth and upwards. Since then it has been the practice to exploit only dead trees and those green trees which carry the characteristically spiked leaves. All trees in either of these two categories are uprooted, regardless of size, the smallest, which contain no heartwood, being burnt. The result of the altered practice, so far, has been to increase the total yield, since enormous numbers of immature trees have had to be removed. There has, of course been a great decrease in the average size of the billets into which the stem and branch wood are cut. This increased yield cannot go on for ever, but considerable work has been and is being done to introduce sandal artificially in localities remote from the disease zone against the day when the species starts to disappear from its natural home. In the meantime we work over the existing sandal areas once every three years, removing all trees which have caught the disease since the last time round. There is sandalwood in all four ranges of North Coimbatore, and the work in connection with it occupies the greater part of the District Forest Officer's time.

Extraction of sandalwood starts in June, by which time sufficient rain has fallen to soften the ground somewhat and facilitate the work of uprooting the trees. At the time of our first visit to Hassanur the work of enumeration was in progress in the coupes from which extraction was due to start 3 months later. I spent several days supervising and checking the enumeration. The latter is done by Foresters of which there were a reasonably large number in this district. Every dead and diseased tree in each coupe is blazed and a serial number is painted with tar on the cut surface. The approximate position of each numbered tree or each group of trees if they are thick on the ground, is marked on a large-scale map. In addition, as the work proceeds, an enumeration register is posted in considerable detail. This register contains the serial number of each marked tree, its girth as measured at breast height, its approximate height, its description, such as "dead" "fallen" or "spiked" and its direction and distance either from a fixed point on the ground or from another numbered tree - usually the latter. The posting of the enumeration register is usually quite well done, since the Forester knows that in all probability the work of extraction will also be done by him and that the ease with which he finds the marked trees some months later will depend on the care with which he describes them and their situation. Supervision is mainly necessary to see that no dead or diseased trees are missed and that no healthy trees are included in error.

Hassanur is a very pleasant spot. There is a comfortable forest rest-house on high ground above the road, with the quarters of the four local subordinates a couple of hundred yards away. All around is forest. The latter was not looking at its best for our first visit since most of the trees are deciduous and were then leafless. But there was enough scattered sandal and a few other evergreens to brighten the temporary drab effect, and at intervals there were splashes of brilliant red where the Butea Frondosa tree (often called the Flame of the Forest) was in flower. The small village of Hassanur, with its cultivated "enclosure" was a mile away. There was next to no traffic on the road, and a delightful quiet reigned. The days were warm, but not unduly so, for most of this large plateau is well over 2,000 feet above sea level, Hassanur being about 3,000 feet, and some of the other camps still higher. The evenings were chilly and the nights cold enough for a couple of blankets. It is one of the great advantages of forest life in Madras that every district has its hills, where one can escape for at least a part of the summer season. In several districts (as in this one) most of one's work lies in the hills.

From Hassanur we went north for my verification of the Mysore boundary. These political boundaries - between British India and the native states or foreign territory such as Pondicherry - have to be inspected once in 3 years. Where they adjoin Reserved Forests the work of verification falls on the District Forest Officer and as they usually run through remote country which nobody wants for cultivation, a good deal of their length lies in Reserved Forests. Occasionally a river forms the boundary, but usually the latter is a broad cleared line, which almost always runs from the top of the highest hill in the neighbourhood, down its steepest side, and up the steepest side of the next peak, and so on. A perverse practice but it must be admitted that the peaks make good land-marks, and ones with which nobody is likely to tamper. If there is any considerable length of such boundary in a district, it is divided into three sections, and one section is inspected every year. So it is in this case. My predecessor, before he knew he was being transferred, had arranged to do the job while staying with a local coffee planter, since there were no facilities for camping within reach of the section due for verification. The invitation was now extended to my wife and myself.

This coffee planter's estate lay in Mysore territory, about 25 or 30 miles north-east of Hassanur. Some 6 miles north of the latter, one crosses the Mysore boundary. The road on the British side was bad enough. Across the border it was worse. The last 10 miles or so were by a branch road which served nothing much except the group of 3 or 4 coffee estates for which we were bound. This road climbed fairly steadily from something less than 3,000 feet up to about 4,000 feet. The gradient was easy enough and the general surface better than the main road. But drainage on the hill portion was affected by a cheap and nasty device known as a "water table". Every hundred yards or so there was a very hard earthen bund or dam, raised about 9 inches above the general level, running across the road, to carry off storm water. A motor cycle having no great clearance, we were continually scraping some part or other in crossing these water tables and had to proceed very slowly to avoid serious damage, especially where, as often happened, boulders had been incorporated in the bund, either by accident or to give it strength. The estate, when we reached it, proved to be a delightful, cool retreat, and our host - who was a stranger to us - the soul of hospitality.

Coffee, I think, is always attractive. In the first place it is shady, for a fairly heavy cover of tall trees is required to protect the bushes from the sun. The bushes are evergreen, with shiny dark green leaves. Easy on the eye at all times, they look their very best when profusely covered with the reddish berries of a good crop. Further, although a certain kind coffee can be grown at sea-level, the better quality thrives in South India only at an elevation of about 2,500 to 4,500 feet, so the coffee planter spends his life in a cool climate. This estate was about 4,000 feet above sea-level, and was cold enough for fires at night, although we were then well into the hot weather. Here we spent three very pleasant days.

From our host's estate to the nearest point on the boundary was about a mile. There were ten miles of line to be inspected in this section. This involved some steep and rough climbing, but nothing like the difficulty I found on a similar job in South Kanara eight years later when I was less agile. There is a printed boundary description which points out each mark along the line, and the direction and distance to the next. One checks the direction with a compass, and the distance, if necessary, with a surveyor's chain. But the marks are often unmistakable and unalterable, so that a rough check of distance by pacing is sufficient. A tall cairn of stones marks every bend in the line. In long straight stretches there are intermediate cairns on the top of a rise so that from each cairn, one can see the one on the other side. As close to the cairn as possible, there is a survey mark chiselled on bedded rock, or failing that on a stone firmly planted for the purpose. Bedded rocks are preferred, and in these mountainous areas they are usually available. At important bends, the words "MADRAS" and "MYSORE" are engraved on stones with a pointer to the appropriate side. Finally each cairn or survey stone bears a serial number. The clearing of the boundary line is the joint responsibility of the two governments. Where it passes through forest it is usual to maintain a broad line, which will stop a fire spreading from one side to the other and thus prevent unpleasantness between the two administrations as to the responsibility for the fire and for any damage it may cause. In theory each government clears an equal width on its own side of the centre of the line as demarcated. The practice varies. In some places each party clears its own half. At times I have had the entire clearing done by my staff and I have been paid half the cost by my opposite number across the border. At other times, I have had the entire line cleared without any such sharing of the cost because the fire season was approaching and the other side had not started work. Before doing any work on the line, we always notify Mysore so that they can, if they wish, send representatives to watch their interest. Repairs to the loose stone cairns are often necessary as wild elephants frequently treat them as playthings.

I completed the boundary inspection in two days, spent the third morning looking round the estate, and we returned to Hassanur in the afternoon after a most enjoyable visit. Our host was a great Shikari. His walls were covered with shooting trophies, and his stories of his varied experiences were very entertaining and often thrilling. He bore the scars of some of his adventures on his face and arms. He had once been mauled by a wounded tiger and at another time by a wounded bear. In a hand-to-hand tussle with the latter the only way he could manage to save his face from its claws was by pushing his left arm down the bear's throat. He came out of that incident minus two fingers and with a badly lacerated arm.

From Hassanur we went to another forest rest-house some 12 miles away to the south-east. There we spent a week. This place was another centre of sandalwood work, and I continued to check enumeration. I also supervised the burning of heaps of small diseased trees which had been uprooted, but contained none of the heartwood which alone is saleable. I missed my stolen shot-gun here, for the locality was alive with peafowl.

This completed our first tour on the plateau, for there was only a week of the financial year left, and there was a good deal to be done down below at Satyamangalam. But we resolved to come back to the hill-tops as soon as possible for we had found the country wholly delightful.

Satyamangalam was hot and extremely dull for my wife since my work there was of an indoor nature. Sometimes we went out of an evening on an inspection of the firewood coupes in the plains forest a few miles away, but this was the only relaxation while I did the annual inspection of the two range offices and the sandalwood sale depot.

In the forest department, everybody inspects the office of each of his immediate subordinates once a year. The Conservator of the circle inspects all the district forest offices. The District Forest Officer inspects all the range offices. The Range Officer's subordinates have no offices in the ordinary sense of the word but some of them maintain cash and timber accounts and are responsible for stock in forest depots, so he also has his periodical office inspections; in his case these are usually quick.

The inspection of a range office is a boring job. Except in a light range, it takes at least two days, working from early morning till late in the evening. It involves scrutiny of cash and timber accounts, inspection and devaluation of dead stock which includes everything from an axe to a caterpillar tractor. I had two of these offices to inspect in succession and was heartily sick of the job before it was finished. But I learnt a lot and felt that I knew what to look out for the next time.

In the sandalwood sale depot, the inspection consisted of scrutiny of the registers, and comparison of the stock with the books. The sales of the year were over and the stock consisted of about 20 tons which had arrived too late for auction. Sandalwood is divided for sale purposes into about 15 (?) different classes depending on the girth and straightness of the billets and the weight of the root pieces. Each class is stacked separately in the stores of which all windows are barred and all doors are locked. There may be several outer doors leading into the premises, but there is one inner chamber with only a single entrance. Its door is both locked and sealed and may only be opened by what is called the "double lock officer" or the District Forest Officer. In this inner sanctum is kept the finished article from the time of "final cleaning" until it is sold and delivered to the purchaser. For purposes of inspection all the wood pieces had to be counted out, carried to the outer premises, weighed on a beam scale which took about 2 cwt. [About 100 kilograms] at a time, and counted back to store, locked and sealed. It was a tedious job, and the strong scent of the sandalwood, both in the stuffy atmosphere of the inner store and while weighing it in the yard under the hot sun, was almost overpowering. I was happy to know that this performance only happened once a year as far as I was concerned. I was prepared to sympathise with the depot staff who live amongst this sort of thing, till they assured me that they liked the smell, even in this concentration. Of course a smell which costs £100 a ton ought to be a good one.

On return to headquarters it took me some time to get up to date with my office work, which had got into arrears while I was inspecting the range offices and the depot. Normally one can keep more or less abreast of office work while on tour. Correspondence and files are sent out from headquarters daily. Each batch may take up to 3 or 4 days on the way, but once the first lot arrives there is a steady stream. Occasionally, as after moving camp further afield, two or even three bundles all arrive at once. There is then nothing for it but to take a day off outdoor work, and wrestle with the lot.

We moved into our own bungalow shortly after returning from the first tour. Government residences in Madras are completely unfurnished, and my bachelor furniture did not make much of a show in the spacious quarters we were now occupying. We bought a few fittings from the outgoing tenant, and had the rest of our requirements in the way of wood work made by the local industrial school, which is run by a French Jesuit mission and turns out excellent work at a reasonable cost. My wife had a native tailor in to make curtains and loose covers and what-not and the place soon looked like a home.

For a plains station Coimbatore has a very good climate. There is little rain, the air is dry and the temperature never rises unduly. The months of April and May however are somewhat oppressive, often with thunder in the air, and we set off for our hills again as soon as we had made our bungalow presentable. This time we went to the westernmost of the three ranges on the Mysore plateau, up the same ghaut road as before. This range was badly served by roads in those days. There was a cart-road of sorts for some ten miles from the top of the ghaut. Thereafter there were only the roughest of cart-tracks. We left the motor bicycle at Hassanur, and proceeded on a round tour on foot - or at least I went on foot. Elsie walked when she felt like it, and was carried on a chair with arms, borrowed from the Hassanur bungalow, with two long bamboos lashed to the legs under the seat and stretching out several feet fore and aft. This was carried on the shoulders of four coolies; not because Elsie is any great weight, but because the coolies in these hills are not used to carrying the heavy loads that coolies often carry elsewhere. It was a most uncomfortable contraption. It made my wife very stiff behind the knees from having her legs dangling all the time. And we could never get four coolies of a size, so that the chair always had more or less of a list to port or starboard, and as likely as not, a slant to the front or rear as well. In practice, therefore, it was usually empty, but it accompanied us on all moves from camp to camp during this tour and on several later tours on the plateau.

Our first stop was at a rest-house about 8 miles from the top of the ghaut. We made a bad beginning. I thought the baggage carts would arrive comfortably by the afternoon of the day we moved. But they made very heavy weather of the bad road, and didn't turn up until about 3 a.m. next morning. We had brought our lunch with us, and ate it light-heartedly at the normal time. But we had neither tea nor dinner, and when darkness fell as it does about 7 p.m. we just sat in the dark, on chairs with straight backs and were thoroughly uncomfortable. As time went on we despaired of the carts arriving that night, so we settled down to get such sleep as we could. There were no beds in the bungalow so we lay on the dining table. Its hardness made sleep difficult, and besides we were very cold, having nothing but a jersey each to add to the light clothes we had worn on the march. We were too relieved to be angry with our servants and the cart men when they rolled up 3 hours after midnight. Bread and cheese went down very well, unusual though the hour was, and whiskey gave a comfortable glow. By the time the carts were unloaded and our camp beds set up it was approaching dawn. The next day was observed as a holiday.

We stayed about 3 days at this camp. There was nothing much to do since it was outside the sandal zone. But it was a very pleasant spot, and very cool, being about 4,000 feet above sea-level. By walking about a mile one came to the outer rim of the hills, and could look out over the sweltering plains below. I inspected some of the bamboo areas below the top of the outer slopes, and helped to put out a forest fire. It was a time of year when fires were common, but comparatively little damage was done owing to the system of "early burning" which had been started in many parts of Madras a few years previously. This is a simple system and consists in deliberately firing the grass early in the dry weather before it is thoroughly dry, thus getting rid of a great deal of inflammable material at a time when the fires can be kept under control. Fires which occur later in the season, when everything is as dry as tinder, are thus greatly reduced in extent and severity and can usually be extinguished with comparative ease. It is not, of course, an ideal method, since there is bound to be a good deal of scorching of young seedling trees amongst the grass. But the only completely effective system, namely that of a network of cleared fire-lines, is not possible, either physically or financially, in the thousands of square miles of forest which produce little return in money, but which we have to maintain in the interests of water catchment and regulation of stream flow. It is only in plantations and other areas when concentrations of valuable trees are found that we maintain interior fire-lines.

Our next march of some ten miles took us to a considerably lower level, about 2,500 feet, and into the sandal zone again. The sandal in this western part of the plateau was, at that time, free from disease, thanks no doubt to the higher belt of non-sandal type of forest through which we had just passed. Here the normal type of working was in progress, exploitation being limited to big trees and those which had died as a result of fire, or from natural causes other than the spike disease. The enumeration of such trees had been completed, and I checked it here and there. The marked trees, being few and far between, were often difficult to locate. I kept a weather eye looking for any signs of the disease which might have been missed by the enumerators, but was relieved to find none. The area was, however, attacked within the next few years.

We camped at three more forest rest-houses in different parts of this lower part of the plateau before returning across the ridge to Hassanur. In addition to inspecting sandal areas, I did several odd jobs such as inspection of repairs to cart-roads and forest buildings, and of the interior Reserved Forest boundaries round village enclosures. I also checked cattle and sheep against grazing permits. Bears were fairly plentiful in several places, especially near the outer edge of the hills where there is a good deal of rock which contains the caves in which they live. The bear in question is the black - or "sloth" -bear. He is a nocturnal feeder and is seldom seen by day. I often used to go out at first light in the hope of coming up with one on his way home, but never succeeded. Near one of the camps there was what remained of an old road call the "Sultan's Battery" road, made in the time of Tippoo Sultan (the Tiger of Mysore) who lived from 1735-99, for the haulage of his artillery. For several miles the road was an avenue of big trees, and the locals said that when the fruit ripened and fell, hundreds of bears could be found there at night. I planned to return in the fruiting season, at a time of full moon, but was prevented by work elsewhere. I had a rifle at this time, but my shotgun which had been stolen in Pollachi range was still missing. I got it back, however, before my next tour in June.

We sometimes got excellent mutton in this locality. We were never able to buy less than half a sheep, but as the cost of this handsome portion, on the spot, was only about two rupees, one could afford to be extravagant. The climate was cool enough to hang the meat for about a day. After that all of it had to be cooked. We ate what we could and gave the rest to the servants. In most camps our meat was the tough village chicken to which I have already referred. Later, when I had a shotgun, I often managed to pick up a jungle fowl or a brace or two of partridge, or some green pigeon, all of which are very good eating. Living, in these hills, was very cheap, but there was little variety of local food available. The population was extremely small, and one could often walk ten miles without seeing a soul other than one's own retinue. There were very few villages. There were, however, cattle pens where cattle were collected at night for protection against tigers. When out of reach of a village, it was the graziers in charge of these cattle who supplied our milk. They would never accept payment on the grounds that if they sold the milk the tigers would kill the cows. I cannot say whether this was the real reason, but it is the fact that they refused payment. The cattle belonged to owners down in the plains. The distance was too great to send down the milk, which was therefore made into "ghee" (clarified butter) and sent down in that form.

Perennial water is very scarce all over these hills. Few streams flow throughout the year, and in the hot weather cattle have to depend on the very odd jungle pool in which a little brackish water remains. Water-holes, scooped out of the sand in dry river-beds, give a small supply in some places. About my time the forest department made a few small artificial "tanks" for catchment and storage of monsoon water in forest grazing grounds. Further work on these lines has been done since, with the co-operation of cattle owners. In places, also, the system of rotational grazing has been adopted, and at the time the second Great War broke out a forest officer who had made a special study of grazing problems in Wales was in charge of this district and was endeavouring to develop its possibilities from the point of view of cattle and sheep rearing in forest areas which are at present largely unproductive.

We spent the last week or two of May in Coimbatore, and went out on tour again at the beginning of June with the Conservator of Forests. This was Hugo Wood's last tour but one before his retirement. (He naturally left his beloved Mt. Stuart last of all.) At Hassanur it was raining and sandalwood extraction had started, but he showed little interest in this work. The story goes that in his early service, when it was suggested that he should be sent to a sandalwood district, he objected strongly and retorted, in his deep gruff voice "I did not come 6,000 miles from home to grow a bloody parasite." Nobody, however, was more alive than he was to the value of the sandalwood to the Madras Presidency, and much though he may, in his heart, have despised the parasite, to him is due the credit for the success which has attended the artificial regeneration of sandalwood during the last 20 years. Others have improved upon his methods, but it was he who first obtained real success, and it was he who first focused attention on the need for increasing the sandal.

In the years before it was realised that the tree cannot grow without its hosts, much time and money were spent in trying to grow sandal on cleared ground. For years after the fact of its parasitism had been established, attempts to grow the tree artificially continued to be an almost complete failure. In nearly every district where there are dry hills resembling the natural home of the species, one reads in old records of the thousands of rupees which were spent on these attempts. "Dibbling sandal seed under bushes" is how the work was usually described. About 1922 Wood had an idea. It might work or it might not, but it would cost next to nothing, and would leave no variation of locality untried. He issued a general order that every Forest Guard in all five districts of his Circle would personally raise at least one nursery of sandal in his beat. I think the only locality he excepted was Mt. Stuart, where he had bigger fish to fry. These nurseries were to be very small, just one small bed, close to perennial water, and also, if possible, close to the Guard's headquarters. The only cost would be the collection and distribution of seed. This was a small item since the tree fruits in profusion. There was to be no interference with the natural vegetation surrounding these tiny patches, so that host plants and trees would be available. All the Forest Guard had to do after sowing the seed and fencing the plot against deer and cattle was to water the bed daily until germination and to keep on watering every day or at frequent intervals until any seedlings which resulted had become established beyond possibility of failure. When passed as established (which would probably take two years) the centres were to be left to their own devices, and new centres started elsewhere. There was no idea of raising seedlings for transplanting. All that Wood wanted was a large number of these centres, even if each eventually contained no more than a single tree. They were to be propagation centres from which natural regeneration would spread, through the agency of birds which eat the fruit and void the hard seed anywhere within a radius of several miles.

The scheme was a signal success. Only where the Guards neglected the regular watering was there complete failure, and few indeed were the Guards who dared to risk the Conservator's displeasure, for he had a tremendous reputation for being, to put it mildly, outspoken. It was these sandal centres that he wanted to see during this tour, and he was, on the whole, very pleased with them. I trailed along with him, walking 15 or 20 miles a day to odd corners to see a few of these little patches of sandal, at a time when I felt I ought to be supervising the important work of uprooting the trees which were to bring in a great part of the year's revenue. But in the last few months of his service I do not believe Wood cared two hoots whether we extracted 150, 200 or 250 tons. He was taking the long view, making provision for the distant future, and he wanted me also to acquire the habit of looking ahead, as the forest officer must do if the forests are to survive. He said little on the subject, for he was a man of few words. But his views were obvious, and his example as a forest officer can never be forgotten either by me or by those of his contemporaries who were fortunate enough to come under his influence.

From Hassanur we went with the Conservator to Geddesal, a camp to which we had not been before. It is a march of about 12 miles mostly up hill by a narrow, rough forest road which in those days was unfit for motor traffic, but has since been widened and improved. This camp is the highest on the plateau, being about 4,500 feet above sea-level, and it is the only one in which I remember having had fires at night. The weather was showery and the hills were often clouded in a thick, chilling mist. There were tall blue gum trees round three sides of the rest-house, and the wind whistled eerily through the leaves at night. Hugo Wood had arrived some hours before us. He was a fast walker, and our leisurely progress, complete with chair, was not to his taste. We fetched up about 5 p.m. to find tea ready on a table outside the bungalow, and a good chital (or spotted deer) stag lying dead beside it. Hugo had come across the stag by chance a mile short of the bungalow, had shot it and the body had just been carried in. We had the tongue and the liver for dinner that night, and a good haunch of venison after it had hung for a couple of days.

The forests about Geddesal are of no economic value. The place is too remote to work either timber or bamboo profitably, and it is too high for sandalwood to grow. Its only importance is as a water catchment area, and several perennial streams originate up here. In a valley about three miles away Hugo had started small plantations of both teak and rosewood when he was in charge of the district some seven or eight years previously. We went to see these, and found them in very poor shape. They had been neglected since his time, but in any case the locality was too bleak and windswept to expect success. The soil was first class, and the rainfall the heaviest in the district, so it was worth the initial attempt, but not worth persevering with as Hugo admitted with reluctance for he was not used to failure.

We spent several days here on general inspections with no particular object except just to see the forests. Every evening from about 4 p.m. till 7 p.m. when it got dark, I used to go out after deer, and Elsie came with me. If it came to stalking I went on ahead and came back to the spot where I had left her when the stalk failed - as it always did on this trip. There was a big herd of deer in the locality, with one very big stag in it, as well as several other shootable heads. But I never came within range of anything but does or immature stags. One evening we surprised a pack of about 30 wild dogs which had just pulled down and disembowelled a doe, which I had to shoot, as it was still alive. They slunk away and I went after them. I fired several shots at long range but did not succeed in killing any. These red dogs can carry a lot of lead unless it gets them in a vital spot, and they make a small target for a rifle. They do a great deal of damage amongst deer. We were in this locality again about two months later and found the whitened bones of deer in many places, and what remained of the herd had cleared right out of the valley.

After the Geddesal camp we returned to Hassanur where the Conservator left me to get on with the sandalwood extraction, which was then in full swing. Coolies uproot the marked trees by digging out the soil round the roots. Pick-axes, crow-bars and "mamotties" (short-handled hoes with large, heavy blades) are provided for this purpose, but the cooly often prefers to squat on his haunches and rootle away with a heavy and almost straight-bladed bill-hook. The smallest rootlets are cut off and left in the ground, but all parts of the roots containing heartwood down to the diameter of a half-rupee have to be extracted, and the same limit is observed in the case of branchwood. After uprootal the tree is "rough chipped". This process consists in cutting off the white sapwood. The orders are that a thin film of sapwood should be left over the dark-coloured heartwood, but in order to see where the heartwood begins, it is necessary to expose it in places, entailing a little wastage. The object of rough-chipping in the forest is to save the cost of transporting the useless sapwood. The trees are then carried from the coupes to the forest depots, of which there is one in each centre of work. At this stage they have always reminded me of skeletons; the tree stripped of its bark and of perhaps 2 inches depth of sapwood all over stem, branches and roots, looks very naked and emaciated. When possible the trees are carried away in one piece, complete with roots and branches. But when they are too big to be carried by one or two men, they are cut into sections. The root is sawn off at the root-stock and the stem is sub-divided as necessary. Any sections so cut are in multiples of 3 feet, since this is the size of the billet as presented for sale. Branches are cut from big trees to reduce the size of the load. Every cut surface is hammer-marked by the Forester in charge, using a Government hammer with embossed seal. He also writes on each cut surface the enumeration number of the tree and a letter and sub-number to indicate whether the cut pieces are trunk, branch or root wood, and the order in which they were cut, taking the junction of root and stem as the starting point. The letters are T (tree or trunk) B (branch) and R (root).

To differentiate between main trunk and main roots and their smaller off-shoots, small letters are used for the latter instead of capitals. There is still further categorisation by combinations of big and small letters into which it would be boring to go into detail. The object of this very elaborate marking, lettering and numbering is to ensure that the whole of each tree has been removed, and to discover whether any piece has been stolen or lost at any stage between the time of uprootal and of storage in the sale depot. The contents of each tree are checked by what is known as "tree-forming". This is rather like playing dominoes. The pieces of each tree are laid out on the ground in the exact position relative to each other that they had occupied while the tree was standing. The letters and numbers on all cut surfaces show where the different pieces have to be fitted into the puzzle. Adjoining surfaces are compared as regards diameter to see that nothing has been stealthily chipped off, and the whole "skeleton" is examined to see that there is no abnormal tapering. In addition each piece is weighed, and the weights recorded. Tree-forming and weighing are done for the first time when the trees are carried into the forest depot. The different pieces of each tree are then roped together and the wood is carted to the sale depot in the plains, under the escort of one or more Forest Guards. On arrival the process of tree-forming and weighing is again gone through, before giving the escort his receipt for correct delivery. The laborious check is also exercised on every occasion that the Range Officer or the District Forest Officer inspects the forest depots.

In the sale depot the wood is "final cleared". Expert coolies chip off all remaining sapwood with axes. All pieces of greater length are cut into 3 foot billets and classified by girth and weight into their sale classes, each class having its own trade name such as "GHATBADOLA", "BAG....DAD", "JUGPOKAL" etc. Chips which contain heartwood are collected in sacks and even the sawdust is collected for sale. When all this has been done, there is the final ceremony of "transfer to double lock". This consists in tree-forming for the last time and weighment of the wood, both done by the "double-lock officer". The wood then goes into the inner sanctum which I have already described, where it is stacked on the floor and on shelves by classes, in lots of ten tons, and is locked up and sealed. Apart from check weighment as part of a depot inspection such as described earlier in this chapter, the wood is weighed but once more. This is when it is weighed out to the purchasers after the annual auction, payment being made on the weight as determined in their presence.

These re-weighments are trouble enough in themselves. But there is the further and obvious snag that no two weighments even agree. And as each separate weighment is recorded in the various timber accounts, the discrepancies have to be explained. The main cause of difference is loss of weight due to dryage. But sometimes, as when wood is transferred in the rain, there is an increase in weight. The latter is all right at the time, but it means excessive loss of weight at a later stage, and must be borne in mind in racking one's brains for an explanation of the abnormal loss. Permissible percentages of dryage have been worked out from the experience of years. Excess loss of weight has to be explained and the explanation accepted, before the loss (which is given a money value) is written off by competent authority. In the case of normal dryage, the Conservator of Forests is the authority, up to a certain limit of value. Above that value, or for abnormal dryage, higher authority has to be sought, and the matter may have to go as high as the Government of Madras, by which time the Accountant General has taken a hand in the game, and there may be hell to pay. The stock phrase "weather exceptionally dry and hot" is sometimes accepted - though I never found any other climatic condition prevailing in Satyamangalam sale depot in the final-clearing season. Rangers often submit the infuriating and meaningless explanation that the loss is "due to re-weighment". Squabbles over "dryage statements" often continue for a year after the wood is sold. Sandalwood accounts are the devil, and I often found myself in hearty agreement with Hugo Wood in damning the tree as a "bloody parasite".

From June to November we spent a good deal of time on the plateau, while I inspected the sandalwood extraction in progress in about half a dozen places. We usually camped in forest rest-houses in pleasant spots. We had only one tent camp on the plateau, but even this was quite comfortable. A District Forest Officer in those days was supplied with 4 tents of different sizes for his own use and one for his servants. On this occasion we used the two largest for ourselves, one as a sleeping tent, and the other for dining and office. The biggest type of tent supplied to a District Forest Officer and which we used here is known as the Swiss Cottage. Its dimensions are 12 foot by 12 foot with a small verandah in front. It has an inner and an outer fly, which make it completely sun-proof and watertight. There is an upright at each end, with a horizontal ridge pole between them, and sides sloping down from the ridge, to end at the top of vertical walls which reach up to about 4½ feet above the ground. This is an excellent tent and is almost as comfortable as a small house. It is too heavy, however, unless it can be carried by cart or on an elephant. Where transport is by pack-pony or cooly headload, only the smaller types of tent can be used.

We made one tent camp in the plains, under shady trees by the river Cauvery, in the east of the district. I have only two clear memories of this camp. The first had to do with coconuts. The distance from Coimbatore was about 80 miles which was a long and tiring journey on a motor bike by the appalling roads of those days. It was very hot, and Elsie, as normal, was covered with the dust that used to pour in over the back of the side-car, and parched with thirst.

We were met at one camp by subordinates with tender coconuts. These give an excellent drink, and one which is always cold, however hot the air. Elsie drank the contents of about three in quick succession and had violent collywobbles for the next 24 hours. Drunk in quantity they affect some people this way. Personally I usually find two at a time are enough. On this occasion I daresay I drank 3 or even 4, but I suffered no ill-effects as I have a pretty strong inside - or perhaps I had laced mine with gin, as I sometimes do. This makes a very good drink, common, I believe, in the West Indies.

My second memory of this camp by the Cauvery is of a very exhausting day. Close to the river there is a small hill, an outlier from the main plateau, rising to a height of about 3,000 feet. I had to inspect a sandalwood area on the top, where we had intended to camp in a bamboo hut which was occasionally used for this purpose. But I found my time to be too limited to make this camp, so had to go up and return the same day. The footpath up the hill was very steep and rocky, and when I had reached the top I was very glad of the change of plan for it was too rough to be any fun for a woman. I went up in the cool of the morning and went all round the small plateau on the top. I should have waited till late afternoon before returning. But I was concerned about Elsie who was still very upset by the surfeit of coconuts, so I staggered down in the blazing afternoon sun, from which the bare hillside gave no sort of shade. I got back extremely tired, but was cheered to find that my wife's collywobbles had abated.

On one occasion we were camping at the foot of the main plateau for my inspection of fuel and bamboo coupes, in a place where there were said to be at least two panthers. I sat up one night, for several hours, in a "machan" over a live goat, hoping to attract a panther. None came, but I heard what I took to be a fight between a wild pig and either a panther or a small tiger. The scrap started within a couple of hundred yards of my tree, and the combatants made a tremendous din, crashing about in the undergrowth, snarling, growling and grunting. It was a running fight and I heard it continue right up a long valley until the beasts were out of earshot. I saw nothing, as it was very dark at the time. There should have been a moon later in the night, but instead a thunderstorm developed, and I got home wet through, after midnight. No signs of the battle were to be seen next day, owing to the torrential rain.

I sat up for tiger many times in this district, both over live bait and over cattle killed by the tigers, but I never got a shot. In fact I saw a tiger on one occasion only. I surprised him, by chance, as he was getting down to his first meal on a cow that he had just killed. He streaked off into the jungle. I sat over the carcass of this cow until it had so decomposed that I could not endure the smell, but the tiger never came back.

Once in the plains of the westernmost range of the district, Elsie and I had the best view that I have ever had of a herd of bison. [Now known as gaur] We were out with a shot-gun, looking for jungle fowl at dawn one morning, about a mile from the Mettupalayam railway station, where one changes to the mountain railway to go up to the Nilgiris. Both the railway and the much-used main road were less than half a mile away. In this very unlikely spot, as we came to a bend in the Reserved Forest boundary, we saw the bison [now known as gaur] filing across the cleared boundary line, about 30 yards ahead of us. We stood like statues and they never saw us at all. It was a pretty sight. They slowly crossed the boundary, in ones and twos. First came the leader of the herd, an enormous bull with big horns, a hump and a great heavy dewlap. Then the smaller bulls and the cows, several of the latter having small calves at heel. The rising sun showed up their dark shaggy hides and the yellow "stockings" which the bison wears on all four feet. There were about 15 of them in all.

This was our second visit to this range. Our first was in July, 1924, when the highest floods within living memory occurred in the many rivers in the west of the Presidency. The sun was shining on the plains of Mettupalayam, the heavy rain being back in the hills. In these circumstances, though we could see that the Bhavani river was running high, we had little thought of a serious flood. One morning, we went to a point about five miles west of the village where we had to cross the river to get to a bamboo coupe which I wished to inspect. We crossed in a coracle, a shallow circular boat made of wickerwork inside a skin of leather, somewhat similar to the coracles still used for salmon fishing on some of the big rivers in the west of England. We made the outward journey with comparative ease. But on our return a few hours later the river had risen several feet and was coming down in a roaring, foaming flood, with uprooted trees and driftwood shooting past in mid-stream. It was a fine sight, but one which made our little boat appear very frail. The river in spate was here about a hundred yards across. We made the crossing safely, but by the time we had got out of the current and reached the calmer water of the other bank, we were about a mile below our place of embarkation. On returning to Mettupalayam we went down to see how the river looked at the big road bridge in the north of the village. It looked grand, but it was only about 4 foot below the roadway, and a group of engineers were sitting close by, watching in gloomy impotence and wondering how soon their beautiful girder bridge would be past history. It rose a further 2 feet, and then started to subside, though the river ran nearly bank-high for days after. The bridge escaped, but several other bridges on this river and many of the rivers of Malabar and the Nilgiris were washed away. Much damage was done also to the Nilgiri ghaut roads and the mountain railway. Late in November we made a short tour on the plateau with Wimbush with whom Hicko [Hicks. 'A' in chapter 2] and I had done our earliest touring in Salem and who had recently come as Conservator to the Coimbatore Circle, on the retirement of Hugo Wood.

On returning to the plains we camped at Satyamangalam for the annual sandalwood sales. As far as I remember we had for sale about 300 tons, of which about 200 belonged to my district, and 100 had come from the neighbouring district of Kollegal. This formed about one-third of the annual yield of Madras sandalwood, the remaining two-thirds being put up for sale in the North Arcot district. It was my first public auction, and it was one of the greatest importance. At that time an appreciable drop in sandalwood prices would mean a debit balance in the budget for the whole of the forest department for that year. I have conducted many big auctions of timber since then, but this, from the money involved, was the biggest one I have ever held. It started about 2 o'clock in the afternoon. There was no preliminary inspection by the purchasers, as in the case of timber. The quality of the sandalwood of any district is pretty consistent, and the merchants know more about the quality than we do. They trust us to the extent of assuming that the usual standard of cleaning has been maintained. There were about twelve bidders. Two were representatives of big European firms, and their powers of attorney were examined. About three of the others were merchants from neighbouring districts who owned distilling plants. The remainder were the Parsees of the Bombay Presidency who handle and control most of the sandalwood trade of India. In view of the big values involved, we collected a big earnest-money deposit, from each bidder before beginning the auction. The earnest money is forfeited in the event of the highest bidder failing to pay the full value of his bid within the time allowed, which as far as I remember, was three days after the sale. The deposit required from each was a thousand rupees. Most of them paid it in a single note; I had never seen notes of such high denomination before, and I have never, at any time, owned such a note myself.

The sale then commenced. I did the auctioneering, writing the names in the sale list of each lot, entering the bids, as they came, against the bidder's names, knocking down the lots in due course, and taking the witnessed signatures of the highest bidders. I passed each sale list, on completion, to the Conservator who had the authority to confirm or reject the sales. He studied them and compared the prices with those for similar classes of wood in previous years, and made up his mind about them. At first the bidding was slow and cautious, but it warmed up after a time, as some of the merchants saw the better classes going to their competitors, and knew that the quality of the best stuff was limited. The wood was offered, by classes, in lots of 10 tons each, and the bid was so many rupees per ton. Starting at a thousand rupees a ton, I took bids in multiples of 10 rupees till this became too slow. Then a rise of 5 rupees was accepted, and finally, to get the last ounce, rupee bids were allowed. By about 6 p.m. the entire stock had been knocked down. The Conservator confirmed all the lots, since the prices were considerably above those of the previous year. In fact I do not think such high prices have been realised since. We were then about the peak of the post-War boom.

Prices declined in the leaner years which followed, partly as a result of the general downward trend, and partly owing to the exploitation of a bastard from the forests of Western Australia which has somewhat similar properties to the true sandalwood, but is of inferior quality and fetches much lower prices. At this sale we realised about Rs 1,600 per ton for the bigger root-wood. The roots yield a higher percentage of sandalwood in oil than the wood of the stem or branches. The average price for the whole stock to the best of my recollection was about Rs 1,500 a ton, bringing a total revenue of £34,000. I cannot remember the cost of extraction but it is well under one-tenth of the sale price, so it is easy to understand why we value the "bloody parasite" though we may dislike the "dick and worry" it entails. I considered the thrill of the auction to be ample compensation for the trials of "tree-forming" etc., and even for the wrangling over dryage statements. An auction with such high stakes involved, and lasting for four hours on a hot afternoon, is pretty exhausting, and we felt we had earned a drink when we got back to the traveller's bungalow, where Elsie joined us in toasting the parasite, and then had to listen to the tale of how clever we had been.

After the auction we returned to Coimbatore. I had seen very little of my office up to this, and I thought that it would do my head clerk no harm to have a spell under supervision for a change. I also wanted to do some cramming for the higher standard Tamil examination, as it was nearly a year since I had passed the lower, and I had given the exams a miss in the previous July. I therefore spent the next six or seven weeks in headquarters.

The staff of a district forest office usually consists of about six to ten clerks, depending on the volume of work in the office concerned. There are the Head Clerk, Accountant, Surveyor, Draughtsman, Timber Clerk, and Permit Clerk, each with a special job, and the rest are available for general work as allotted. In North Coimbatore I think there were about 9 clerks in my time. Sandalwood in a district makes a lot of extra work in the office as well as in the field, and there never seemed to be enough clerks to do the job. This, however, is a complaint common to almost all forest offices. Our clerks work much longer hours than those prescribed by Government, but our office work is chronically in arrears. I think the state of affairs is largely due to the fact that the capacity of a clerk is fixed at the standard reached by the best, and the best rarely come to the Forest Department. They prefer the Revenue Department where the pay is higher and prospects of promotion usually better. We struggle on, periodically putting up a case to Government for an increase in staff, and rarely getting it. After some years one comes to regard heavy arrears as the normal state. Apart from the arrears with clerks I have often had up to 20 cubic feet of files awaiting my own perusal and orders, piles and piles of them on my table, on a bench by the side of the table and overflowing onto the floor. And every file marked with a red slip bearing the words "Urgent" or "Very Urgent". A terrifying spectacle when one first sees it, but I soon learnt that practically all files are so labelled by the clerks and that this marking has no significance. If a file is urgent they mark it with a word coined, I feel sure, by themselves or rather by their forebears as "emergent", and files so classified ought to be given attention at least within three days of receipt. I think "immediate" is a label which is given priority to "emergent", but I am not certain on this point. However, all will be well so long as one knows and remembers that the papers to be dealt with first are labelled with a blue card bearing the printed inscription of "special". This is the stuff that really matters and that brooks no delay.

Luckily there is little of it in a district forest office, and the trees grow just the same.

I devoted most of December and January to my office. During this time I had Tamil lessons early each morning from my accountant who proved to be an excellent "munshi". We stayed in Coimbatore for the Christmas holidays, and I was able to do a good deal of cramming then, since office-work was at a virtual standstill for ten days. I went to Madras for the examination about the third week of January, 1925, and surprised myself by passing. I was well pleased to have the language exams behind me for good and all. I could then sit back and forget what I had learnt, which was, in effect, what soon happened, for I was moved out of the Tamil-speaking country within the year.

After my return from Madras we went out for what proved to be our last tour on the plateau. It lasted about a month, and was delightful. It was still the cold weather, and the air on the hills was very invigorating. We moved in leisurely fashion from camp to camp, there being no urgent work on hand to make us hurry. I got some duck shooting on this tour. At Hassanur there is a small tank of a few acres in extent, by the village, where I got a couple of gorgeous teal one evening, and another couple the next day. From here we moved into the western of the three plateau ranges. Near one of the camps there is a series of three tanks, surrounded by jungle, each about half a mile from the next. Here there were quite a lot of birds, mostly the "whistling" teal, which is a big bird, about half way in size between the ordinary teal and the smaller kinds of duck. I used to get a few shots on one tank; then the birds would fly off to the next, whither I followed, to get some more shots, and so on to the third tank in the series. This game lasted about three days. Then the birds tired of it and disappeared for good. I cannot remember how many I shot, but one day it was more than I could eat, for I remember sending some down to the plains to an English missionary and his wife who lived a lonely life near Satyamangalam. On one occasion I brought down three birds with a single shot - a lucky shot that I have never repeated. On our return journey we spent one night at Hassanur. I went off to the tank in the evening hoping to get one or two of the teal that had been there at the time of our previous visit a fortnight earlier. But far from finding any birds, I could not even find the tank. I thought I had gone to the right place, but there was no tank to be seen. I asked the way of some villagers who were ploughing hard by, and they told me I was in the tank, but there was no water. They were actually ploughing up the tank-bed for growing vegetables which do very well in such situations. The water had been used up in irrigating the small area below the tank and by evaporation during the time we had been away.

We left Hassanur without ever having seen the solitary elephant which used to live in the country between this village and the Mysore boundary. The local subordinates said that he used to chase motor cars on the road, and that when outdistanced he was in the habit of uprooting the furlong stones and throwing them after the car. The latter seemed unlikely, but it is true that an elephant or elephants frequently pulled up milestones and furlong stones on this stretch of road. I have never met a wild elephant while motoring, and I have no wish to do so. A few years ago a European couple had this experience in the hills of Travancore. The elephant attacked the car, but fortunately not before they had had time to nip out, and disappear into the jungle. He drove one of his tusks through the radiator and I am sure the heat did not improve his temper. The car was a scrap-heap by the time he had finished with it. The insurance company paid up, though I believe they hedged for a bit under the exemption clause in respect of "damage due to acts of the King's enemies".

In February we held auctions for the lease of the fuel and bamboo coupes for the year commencing in April. I had to hold such auctions in all four ranges. This entailed some dull touring, going from one range office to another to hold the sales. I had done the annual inspection of two of the range offices before Christmas. I now inspected the other two, and I also inspected the sandalwood sale depot. During this uninteresting tour I had a letter from the Chief Conservator to say he was having me transferred to South Coimbatore about the middle of March, and that I was to do a short tour with the District Forest Officer whom I was relieving, in order to acquaint myself with the progress of work at Mt. Stuart before taking charge. This was a bolt from the blue, and a most unwelcome one. I had just completed a year in North Coimbatore, and had got to know my way about, and was looking forward to several years in which to work out various new ideas which had occurred to me for improving the management. Both Elsie and I loved our hills and the free vagabond life we were leading. I knew what sort of job I was going to, and I knew it would attract me, but I would have preferred to let it keep for some years until we felt the need of a change of scene.

According to custom I had left the inspection of the current year's section of the Mysore frontier to be done in March. This baby I passed with malicious glee to my successor.

Chapter VI

A HILLS TIMBER DISTRICT

We returned to Coimbatore a few days after the transfer bomb-shell and looked up our neighbours of South Coimbatore whose bungalow was a couple of hundred yards from ours. John Connolly was just back from Mt. Stuart. He had had a letter from the Chief Conservator similar to mine, and was furious about it. In the nine months that he had been in South Coimbatore he had become so keen on the district generally and on the teak planting in particular that he never wanted to leave it. He also had a young wife who shared his sentiments. So we held a joint indignation meeting and fixed up the joint tour to Mt. Stuart. The latter was a stag party. Mrs Connolly had to pack up, so she stayed with my wife while they both dismantled her bungalow. As my transfer did not involve a changed headquarters I had got permission to retain my bungalow. This saved a lot of trouble; it was also the better of the two houses.

About the first week in March 1925 Connolly and I went out to Mt. Stuart together, in his car. The new road up the hills had been opened some time before, so we made the journey in great comfort, only having to walk the 2½ miles or so from the top of the ghaut to the rest-house. Having been here for a visit in 1923 I knew the nature of the work, and about three days were enough to show me the state of progress of the various jobs on hand. Everything was ship-shape and I foresaw no difficulties ahead. Little did I know what Fate had in store for me. The Teak plantation of 1924, most of which had been planted in Connolly's time, was in a most flourishing condition. The unusually heavy rain, which had caused disastrous floods elsewhere that year, had accelerated the growth of the young Teak. We walked back and forth through this plantation in all directions, and could scarcely find a single plant missing, although the area had been further increased from the 100 acres of the 1923 plantation to 200 acres (?150) for this youngest one. The dragging of timber was almost finished for the year, and the elephants were about to start their annual hot-weather rest. Haulage of timber on the tram-line was in normal progress, and so was carting down to the plains. In fact everything in the garden was lovely.

We had one mild excitement during the camp when a bull bison fell in an elephant pit, and had to be released. This is done by felling small trees, cutting them into billets and filling up the pit with these and branch wood until they reach such a height that the animal can scramble out. The bison did not realise what was being done for him. He took each piece of wood as a fresh insult, and tried to toss it back to us, bellowing angrily all the while. We concentrated on one corner of the pit and after about two hours the pile at this point was within a few feet of the surface of the ground. There were two or three coolies and subordinates on the job, and we all withdrew to the far side of the pit and shouted at the bison. He scrambled up the sloping pile of wood, and after a few futile attempts, succeeded in rolling himself out on his side. He got to his feet and turned towards us looking angry and puzzled. But a shot in the air with Connolly's rifle, and the ululations of the crowd, quickly made up his mind for him, and he turned and galloped off into the thick jungle.

Bison, sambhur and spotted deer frequently fall into our elephant pits. They are always supposed to be released but it is feared that occasionally, when nobody of importance is likely to hear of it, an odd sambhur or deer is killed for its meat. The bison, however, is spared, being akin to the cow, which is sacred to the Hindu. Dangerous animals seldom fall in though in his short time in this district Connolly had had to shoot two bears and a half-grown tiger in the pits, little though he liked taking them at such a disadvantage. These unwanted falls are a great nuisance and a considerable addition to the cost of elephant capturing. For not only do the pits have to be filled up to release deer and bison, but they must be cleared out again and re-covered for the deception of the elephants, for which they are intended.

On our return from this joint camp I spent about ten days in headquarters clearing up arrears of office work. I handed over charge of the old district and assumed charge of the new on the same day. The two officers combined for the purposes of a group photograph. Transfer of charge between officers used always to be an occasion for a photograph, arranged and paid for by the staff of the office. Dreadful photographs they usually were, taken by semi-skilled operators, and badly produced by up-country studios. Indian clerks, on these occasions, focus on some distant object with a fixed stare, and their eyes in the finished product seem to be starting out of their heads. The officers (and their wives if living in the station) may adopt an easier pose, but when the photographers have done their worst the result is scarcely recognisable. The photo on this occasion was even worse than usual. The combined staff of the two offices made a group of unwieldy proportions for the cameraman, and there were, in addition, three officers and their three wives, for my successor was of course included in addition to Connolly and myself.

Following our joint tour, Connolly had just made a last trip to Mt. Stuart for the purpose of burning the clearing for plantation of 1925 from which job he had just returned. He said it had been a poor burn owing to unexpected rain, but neither of us thought that this would mean anything worse than a small setback in the time programme.

After transfer of charge, the Connollys stayed with us for a couple of days before going to Ootacamund, where he was due to take over the post of Forest Research Officer. As soon as they had gone, Elsie and I set off for Mt. Stuart. We were prepared for a longish camp, and we got it.

The clearing for the new plantation was bigger still than the 1924 plantation. It was intended to be 250 acres but a resurvey showed that owing to an error in laying out the boundaries, it had grown to 261 acres. This was, by a long way, the biggest single area of Teak plantation ever attempted in Madras before or since. In fact from 1926 onwards the annual planting area in the Mt. Stuart forests was reduced to about 150 acres, since an examination of the locality by a working-plans party showed that the area suitable for Teak planting was limited. If we proceeded at the rate of 250 acres a year, it would all be planted in about fifty years, whereas the policy was to spread the work over at least 90 years, so as to have a constant annual yield of big Teak in the distant future, when the plantations now being made should become ripe for the axe.

The new clearing was five miles by the tram-way, and about three miles by various short-cuts from the Mt. Stuart rest-house where we made our first camp. It was about the 20th March that I made my first inspection of the work. The full significance of the situation did not strike me at the time, nor, in fact did it do so until two or three weeks had elapsed. In planting Teak in these clearings on which the natural jungle had been felled, a good burn is half the battle. After the saleable timber has been removed there is still a great deal of inflammable material left in the way of undergrowth, bamboos and trees of unsaleable species. The area is cleared by cutting all this useless stuff, leaving it to dry, and then burning it. The fire clears the ground for planting, leaving a good deal of ash to serve as manure for the young Teak. It also greatly reduces the subsequent growth of weeds both by burning such as are growing at the time and by killing the seed which lies dormant in the ground. When conditions are favourable a great deal of the unmarketable material is consumed at the first burning, in which fire spreads over the whole area, and burns out in two or three days. What remains has then to be collected, piled in heaps and re-burnt. These heaps are made, as far as possible, on patches untouched by the original fire.

In the present case the first burn was started on the 15th March, which had been the usual date in previous years. Light showers are expected any time after the middle of March, but not earlier. This year, unfortunately, was an exception to the rule, for there had been rain a few days before the fire. Patches up to ten acres or so, here and there, had burnt quite well, but on the whole the first burn was a failure, and subsequent attempts to get fire to spread through the clearing were unsuccessful. There was nothing for it but to heap and reburn over virtually the whole of this area of nearly half a square mile, and this work had already started at the time of my arrival. Elephants are employed to pile the bigger trees for burning. I therefore had to postpone the departure of the elephants for their annual hot-weather rest, and eventually had to cancel their holiday altogether.

To make matters worse the weather behaved abominably. Instead of the usual thunderstorms at intervals of a week or so, we had heavy showers nearly every day from the time the piling started, until the South West monsoon burst in June.

This frequent rain made burning of the heaps difficult, but worse still it promoted rapid growth of woody weeds and of bamboos which involved a vast amount of new cutting, in addition to the cutting of branches from the felled trees and of the bamboos which were lying on the ground in whole clumps which had to be broken up before they could be piled in compact heaps. Another consequence of the delay in burning was that the whole planting programme was upset. Normally the whole area is burnt in two or three weeks. Then it is marked out with small bamboo stakes or pegs at the planting distance - in this case 4½ foot by 4½ foot - and the seed is sown at each stake. By the time the South West monsoon starts in June there should be germinated seedlings at a large proportion of the stakes, so that the monsoon work consists only of planting seedlings whose germination has failed, and weeding the clearing periodically. All these operations were now delayed owing to the failure in burning.

We did our best. As soon as 5 acres or so had been completely burnt, we did the staking and sowing piecemeal. But it was heartbreaking work, and it got more and more difficult, for as time went on the rain grew heavier and the re-growth of jungle stronger. Once the monsoon started, almost all stages of the work of Teak planting were in progress concurrently in some part or other of the clearing - cutting and heaping, burning, staking, planting and weeding. To cut a long story short, we did not burn our last heap until late in October, and did not complete the planting until the first week of November, after which there were only the light rains of the North East monsoon to enable the seedlings last planted to get established.

The South West monsoon of 1925 was lighter than usual at Mt. Stuart. Had it been normal, the task of burning during the rains would have been quite impossible. As it was, it often looked hopeless. But I refused to be beaten by weather. Had I, at that time, had the experience of Teak planting which I was to acquire within the next four years, I should not have persisted. But the confidence and obstinacy of youth kept me at it. When the Conservator (Wimbush) came out to see the work in June, he suggested that I abandon the half of the area which still remained to be burnt. He did not however insist on the point, when he found I was so keen to make a job of the whole show. But this undoubtedly would have been the best course. My argument was that about Rs 15 per acre had already been spent on the part he proposed to abandon, and that this money would be completely wasted, for even I, in my inexperience, knew that it would be impossible to plant Teak successfully on an area that had been left to secondary jungle for a year. But in persevering to the bitter end there is no doubt that it was a case of throwing good money after bad, since the parts which were planted late in the year did not get a proper start. A large percentage of the late plants died in the ensuing dry weather, and even though replanted in 1926 such plants never came on properly and eventually turned out to be practically a failure.

Between April and November I was never away from this plantation for longer than about a week at a time. In fact I might say that Mt. Stuart was my headquarters, from which I dashed into Coimbatore now and then for a few days in the office, or else I paid a fleeting visit to some other part of the district. Fortunately the office work was light in those days. I used to spend the whole day out of doors, and was able to deal with the office work in two or three hours each evening. Most of my time was spent in the new plantation, supervising the work and urging the coolies and subordinates to greater efforts. Occasionally I spent a day or half a day supervising the various other works which were going on in the locality.

During our first camp of three weeks or so, we lived in the Mt. Stuart rest-house, and I walked to the work each day, taking my lunch with me. But the homeward journey was practically all uphill, and at the end of a long day I found it rather a trial. The next time we went out on tour, we took with us enough camp furniture, stores, extra clothing, etc., to make a comfortable semi-permanent camp in some bamboo huts which had been built in the previous year, within a stone's throw of the new clearing, and here we settled down to the simple life which was to last, with only brief interludes for the next five months. Many a wife might, with some reason, have considered this primitive existence as grounds for divorce, but mine was as interested in the work as I was. Except when the rain was too heavy to remain out for fun, she amused herself in planting Teak seedlings, and must have done a good deal of work (unpaid) in the months we spent out in the blue. Only on two or three occasions did she elect to spend an extra week in Coimbatore, on her own.

Ranger with 17 month old plantation.

We had three bamboo huts all in a row, and used one as a living room, one as a bedroom, and kept the third for visitors, if any. As far as I remember, the spare hut was used only once, for this jungle camp was not everybody's cup of tea. These huts were about 15 foot by 12 foot, with a bathroom (so-called) screened off in one corner. The sides and doors were of split bamboo, the floor of beaten earth, and the roof thatched with coarse grass. The elevation of the locality was about 2,000 feet, so the climate was cool enough in the hot-weather, and definitely chilly in the rains, especially as we could not have fires indoors without smoking ourselves out. There was of course always a fire in the bamboo kitchen at the back, but servants don't seem to mind smoke. Or if they do they have to put up with it.

Many of the timber operations at Mt. Stuart were seasonal. To get the best prices the logs had to be as fresh as possible. In actual fact a log that has been air-seasoned for a year is a better proposition for the buyer than a green log. But the timber merchants set much store on appearance, and seemed to have the idea that a dry-looking piece of timber was second-hand. Felling the forest started in June, at the end of the hot weather, and was usually completed about November. The timber of the year's felling was transported to the sale depot by the end of March. Elephant dragging also started in June, as soon as the first trees had been felled, and went on until February or March. Haulage on the tramway was in progress throughout the year except during the hottest months of April and May, when the draught cattle were rested. From the end of the tramline, at the top of the hills, it was possible to cart the timber down at any time of year, since the whole road was metalled. In practice, however, to save wear and tear on the road during the period of heaviest rain, no cutting was allowed between June and October.

Two kinds of felling were in vogue. In the area next to be planted with Teak, all saleable trees were felled and removed. This was the first felling of the year, and was completed as quickly as possible, to give time for dragging, and then for the heavy work of cutting the unsaleable trees, bamboos etc. which, after drying had to be burnt on the area. In addition there were what was called the "selection fellings". In localities which were not due for clear-felling and planting for many years, trees which were considered mature were exploited. One such area was worked each year, and all trees of 7 foot girth and upwards, of species which could be profitably sold, were felled and extracted. The selection fellings were commenced as soon as timber felling was completed in the area to be planted. All felling was done by axe. A few of the axemen were local hill people, but most were from the neighbouring district of Malabar where expert axemen are always available in large numbers. The only point in supervising felling is to see that the trees are cut close to ground level to avoid wastage and that other trees are not broken when the felled trees come down. After felling the branches are removed and the trees cut up into logs of suitable size for carting. This sub-division was also done by axe, although a saw would have been more economical. But the thick end of each log has to be roughly tapered, to allow the log to ride easily over the ground in dragging, and this taper can only be given by axe. Supervision of the felling and logging operations was full-time work for an assistant ranger. The logging was important because straight logs fetch the best price, and all the trees do not grow straight. It requires skill to sub-divide crooked trees in such a way as to make the most of them.

I often watched the elephants at work, after dragging started. I had a guilty conscience where the elephants were concerned, having done them out of their annual holiday, and I wanted to ensure that they were not overloaded or ill-treated. About twenty elephants were employed at Mt. Stuart at that time. In normal years they had two months' rest in the hot-weather. In April and May the streams at Mt. Stuart are very low, and the water dirty and poor. Good grazing is scarce. It was therefore the custom to send the elephants to the "Grass Hills" for a two months' holiday. The hills are far back in the Anamalais, 30 miles or so from Mt. Stuart, at an elevation of 6,000 to 8,000 feet. They are above the timber-line, and enjoy a magnificent cool climate in the dry weather. The grazing is excellent and crystal-clear water is abundant. The usual hot weather exodus to these delightful hills is not only a boon to the elephants, for the District Forest Officer himself always spends at least a week there during their visit, to see that all is well with them. For him, too, this is more or less of a holiday, in a beautiful and healthful setting. And if he is keen on stalking, he spends a good deal of his time after the local "ibex" [Nilgiri tahr. See p177] a wild goat which lives among the crags of the mountain peaks. Bison, too, are very plentiful in the locality. From a selfish point of view my wife and I were very disappointed to miss this annual treat.

The timber, after logging, was dragged to one or other of the two branches of the tram-line. In my day the lead for dragging was anything up to a mile. (Now that the plateau is served with roads, the elephant's work is greatly reduced.) The elephants wore harness for dragging. The weight of the load was taken on a breast-band to which were attached the chain traces whose other ends were fastened to the log through a "drag-hole" cut in the butt-end. Badly fitting harness, and unoiled leather parts caused galls and abrasions, and constant examination of the harness was necessary. The dragging capacity of each elephant was fixed according to its size and strength, and as the cubic contents of each log are engraved by chisel on the log itself, there should be no excuse for overloading. But the mahouts cannot read, and the Forester or Forest Guard in charge, may be lazy; and even if energetic, he cannot be everywhere at once, to see that the correct loads are given to each animal. For one reason or another, overloading can and does occur. And so does under-loading, which is also to be avoided as far as possible, if working is to be economical, and extraction costs kept low.

Transport of timber by the tram-line was known as "tramming", and there was a "tramming ranger" in charge of the work. In theory it was extremely simple. Elephants lifted the logs on to the bogies, the teams (usually one pair of bullocks and one pair of buffaloes) were yoked up, and off they went on the eight mile trip to the terminus at the outer edge of the hills. In practice it was the very devil. At least half the distance was uphill, and the gradient in places was over steep. The line had been in use, I think, for over 30 years. The rails were worn, the steel sleepers weak and often buckled and the fish-plates loose. Running repairs were the full-time work of a fitter, but what was needed was a completely new line. The rolling stock also was old and decrepit. Wheels came off, axles broke, brakes failed when wanted, or jammed on when not required. In the very hot wet weather the draught animals got bogged in the deeply worn tracks on either side of the line in which they had to walk. Derailments were very frequent, and usually happened on a high embankment, down which the logs would roll into the thick jungle below. It required elephants to retrieve such logs, and elephants could not be spared each time a tram was derailed. So the practice was to collect the logs periodically. Often they would lie for months before collection. In this stage they were given, in the register, the delightful title of "errant logs". How I cursed these sinners at the annual stock-taking, when all timber had to be checked. It meant days of poking about in the rank undergrowth to find them. Some, in fact, could never be found at all; decay and the white-ant removed the strays, if errant too long. About 20 pairs of bullocks and 20 pairs of buffaloes were employed. The leaders of each team were bullocks as being the more intelligent; not that much intelligence was asked for, since once yoked and put on the tracks there was nothing to do except go forward or lie down.

Buffaloes kept very fit as a rule. The bullocks went down a lot in condition in the hot weather. The elephants, too, lost condition if they missed their annual holiday in good grazing grounds, as happened in 1925. There was, besides, a good deal of sickness amongst the elephants, usually due to intestinal parasites. Work had gone on in the same locality for years on end, and much of the ground was contaminated, especially near the few dry-weather watering places. An Indian assistant surgeon of the Veterinary Department was permanently stationed at Mt. Stuart, to attend to the health of the elephants and draught cattle. The presence of this technical assistant did not, however, relieve the District Forest Officer of his responsibility for the welfare of his livestock.

The timber sale depot was at Pollachi, an important market town and centre of the ground-nut trade, midway between Coimbatore and Mt. Stuart, and about 25 miles from each. An auction was held once a month, and I used to leave the Mt. Stuart work and return to Coimbatore for a few days round about the date of the sale, holding the auction either on the way in to headquarters, or when going out on tour again. The boom in the timber trade caused by the war was now over, and both demand and prices had begun to decline. It was fairly easy to sell fresh stock of Teak and Rosewood at reasonable rates. But the older stock, and the timber of species other than these two was difficult of disposal. The cost of transport from Mt. Stuart was very high. Starting with long leads for elephants dragging, there was then the inefficient tramline, and finally a journey of some 25 miles by cart, part of which was over a ghaut road, which is always expensive. Carting was made still more costly because we had to compete locally for carts with the very profitable ground-nut trade. The principle we worked on was to consider overhead charges as a burden only on the Teak and Rosewood, since they could always stand it and still show a profit.

In the case of other species, we extracted only timber which could be sold at a price exceeding the actual cost of felling and transport. This, however, was a tricky business. Unless one left a very cautious margin, there was always the danger of the work becoming unprofitable owing to a fall in price in the interval between felling and marketing. When this happened one had either to sell at a loss, which nobody likes to do, or else to hold the stock in the hope of the price improving. In 1925 there was a very large stock of inferior species in the depot. Some of it had been there for years, owing to the reluctance to sell at a loss, and the timber was rapidly deteriorating. I soon realised that we must cut our losses in respect of the old stock before it became completely useless, and I started to do so. But with fresh timber always coming in, it became increasingly difficult to get any sale at all for the old stuff. The next step was to restrict the felling of everything except Teak and Rosewood, and this helped matters in the next few years, but even so a great deal of the old stock eventually proved unsaleable even as firewood. With the depot in this state, the monthly auctions were depressing affairs. Now and then I had a bit of fun when two deadly enemies would bid against each other until the lot was eventually knocked down at double its value. But the laugh was more often against than with the Government, and on the whole I found the auctions dispiriting, though I kept my feelings to myself, and did my best to keep the bidders in a good humour by means of such wise-cracks as occurred to me.

Elephant capturing was always a welcome change in the normal routine, and we saw more of it than usual in 1925. We caught ten or a dozen, chiefly through siting the new pits in a locality where no capturing had been done for many years and the elephants had therefore become rather careless. Early in the dry season when good grazing and water become scarce, most of the wild elephants leave the Mt. Stuart forests for the better pastures of the higher hills and deeper valleys. They return about the beginning of the south-west monsoon in June, and this is usually the best time to catch them. They follow fairly regular routes, year after year, and our pits are dug along these routes, or in other restricted localities known to be specially popular.

When pits are dug on one of these routes, they are usually placed three in a line, with the central pit in the actual pathway, and the others placed one on either flank. The idea of this grouping is that if the leading elephant falls in the central pit, the herd will scatter to either side, and one or more may be caught on the flanks. Sometimes there may be as many as five pits in such a group. The pit is about twelve feet square at the top, ten feet square at the bottom, and ten feet deep. In the bottom of the pit small brushwood is piled to a height of 4 feet to break the fall of the animal. The excavated earth is carried some distance away, and covered with branches and leaves since new earth makes the elephants rightly suspicious. The mouth of the pit is covered with a layer of saplings or bamboos and earth, and finally with such fallen leaves as are found on the solid ground around the pit. The camouflage is very cleverly done as a rule, and it is never safe to go into a capturing area without a local guide who knows the exact location of every pit.

A true story is told of a Chief Conservator inspecting pits on one occasion. On being shown the first one, he said the covering was disgracefully done, that any fool could spot the pit a mile off, and he strode off in disgust. A few yards away he disappeared from sight, he had fallen into the next pit. His language, I believe, almost ignited the bedding of brushwood which had saved his neck, though nothing could save his face.

Cleverly though the pits are disguised, it is very rare for an elephant to be deceived by day. In nearly twenty years I have never heard of a fall except by night, and dark, wet nights are the best, from our point of view. In the season when falls are expected and the pits are covered, a watcher goes round all pits at daylight every morning, and if he draws blanks (as is usual) he spends the next few hours titivating the coverings where they have been disturbed by wind, birds, or light animals. Should he find one or more falls, either of elephants or other animals, he returns post-haste to the range headquarters and makes his report.

The Range Officer then makes his arrangements. If there is a wild tusker to be dealt with, the first thing is to send several tame elephants to the spot to prevent the wild one escaping. By digging with his tusks at the sides of the pit, any big tusker can, in time, dig himself out. Cow elephants, however, are helpless, having no tusks. Axemen are collected for cutting small trees and branchwood, and a party of thirty or more proceeds to the spot with the capturing ropes. In the elephant camp a compartment of the kraal is cleared and got ready for the new recruit, and a supply of fodder and water is laid on.

Most of our tame elephants are trained to assist in capturing, but it is the biggest tuskers which are usually used, as being the most reliable should a dangerous emergency arise. They have always given me the impression that they enjoy the task of depriving their wild brothers of their freedom. They understand the job thoroughly and will, of their own initiative, suitably counter any attempt by the wild elephant to escape or give trouble. The number used to assist in capturing depends on the size of the animal in the pit. If the latter is small, three are enough. But we usually bring out five or six. It is useful to have a reserve. Sometimes when a calf falls in a pit the mother hangs around and is apt to make trouble; the tame elephants then come in handy.

The tame elephants stand round the pit, facing inwards with their mahouts sitting on their necks. Roping them commences. The ropes are about four inches in diameter, and are made, by the jungle folk, out of a fibre which they plait together. When fairly fresh they are unbreakable, and we take good care not to use old ropes. The neck rope is the first to be used. A noose is made with a wooden peg driven through the strands of the rope and securely tied in position, to serve as a stop and prevent the noose tightening to such an extent as to throttle the elephant. The position of this stop is determined by calculation. The height of the elephant is measured by noting some mark or other on one of the walls of the pit at the height of his shoulder, and measuring this by dropping a bamboo into the pit when the animal is facing the other way and noting where this mark comes on the bamboo. A certain ratio - which I have forgotten - exists between the height of an elephant and the circumference of his neck, and the correct circumference of the noose is then calculated. Three or more men hold up the widened noose on the forks of bamboo poles above the elephant's head, and if the elephant does not raise his head and trunk at this gesture, a long white or coloured cloth is flapped at him, to tease him, and get his head up. The noose is then dropped over his head, trunk and tusks, and tightened up to the stop by a gang who are hanging on the slack of the rope like a tug-of-war team. It would be more correct to say that the above is the intention of the manoeuvre rather than its usual result. The elephant takes strong exception to the dropping of a noose over his head. He butts it off, or seizes it in his trunk and worries it, trumpeting savagely the while.

The operation is particularly difficult in the case of an animal with big tusks, and I have seen repeated attempts continue for two full hours before the noose had landed and been pulled tight. Only once have I seen the first throw turn out lucky. It is usually a case of patience and perseverance. When the noose has been tightened up to the stop, it has to be bound with light cord at this point to prevent it slipping loose in the subsequent struggle. The elephant is manoeuvred into one corner of the pit by means of the rope which is pulled by the tame elephants and encouraged by prods from the bamboos of the men. The end of the rope is given a couple of turns round a nearby tree. The elephant's attention is diverted to one side, again by teasing him with cloths and bamboos, while a brave man kneels at the edge of the pit with his head and torso down, while he binds the joint of the neck noose. This is definitely dangerous work, and it is constantly being interrupted by the elephant. The brave man's belt is firmly held by his wife's brother. This is his guarantee of safety. A careless friend might let him slip or be pulled into the pit; an enemy might drop him in on purpose, but his wife's brother will have to support the widow should the worst happen. The brother-in-law therefore watches the proceedings like a lynx, and jerks the binder back out of danger whenever it threatens.

When the neck-rope has been securely fastened, a similar but easier operation is performed with the leg-rope. This is a plain running noose without a stop, for on the leg it can do no damage beyond causing abrasions, which are inevitable. The noose has to be put round one of the hind legs. It is opened wide and dropped near one of the hind feet. The appropriate leg is prodded with bamboos until the elephant lifts the foot, when the rope is moved by means of the bamboos into such a position that the foot is likely to be encircled when put down again. The rope is usually kicked about a good deal before it can be got in position and pulled taut. But the job is much quicker than fastening the neck-rope.

The next stage is to fill the pit with billets and brushwood, as in releasing bison or deer. The elephant objects with more effect than the bison. He kicks the billets about, tosses them on his tusks, and sometimes throws them back with his trunk. As the pile rises, the elephant rises on it. The spare end of the neck rope is now coiled round the body of the biggest of the tame elephants, who also holds it in his mouth. Another big elephant takes the end of the leg rope in his mouth. The other elephants of the escort stand by.

When the pile of brushwood is high enough the elephant struggles out of the pit, and usually lets loose a bellow and bolts for freedom. Sometimes he stands in a somewhat dazed manner looking round at his enemies and wondering whom to attack first. In either event the result is the same. The elephant on the neck rope closes in and holds the rope close up to the head of his wild brother. Another escort elephant closes in on his other side. The elephant on the leg rope pulls it tight and keeps it tight; so tight as to lift the hind leg completely off the ground, when necessary. The other elephants also close in. The captive is now hemmed in on both sides, and is prevented from going forward by the pull on his hind leg. In this position the noose round the hind leg can be safely bound in position with cord by a man squatting under the belly of one of the escort. A second rope on a chain is put round the neck if the captive is a very big animal; this is done by the mahout on one of the elephants which has closed in beside the captive. The rope round the body of one of the escort leaders is also shortened and made secure.

The wild elephant usually struggles a lot to start with, but in time he seems to submit to the inevitable. Under this close escort he is marched off. When he stops he is pulled forward by the neck rope and is butted in the hindquarters by one of his "friends". When he tries to run forward he is held back by the leg rope. Efforts to move sideways are countered by the escort animals who bump him back into position. The march home may be anything up to five miles or so. The first part of the way is always through jungle, where trees and other obstructions have to be avoided. As soon as possible he is taken on to a forest foot-path or possibly cart-road, where the going is easier. If a stream is crossed he is allowed to stop and drink and to spray himself (and everybody else) with water through his trunk. On one such march at Mt. Stuart, when we had a good four miles to go with the captive, one of the elephants accidentally disturbed a hornets' nest in a tree along our route. The hornets attacked us furiously and nearly everybody was stung. Luckily the elephants did not suffer, though I feared they would, and I had an awful vision of a stampede. I got three or four stings on one leg, and it swelled up to twice its normal size that night, and did not subside for two days. I was glad that this happened on one of the rare occasions that Elsie was in Coimbatore, otherwise she would also have been stung.

On reaching the elephant camp the captive is put through the operation called "enkraaling". The kraal is a strong wooden cage, divided up into a number of compartments, each to take one elephant. The horizontal bars of the sides and ends are about one foot apart. To admit the new captive, the bars of one side or end are pulled half out through slots in the uprights, leaving an entrance about six feet wide. The spare end of the neck rope is unwound from the body of the escort elephant to which it has been fastened and is passed through the entrance, and out through the bars at the opposite side or end of the compartment, where it is pulled, either by men or elephants. At the same time the captive is shouldered at the sides and butted in the rear and by combination of these different efforts he is worked up until he faces the entrance, through which he is finally pulled and butted. The horizontal bars are hastily pushed home behind him, and he is a prisoner. The neck rope is cut off by a man who climbs up the bars of the kraal for this purpose; the elephant's movements are restricted at this time by maintaining pressure on the ropes. The leg rope is then cut off at the noose by a man standing outside. The horizontal bars are made secure by driving wooden wedges where there is play between the bars and the grooves through the uprights. Here the elephant remains for anything from 3 weeks to about 3 months, and where he receives his early training. The youngest captives can usually be removed with safety in 3 or 4 weeks. The older elephants spend a considerably longer period in the kraal, since they take less kindly to captivity than do the young ones.

Captures during our time at Mt. Stuart usually came singly. But on one occasion we had three falls together in one group of pits. Elephants over 30 years of age (which Indians with long experience of elephants are adept at estimating) rarely do well in captivity. The older elephants which fall are therefore released, by filling up the pit and scaring them off by shouting and firing shots in the air. During the monsoon of 1925 a colossal tusker fell in one of our pits. He was known to be a "rogue", and was the biggest elephant I have ever seen. I ought to have shot him in the pit, since he was highly dangerous. But a local man of means offered to buy him from Government for Rs 5,000 if I would capture him and deliver him roped at the pit side. His idea was to sell him as a temple elephant, for which very big prices are often paid, but I was very doubtful if he could ever be made safe and tame. However, I did not see why I should do Government out of Rs 5,000, when it was offered, so I decided to get on with the job. I was not very happy about it, for the brute was so very big and fierce that there seemed to be some danger of injury to my men or elephants, or both. The roping took all day. The tusker was taken out late in the evening. He was so powerful that he pulled five or six of our strongest elephants all over the shop by the ropes which were meant to control him. He therefore had to be tied to trees. Next morning he was found dead, presumably of heart failure caused by terrific struggles against the neck rope which bound him to a tree. I was full of regret that I had not shot him in the first instance.

In the dry weather malaria is very bad at Mt. Stuart and on the plateau below it. The Kaders and Mulcers, who are the indigenous tribes of these hills, suffer from the disease from the cradle to the grave, but their systems have become so accustomed to the fever that its severity is very much less with them than it is with the plainsmen or Europeans who only visit the locality. Except for a handful of local hill-men, all the forest subordinates are natives of the plains, and malaria had become so serious in their case that in 1927 the headquarters of the range were moved to Topslip, at the outer edge of the hills. This was a much healthier locality, which had been improved by drainage, jungle clearing and other anti-malarial measures. I got malaria early in the hot weather of 1925, and it recurred every three or four weeks for the eight months I spent in the district. At that time most forest officers regarded this recurring fever as an inevitable part of their job, so it never occurred to me to consult a doctor. I used to have one day of fever and ague, when I stayed indoors, then a day without fever when I did my normal work, though feeling rather shaky. On the third day the fever and shivering returned, and that was the end of that particular bout. I took quite a lot of quinine and aspirin when the attack was on me, and it was not until after I had left the district that somebody suggested that I should continue to take quinine after the attack had passed. This I did for several months together which was probably excessive, but it killed the malaria in my system, and I have been fortunate enough since to avoid fresh infection, though I have often been in much worse places than Mt. Stuart. Malaria causes an enormous loss of efficiency in the forest department, both in the case of subordinates and of the labour force. Modern research has proved that it is possible to make a restricted locality completely free from the mosquitoes which carry the disease. But in the case of forest work it is practically impossible to establish permanent residential areas and keep the personnel from spending occasional nights elsewhere. There is always some work to be done in remote places which necessitates camping on the spot. By adopting such measures as are practicable the incidents of malaria have been much reduced, but it remains a very real scourge.

In 1925 our most fruitful area for elephant capturing was close to the new ghaut road and near the foot of the hills. A herd of elephants remained in this vicinity for months. There was no timber traffic on the roads during the rains, and I decided not to disturb the country with my motorbike either. For most of our Mt. Stuart tours therefore we left the machine at the rest-house near the foot of the hills, while we went up and down on foot, using the old road a couple of miles to the east. I used to walk all the way, while Elsie had an elephant in attendance, and used to ride or walk at her pleasure. This elephant rejoiced in the inappropriate name of Phyllis, in honour of the girlfriend of one of my predecessors in the days when no discretion was exercised in the naming of elephants. Now Phyllis (the elephant) had an obscure affection of the skin. She was all right while she took things easy, but whenever she was given any hard work, such as dragging timber, she broke out in spots. Very convenient this was for Phyllis, and a less exacting method of dodging work than that of inviting pregnancy, as adopted by Kitty, and another lady elephant in my next district. Since her trouble was thought to be contagious, Phyllis was segregated from her fellows and lived on the fat of the land at the foot of the hills.

She was therefore always available for occasional light work like carrying the District Forest Officer's wife or half a ton of straw for the bullocks, or some such trifle. She was an excellent riding elephant, a fast walker with easy paces. Most elephants give the rider a spine-jolting bump each time they put their ponderous forefeet to the ground, but Phyllis was handy with her feet. She was, however, a coward. All cow elephants are apt to be timid when on their own, but Phyllis was unusually nervous, possibly as a result of her continued isolation. On one occasion when we were returning from the plains, we encountered a solitary wild elephant, at a place where the tram-line passed through some very thick bamboo jungle. Elsie was riding Phyllis along the tram-line, and I was tagging along a few yards behind, keeping pace with difficulty, for Phyllis, as I have said, was a fast walker. Suddenly she put on all brakes, held her trunk straight up in the air, trumpeted in fear, turned about, and was off back along the tram-line at the rate of knots. The Range Officer and one or two or the subordinates were walking with me at the time, and we all gave chase in an attempt to catch the stampeding Phyllis. It was all right while she followed the track, but I had awful visions of her taking to the jungle and leaving Elsie, like Absalom, among the treetops. Our pursuit was futile, for we were left far behind. The mahout however managed to stop her after she had gone about half a mile. Those of us who were on foot had seen nothing unusual, but when we got back to Phyllis we learnt that it was a wild elephant that had upset her. We therefore approached the spot again, and shouted at the elephant, which was standing in a swampy hollow about forty yards from the tramline, but he declined to move. He did not however show signs of being unfriendly. We tried to persuade Phyllis to pass, but she jibbed again and would not go closer to the spot than about 200 yards. The jungle was too thick to make a detour, and I had no firearm with me at the time. So the Range Officer sent back to Mt. Stuart, about a mile behind us, for his gun, and when it came he fired a couple of shots in the air, and the wild tusker sheered off. We passed the spot, and after half a mile or so, since he did not reappear, we had no further need of the gun, so I sent the Range Officer home. Before parting, while I was standing talking to him about some work I wanted done, I noticed he was holding his blunderbuss - a heavy rifle of antique design - rather carelessly. In fact it was pointing more or less at my middle. I remarked that I hoped it was not still loaded, but at the same time I stepped to one side; as I am rather fussy about gun etiquette. As I moved, the weapon went off in his hands. The bullet must have missed me by inches. The poor fellow was so full of apologies that even when I recovered speech I could not be too severe with him. He was a first-rate ranger, one of the best I have ever had, and I shall never forget his hard work and co-operation during that very trying year at Mt. Stuart. Neither, am I likely to forget this careless gun handling, nor for the matter of fact is he.

Having had so much trouble and worry with the 1925 planting, I made up my mind that next year I would make a plantation the like of which had never been seen before. I selected an area of the best soil I could find in the locality. When the saleable timber had been extracted, we started to fell the rubbish. I insisted that all undergrowth and bamboos should be cut first, and the unsaleable trees last. The effect of this procedure is that the cut bamboos and small stuff are pressed down by the weight of the trees, making a compact mass for burning. I was determined to have a good first burn - and it was, though I was not there to see it.

Before my time the timber from Mt. Stuart was carted out in the form of round logs. Often the logs were too heavy for carting and they were then sawn into halves, longitudinally. I had a poor opinion of these "half-rounds", from all points of view. It meant importing expensive sawyers from Malabar, and the employment of elephants to "hoist" the logs above the ground for sawing. The exposed heart of the log tended to develop cracks, especially if stored in the sun. Worst of all, the hollows, hidden defects, shakes (a "shake" is a crack in growing timber) and what-not, which in the entire log are decently concealed from view, were now revealed in all their ugliness to the critical eye of the purchaser. In the previous year, Connolly had started to "rough-square" some logs as an experiment. The rough-squaring was done by axe, and cost a very little extra. It reduced the weight of the timber for transport, without wasting anything appreciable in the way of convertible timber, since large outer slabs have in any case to be sawn off before a log can be cut into planks or scantlings. I found I got considerably better prices for Connolly's rough-squared logs, and I went in for this improved form of conversion in a big way. It was later adopted with excellent results in North Malabar, where carting is even more expensive than at Mt. Stuart.

Owing to the difficulty we had with the plantation of the year at Mt. Stuart, I saw little of the rest of the district. Pollachi Range in which I had completed my training in 1923, lay on our way between Coimbatore and Mt. Stuart, so I frequently stopped at the fuel and bamboo working. We had one very pleasant trip to the hill range lying to the east of the Mt. Stuart range, camping at a bungalow perched on the side of the hill at about 3,000 feet elevation, with a magnificent view over the plains to the north. This range adjoins the tea-planting district of the Anamalais, and we went about thirty miles back into the tea district on one occasion to see some forest land which a tea-planter wanted to add on to his estate. This is a common weakness amongst tea-planters, and the forest officer has a lot of such extra inspections wished on him, where his boundaries march with the tea estates.

I paid, I think, two flying visits to the dry, scrub forests in the eastern range of the district. I should have liked to go there more often, for I imagine various abuses must have been in practice. There was a tendency to keep the best subordinates for the most important ranges, and to send the bad hats to these scrub forests, where it was thought they could do the least harm to Government property.

Despite the heart-breaking task of burning a clearing in the rain, I had very soon become so interested and absorbed in the new district that I should have been most unwilling to return to the sandalwood district which I had been so loath to leave a few months earlier. Elsie, luckily, felt the same about things. We bought a car in October, and thus ensuring more comfortable touring in future, we settled down to a life of what we thought would be undisturbed content.

In November, however, the second thunderbolt of the year descended on us, hurled by the same lord of Olympus. Another demi-official letter from the Chief Conservator to say that he had proposed to Government that I should be transferred to the newly created Working Plans Circle, to prepare a working plan for the Nilambur district of South Malabar. My headquarters were to be in Ootacamund, the best hill station in South India, if not the whole of India. But this seemed little compensation for the loss of the district which we had found so attractive and whose delights we had only begun to explore. There is good shooting of many kinds in South Coimbatore, but I had been so busy up to date, that I had not done any at all. It was all in the future, and there was no future for us in this district.

We had rather short notice to move. Elsie began packing up at once, while I made my final trip to Mt. Stuart on my own. The new plantation was at last completely planted and weeded, and though the plants which had been put in last were on the small side, the whole area was in a thriving state. The weeding of the earlier plantation had been done satisfactorily. The preparation of the area for planting next year was well advanced, and timber operations were in normal progress. I was well satisfied with the "baby" I was passing on, but it was a precious infant and I hated leaving it.

During this final camp in the bamboo huts by the new plantation, I was joined, for one night, by Mike Williams, [He was a year senior to Browne and known as Mike in his first marriage but as Charles in his second marriage. He was D.F.O. at several districts from Vizagapatam in the north east of the Madras Presidency to Wynaad in the north west between 1922 and 1939, Principal of the Forest College in 1924 and Conservator in 1940] who as Principal of the Forest College had come out to plan a tour for his students. I occupied our usual hut and he had the one at the other end of the row, with the dining hut between us. It was a wet and windy night and I had been in bed some hours when I was wakened up by the noise of a crash just outside. I immediately thought that wild elephants were having a rough game with the huts, as they sometimes do, so I picked up my rifle and rushed out. What I found was a freshly fallen tree. The crown was on the ground just in front of the huts, and the trunk lay dead in the centre of the space of about eight feet that separated my hut from the dining hut. No part of the tree had touched either hut, though if the most expert axeman had been employed I doubt if he could have felled it with such dead accuracy as to do no damage. Cold though the night was, I found myself sweating when I saw what a close shave it had been. Williams, who was a sound sleeper, had not heard the noise, and was a trifle unsympathetic when I woke him up and told him what had happened.

This is the only adventure I have had with a falling tree, though I have often wondered why forest officers do not more frequently come in the way of falling timber. The only real accident I remember, in which a tree and a forest officer were concerned, was when Dyson was impaled on the broken steering column of his car. He was driving to a tea estate in the Nilgiris along a road with big Bluegum trees [Eucalyptus] on either side. Felling was going on, but he did not know it, and the felling coolies had not troubled to warn traffic on the road and to stop cars when necessary. His car came along just as a tree was felled across the road. The tree came down on the front half of the car, doing such extensive damage that the vehicle was not worth salvaging. The steering column snapped, and one jagged half was driven through Dyson's thigh. He was pinned down in the driving seat. His peon who was in the back of the car was injured, but not too seriously, and was able to get out. The felling coolies, seeing the damage they had done, took to their heels instead of coming to the rescue. The peon had to walk about two miles before he could get help. It was an unfrequented road, and he had to go to the estate for which they were bound in any case, before finding anybody. Meantime Dyson sat impaled, bleeding away, unable to help himself, and not knowing whether he had severed an artery. He had not, fortunately. But he must have had a most anxious and painful vigil of one and a half hours or so until his planter friend was fetched, to release him and take him off to hospital. No serious damage was done, but it was a painful wound and took considerable time to heal.

Having said goodbye to Mt. Stuart I returned to Coimbatore and lent a hand with the packing. I handed over charge about the last week of November, and we went off to Ootacamund, in the Nilgiri Hills, about fifty-four miles north of Coimbatore.

Chapter VII

WORKING PLANS

A forest working plan is a treatise which lays down, in detail, the system of future management to be adopted in respect of the particular area of forest for which the plan is prepared. It is divided into two parts which are aptly described in the titles by which they are universally known. The first part is the "Summary of facts on which the proposals are based" and the second is "Future management discussed and prescribed." Part I is usually a work of very considerable length. It gives, in detail, the past history of the forest, the systems used heretofore and their results, and a description of the locality from all points of view such as topography, climate, soil, flora, fauna, lines of communication, etc., etc. It discusses the various kinds of forest produce, markets, prices, and so on, and contains a mass of statistics regarding growth and yield. The first part contains, in fact, everything which can have any possible bearing on the present condition of the forest, or which can be a guide in the future management. In striving to omit nothing which is in any way relevant, it almost inevitably happens that a good deal of matter creeps in which has no real bearing on the subject, and the serious reader of a working plan turns with relief to the second part, which is much less ponderous.

Part II lays down the general future policy in all its aspects, and then makes exact and detailed prescriptions for all works to be done for a limited number of years - usually ten - in the immediate future, after which the plan is due for revision. Such maps as are necessary for management are prepared, and "control forms" are prescribed in which the various works as actually carried out each year are to be entered for comparison with the corresponding prescriptions of the working plan.

Late in 1925 a Working Plans "Circle" was formed in Madras, with a Conservator of Forests in charge. This was a most important step in the post-War development of the forests. It was, in fact, an essential preliminary to systematic development. Earlier management, with a few notable exceptions, had been of a somewhat haphazard and opportunist nature, as was inevitable when many district were without plans and when most of the few working plans in existence had been prepared by District Forest Officers in addition to their normal work, which is, in itself, a full-time occupation. Now there was a Conservator, with no territorial responsibility, able to devote his whole time to the problems of the future and to the guidance, along suitable lines, of the

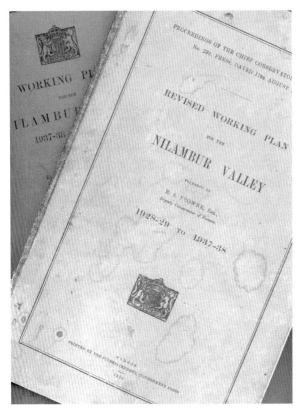

Working Plans for Nilambur.

special staff allotted for the preparation of the working plans.

Five Working Plans Officers were appointed, in the first instance, to work under the Conservator of the new circle. The Chief Conservator chose them from amongst his youngest officers, for several reasons. One was that the work was considered to be the most arduous in the department, and therefore the youngest and fittest seemed most suitable. It involved almost continuous absence in the jungle, far from the comforts of a home; hence again the young officer, who is, at least in theory, a bachelor. (I was the only one to be married at the time.) A further reason which I feel sure carried some weight was the assumption that the young officer had not had time to acquire any very strong convictions of his own, and was therefore more likely to do what he was told, without argument, than the older forest officer, who is commonly and often distinctly self-opinionated.

In Ootacamund we started off by house-hunting, and eventually arranged to rent one from the following March. I had decided that my early work would all be in the jungle, and that we would therefore have no use for a house before the hot weather.

After about a week in the hills we went down to South Malabar to make our first acquaintance with the Nilambur Valley for whose forests I had to make a working plan. Nilambur is only sixty miles from Ootacamund by the shortest route, but there had been a number of bad landslides on this hill road during the floods of 1924, and it was some years before it was cleared and opened to traffic. We therefore took the next shortest route, of about 145 miles, via Coimbatore.

Most of the road in the plains was then in poor repair, and thick in white dust. Being the main road from Madras on the east coast to Calicut on the west, it was crowded with traffic, chiefly, in those days, the lumbering bullock-cart, usually overladen, and slow to make way for a car to pass. Some 40 miles short of Nilambur we took a branch road running north-west. This passed through the beautiful, green country of Malabar, the dark green of the paddy fields in the low-lying ground between the gentle undulations which are characteristic of these inland plains. Here the road was unmetalled, but it was on laterite, a red soil which makes an excellent fair-weather road. The red of the road surface makes a pretty contrast with the green of the surrounding jungle, and the road itself winds its way delightfully through the country, serving a small village here, curving round a low hill there, and generally continuing to avoid a straight stretch of anything more than about 800 (? 300) yards at a time. Traffic on this branch road was negligible, and driving was a pleasure. The charm of Malabar was upon us.

Nilambur is a small inland village, 45 miles north-east of Calicut. It is the headquarters of the Nilambur Forest District, and the home of Teak planting. It is, in fact, the "*fons et origo*" of ordered forest management in India. About the year 1840 an enlightened Collector of Calicut became concerned about the rape of the virgin forests of the locality which had been stripped of Teak to supply the naval dockyards at Bombay. He made up his mind to start providing for the future by making Teak plantations at a time when nobody in India ever thought of planting forest trees, and there was no local knowledge of the subject. His first difficulty was land. The East India Company owned practically no land in South Malabar owing to their generous action after defeating Tippoo Sultan in (?year) [1805] of handing over the reconquered land to any of the old landowning families of Malabar who pressed their claims. No doubt many of the claims were valid but many others could not have been upheld had there been a close enquiry into the titles. The Company could easily have retained considerable forest land for the State. To obtain land for his planting project the Collector was obliged to rent it. The first of these leases was in respect of several blocks of forest land amounting to about (?) acres, most of them close to Nilambur, and it was in the leased forests that Teak planting commenced. The process of acquiring forest on lease went on for many years. The leases are terminable only at the will of Government, so permanency of tenure is secured. In the earlier leases the rent was based on the "stump fee" system, whereby Government had to pay a fixed sum for every tree of the more valuable species which they cut from time to time. Gradually, however, and often in consideration of a loan from Government to the landlord, most of the leases were revised on the basis of a fixed annual rental. With the exception of one or two blocks which were bought outright by Government at debtor's auctions, the forests of the Nilambur District remain leased forests to this day. They are, however, virtually Government property since the forest management is not hampered by their few rights, such as washing for gold, which the prospectors have reserved themselves.

The Collector put one of his Indian Office assistants, Chathu Menon by name, in charge of the planting. The latter, who had been trained amongst the ledgers of the Calicut office to the task of revenue collection, knew nothing at all about trees, but he achieved almost complete success in the second year, and remained at Nilambur for the next twenty years or so as the first forest officer.

The first planting was done in the year 1843 (?1842) in a block of some twenty miles downstream from [..............] which drains the Nilambur valley. The Teak tree is what is known as a "light demander". If denied full overhead light, it may survive, but it cannot thrive until the shade above it is removed. Chathu Menon was unaware of this when he attempted his first Teak plantation. He planted his young seedlings under the shade of the standing jungle, and most of them died within the year. He seems to have guessed the cause of his initial failure very quickly, for in the second year he adopted an entirely different method. This time he modelled his plantation on the practice of converting jungle to rice cultivation. He cut and burnt the jungle and sowed his Teak seed in nurseries similar to those used for paddy. When the monsoon came he transplanted the small Teak seedlings from the nurseries to the clearing. These operations met with immediate and almost complete success, and the method then adopted has been followed in general principle to this day. Planting operations were suspended, for different reasons, from 1894 (?) to 1896 (?) and again from 1912 to 1916, and planting had to be abandoned in 1921 and 1922 owing to the Moplah Rebellion. But apart from these temporary interruptions, a new Teak plantation has been raised at Nilambur every year since (1842?, 1843?) 1844 and at the time that I made my first acquaintance with the district in 1925, a total area of about 6,000 (?) acres had been planted. Since then the area has been expanded by about 150 acres a year. An increasing amount of revenue has been realised by the sale of thinnings from the very earliest years. But it was not till 1916 that the big money began to come in. In that year one of the oldest of the plantations was felled at the age of 72 (?), the axe being laid to the first of the mature trees by a very old resident of the village who, as a small boy, had assisted in the original planting. From then onwards some 70 acres of mature plantation have been felled every year, and replanted with Teak in the following year. The value of the trees on each acre of plantation at the time of final felling is about £200 (?) and the plantations as a whole constitute, for their size, the most valuable forest property in India, if not indeed in the world. It is a property of which the Madras Forest Department is justly proud.

This rosy picture was not, however, the one presented to me on my first visit in 1925. The Nilambur plantations had fallen on evil days, and though the original plantations were doing as well as ever, many senior officers considered that continuity was impossible, and that Teak could not again be grown on the soil that had yielded one crop. This view, if correct, would have meant a calamity, for most of the best and most accessible areas had already been planted, and the maintenance of the high value of the property depended on the re-planting of the same sites. This replanting had commenced in 1917, but by 1925 the opinion was very commonly held that the plantations of the second rotation were a failure, and the replanting of 1926 and 1927 were to do nothing to correct this impression. The problem of the second rotation was recommended to me as the most important amongst my terms of reference in taking up my new job. It was a problem with which I was to be associated for the next 6½ years. Amongst the various reasons to which I finally attributed the failure of the second rotation, I was tactless enough to include that of mismanagement. To this the inevitable answer was "Manage it yourself", and when I came back from leave after completing the Working Plan, I found myself posted to Nilambur again, this time as District Forest Officer. This however is anticipating.

A mile north of the Nilambur village is a hill some 500 feet high, with the bungalow of the District Forest Officer on the summit. It is an excellent site, and in the warm, humid climate of South Malabar the breezes one catches on this hill are more than welcome. The view from the bungalow is [.....................] nothing very much, raises it sufficiently to enable [..............] look down on the whole of the broad forest-clad valley in which it stands, and across the valley to the towering peaks of the Western Ghats. The valley has the shape of a horse-shoe with Nilambur in the open end on the Chaliya River which drains the horseshoe from north to south (?flowing 10 miles.) To the west, between Nilambur and the Indian Ocean, lies a rugged mountain range, rising to about 6,000 feet. It is undeveloped jungle in private ownership, and through lack of communications is very little known. They say in Nilambur that there are people up in these hills whose ancestors took refuge there from Tippoo Sultan, and who, to this day, are afraid to come down, and have no intercourse with the plainsmen below. I greatly doubt whether the latter part of the story is true. But I have always felt that there is a mystery about these hills. In my years at Nilambur I always meant to explore them, but in the ordinary way I could never spare the time, and later on there was the superior attraction of Ootacamund for short periods of leave or holidays, since my family was living there. So this unknown territory remains a mystery as far as I am concerned, and I have never met anyone who has been up there. I still cherish a wish to make this trip, for who knows what one might find? There might even be nuggets of gold waiting to be picked up or lodes of gold in the rock, for there is certainly gold in the sand of the Chaliya River which receives the drainage from the eastern slopes of this mountain range.

Some 15 miles north of Nilambur, at the head of the valley, the ground rises steeply to about 3,000 feet. This is the southern extremity, in this locality, of the vast plateau of North Malabar and the lower Nilgiris which extends to the small province of Coorg, and includes the greater part of the State of Mysore as well as the parts of several districts of Madras which have been mentioned in an earlier chapter. These slopes at the head of the valley are covered by forest. But being privately owned, and within reach of cheap river transport, the forest has suffered from excessive felling, and is in a degraded state. This, however, is not apparent at a distance of 15 miles, except in the muddy waters of the river which tell their own tale of erosion. The distant view is simply the delightful green of Malabar.

To the north-east and east of the horseshoe, and again about 15 miles away, lie the higher Nilgiris, steep slopes rising out of the valley to a crest-line averaging about 7,000 feet, with three outstanding peaks of which the highest is 8,300 feet above sea-level. These are truly lovely hills. Even the lower slopes are steep. The upper give the appearance of being practically vertical. Up to about 2,000 feet the forests are mainly deciduous, with a mixture of bamboos. But though deciduous, this jungle never has a bare appearance, since at the time that many of the trees are leafless the commonest tree of the lower slopes is thickly covered with what appears to be red flowers, but are really small brick-red fruits. The hillside covered with the red-topped trees is a lovely sight. Above 2,000 feet the forest is evergreen. Trees of huge proportions to begin with, but trailing off in size as one ascends above 5,000 feet, and ending in small Rhododendrons scattered amongst the grass and rocks of the highest slopes. This was the view with which I lived for about six years, but of which I never tired. Restful to the eye at all times, these towering hills seem to be covered, towards dusk, in a veil of soft purple. In the early morning, before the sun has risen sufficiently to appear above their lofty summits they wear a mantle of hazy blue. The full moon, as sometimes seen for brief moments in its ascent, balanced on the top of one of the eastern pinnacles, is a sight not to be forgotten.

The Chaliya is the main river of the Nilambur Valley, but it is augmented, about three miles north of Nilambur by the inflow of two other big rivers which rise in the hills to the north-east and east of the horse-shoe, and themselves meet some three miles above their confluence with the Chaliya. These big rivers with their smaller tributaries are the key to the success which has attended Teak planting in this district, their influence being twofold. In the first place the finest soil in the valley is the rich alluvium which they have carried down in the course of centuries and deposited high above the present water level. It is on this alluvial soil that most of the plantations have been made, and it is within 300 yards of the river that the Teak reaches its maximum development. Secondly, and of even greater importance is the facility for cheap transport which the rivers provide. There is no limit to the size of log which can be floated down the Chaliya and landed right in the market on the coast. And the cost of river transport is so low that Teak saplings of 5 (?) inches diameter, or sometimes even less, can be sold on the coast at a price which shows a profit over the cost of exploitation. This last factor makes all the difference to a tree planting enterprise. In most forest planting the difficulty in the way of financial success is the very long period which must elapse before there is any return on the capital invested. And when the return does come, it is apt to look somewhat silly deducting the capital cost plus compound interest for anything from 50 to over 100 years. In the Nilambur Valley, however, with cheap water transport, and a market which takes poles as well as big timber, one can reasonably expect that the cost of planting will have been recouped from profits on small poles by the time of the third thinning of a plantation, that is at the age of [........] years or less. Thereafter there are only the small recurring costs of maintenance to be deducted, while the profit on each successive thinning is greater than from the last, as the trees grow in size and value, until finally there is the rich harvest which is reaped at the age of 70 when the mature plantation is cut down.

On one shoulder of the hill whose crest is occupied by the District Forest Officer's bungalow, there is an unusually commodious forest rest-house known as "the Circuit House". This was our first camp in Nilambur, and it was here that I spent most of the next two years, since it is centrally situated for the plantations, and within reach of a good deal of the natural forest also.

When the Working Plans Circle first started, there was no subordinate staff to assist the Working Plans Officers. Each had to collect a staff for himself and then to train it. Nowadays things are all cut and dried, and trained staff of subordinates moves on with the Working Plans Officer from one district to another, until he or they revert to the regular line, and are replaced by others. I started off by appointing a clerk and two peons. A peon is the lowest grade of

Government Servant. He functions as a runner, and a sort of office slave. No education is required, so candidates are always forthcoming, and I picked up two with ease, one of them being quite a bright young coolie from the Teak plantations. As a clerk I selected a young Malabar man who had recently been employed in managing an "insectary" - which he and many of the locals called the "Buggary" - in which, in connection with investigations which were being carried out by the Forest Research Institute at Dehra Dun, he himself was locally known, in all innocence as "The buggary writer", until I raised his status to "working plan clerk". Field staff had to be obtained by transfer from the regular line. I applied for two rangers, and after some months one turned up. I had not expected the brightest and best, for officers tend to retain such, when told they must spare a man for elsewhere. But I was hardly prepared for what I got, and I took early steps to have him removed elsewhere. He was an elderly ranger of singularly pleasant bearing and manners, who prided himself on his honesty. He was always telling his office how perfectly honest he was, and I, for one, was quite convinced of the fact, for he had not the brains to be crooked.

The lack of field staff was no disadvantage in my early work, for it took me many months to make my preliminary inspections and decide what actual field work was required. With the exception of the Christmas holidays which we spent in Ootacamund, my wife and I toured in and around Nilambur from early December until about the middle of March.

I was attracted, from the first, by the fair and smiling land of Malabar, and was much impressed by the Teak plantations of the first rotation, and especially by the giants which were ripe for the axe. But almost without exception, a very sorry spectacle was presented by the plantations raised in the previous nine years on the sites which had carried the original Teak plantations. Large areas had completely failed. Many others were so understocked with Teak that the latter was in early danger of being completely replaced by faster growing adventitious species of no value. High floods in 1923 and the record floods of 1924 had contributed to the tale of woe, killing the young Teak outright in considerable areas, turning other areas into swamps which killed the Teak slowly, and in one place washing away a complete plantation, trees, soil and all. None but the two earliest of the new plantations was sufficiently stocked, but even these were growing very poorly, owing to the dislocation of normal management caused by the Moplah Rebellion of 1921-22, and the reconstruction which it necessitated.

Coming from Mt. Stuart where the young Teak plantations though in a much less favourable climate than Malabar were all in apple-pie order, and where Hugo Wood's tradition of successful planting was being maintained, I was somewhat intolerant of what I saw at Nilambur, and inclined to attribute more of the responsibility for failure to the management than to natural and other causes beyond their control. If I distributed the responsibility unfairly, it proved to be an advantage to do so. My criticism was directed against nobody in particular, for in the state of flux as regards promotions and transfers in the years which followed the first Great War, no officer with experience of Teak planting had remained long enough in charge of the district to ensure the success of even one year's planting, or to restore the art of successful planting when it seemed to have been lost. To attribute much of the failure, however, to faults of management, was to assume that the trouble could be at least partially overcome by improved methods, or by closer attention to the detail of the methods of the past. In this view I was much encouraged by Tommy Wimbush who had been appointed as the first Conservator of the Working Plans Circle. Nilambur was the darling of his heart. He had been in charge of the district for four years shortly before the War, and in his eyes nothing could ever be far wrong with it. He scoffed at the school who believed that the soil was played out after one crop of Teak. His conviction was not altogether free of what is nowadays called "wishful thinking". But he pointed to a good many reasons which had contributed to the sorry state of the new plantations, and set me to discover others.

During the first four months I made a general inspection of all the plantations, and of the natural forests of the plains and foothills. I inspected all forest works in progress to study the methods in vogue. Having no routine office work to do beyond paying myself, my clerk and my two peons on the first of each month, I had ample time, when indoors, to study the past history and past management of the forests, and the statistics regarding yields, costs, timber prices, etc., etc. Most of the information was available in a working plan - probably the best that India has ever seen - prepared by Bourne, and supposed to be in force from 1918 to 1927. It was a monumental work in five volumes. Unfortunately it was never sanctioned and therefore never put into operation, though some of its prescriptions had been observed. The trouble was that the plan (which included the first yield tables to be made in India) was not completed until 1921, when the Moplah Rebellion had started, and all forest work in Nilambur had come to a full stop. After the rebellion there were several years of reconstruction, in which the dispersed labour force had to be collected again; residences, offices and storehouses destroyed by the rebels had to be rebuilt, and even the working elephants had to be sought all over the forests in which they had been wandering at large - though hobbled - for the best part of two years. In these circumstances it was impossible to put an ambitious plan such as Bourne's into operation. Besides the "rot" had by then started in the ageing plantations. My job, therefore, was to draw up a plan of rehabilitation coupled with such development as could be achieved in ten years, starting out of the chaos which had prevailed for several years after the rebellion.

The nearest of the Teak plantations is about 200 yards from the Nilambur Circuit House, and a large number of them can be reached either on foot or by car from this camp. Some are on the opposite side of the Chaliya, which is unbridged except in one place near the coast. These are reached by crossing the river in a boat and walking. Several blocks of natural forest are also easily accessible from the circuit house. It is a very pleasant camp, looking up the broad river, which is 200 yards below it. One can bathe in the river but its rather muddy waters have seldom attracted me, since there is a delightful bathing pool 8 miles away.

This pool is in the eastern of the two main tributaries of the Chaliya. The water of this river is gin-clear, in striking contrast to the muddy water of the Chaliya itself and of its other small tributary, both of which have their headwaters in private forest where excessive felling on the steep hillsides causes continuous erosion. This eastern river, however, and its feeders, have their origin in a mountain tract whose forest cover has been protected by Government over fifty years. The result, as seen by the absence of eroded soil in the water, is a striking demonstration of the importance of forest conservation in water catchment areas, even though such forests may have no direct financial value.

A rock rises to a height of about 100 feet above this pool, and on top of the rock is the Nedungayam forest rest house. This is the most attractive camp in the district, its one disadvantage being that the bungalow is hot by day being made of wood and situated on the rock which in all other aspects makes an excellent site. Many of the Teak plantations of the first rotation are in this locality and extension of planting is proceeding in the surrounding jungle of the plains and foothills. About 3 miles from Nedungayam the massive Nilgiris rise out of the plain, gently at first but from an elevation of about 1,500 feet the slope becomes extremely steep [.......... ....] a busy one at most times of year. The elephant [......] in this locality [..... ....] usually about 20 [......... ....] June [........ ....] rafts of timber are made up, and started off on their journey [........ ....] or so to the coast. Felling of some kind is usually in progress. Sometimes it is the selective felling of mature trees from [..... .....] forests. At other times timber is being cut on the areas [..... ....] to be cleared for Teak planting. And every year [........ ....] timber thinned according to programme [...... ....] two months annual rest in the hot weather, timber is being [........ ....

.........] elephants being used for [.....   ....] and buffaloes yoked in pairs [........ ....]   Wild elephants [.....] these with [......... ....] Nedungayam that [..... ....] capturing [........] of the district are undertaken. Herds of bison and .... spotted deer are very common. Sambhur, too, are plentiful but they are shyer than the chital and one hears their barking noises more often than one sees them. Small game is less abundant but there are jungle fowl to be had and green pigeon. And in the old forests there are snipe in some of the open grass swamps which [...........] amongst the jungle. For several years, shortly before dark and sometimes early in the mornings, one could see from the new bungalow a sambhur stag, with a small following, come down and drink at the opposite side of the river. Two hinds were usually with him and their fawns, when at foot. We came to regard them as pets, though of course they would not want to be approached for a close-up view. One day a bloodthirsty soldier, on shooting leave, shot the stag from the verandah of the bungalow. There is nothing in the shooting rules to prohibit shooting off one's own doorstep and the stag carried a head of allowable dimensions, so it was absolutely in order, though it seemed none the less a shame. The hinds came no more to this spot; presumably they warned their new husband against it.

The other forest camps in the district consist of huts called "serambis". A serambi is a building raised on stilts. Elevation above the ground level is supposed to lessen the risk of malaria. It certainly keeps the building dry, and what is more important, it raises the fabric out of reach of playful wild elephants, which would be certain, sooner or later, to demolish such a building at ground level in remote places where the serambis have been built. There were five of these serambis and I used them all in 1926 and 1927. Three are on the opposite side of the Chaliya from Nilambur, so kit had to be carried by elephant. Another is about 2½ miles from the main road at the foot of the Nilgiris, and required elephant transport in those days, but now is served by a motorable forest road. The fifth, some eight miles from Nilambur, is reached by a fair-weather road. All of these five are in the plains, and were built mainly for inspection of work in the outlying Teak plantations. Some years later I built one in the hill forests at 2,000 feet elevation. The usual type of serambi in this district is a two-roomed hut, with a projecting platform in front, which is roofed over but has open sides except for the handrails which prevent one falling off. The building is raised about seven or eight feet above the ground on masonry pillars two feet in section. The floors and walls are of wooden planks, and the roof is tiled. The rooms are hot and stuffy in the dry weather, and I always lived and slept on the unwalled platform, except in the monsoon. The serambis are so little used in these days that they have become a home for bats, which are rather a nuisance.

A deaf elephant used to live in the vicinity of one of the serambis where Elsie and I camped several times in our early months at Nilambur. He used to stand, sometimes for hours at a time, on a cleared fire-line between a young Teak plantation and the natural jungle. I found this habit a nuisance on several occasions, for the fire-line was a convenient path to get to the work I was doing at the time, and the undergrowth on both sides was dense, and a detour not easy to make. The first time I saw this elephant, I questioned whether he was deaf as the subordinates assured me he was. We approached to within about 100 yards. The animal was standing at the side of the line, in the shade of a tree, with his hindquarters towards us, flapping his great ears, but otherwise motionless. The wind, if any, must have been from him to us. To prove his deafness the three or four men I had with me all shouted together at the tops of their voices, but the elephant took no notice whatever. They all said he was harmless, but when I suggested that we walk past him, they laughingly objected. I had no such intention myself. The elephant was a solitary tusker, and an elephant apart from his herd is never to be trusted. He had not been proscribed as a "rogue", so he could only be shot in self-defence. I had a rifle with me, but I am neither sufficiently brave nor so deadly a shot as to go trailing my coat before a wild elephant in order to provoke an attack from which I could defend myself. We therefore made a careful detour on this and other occasions when we found this peculiar elephant blocking the thoroughfare.

A complete change to the usual forest camping was provided by an occasional trip to Beypore, at the mouth of the Chaliya river. Here is the sale depot to which the bulk of the Nilambur timber is floated. It is seven miles south of Calicut, and about 46 miles by road from Nilambur. The depot is on an island of about 40 (?) acres in the estuary of the river, and is reached by ferry-boat across nearly a mile of water from the lock-up garage where one leaves one's car. Except for the foreshore facing the Indian Ocean, the island is covered with coconut palms, which grow very well in the sand of the island. A good deal of the bigger timber is stored in the salt water of the estuary, protected by a boom. But the poles, and any big timber for which there is no space in the "log pond", are dragged out and stacked on the sand, under the shade of the palms.

The forest rest-house at Beypore is a comfortable three-roomed building on the outer fringe of the coconuts, with an unbroken view to the front over about 200 yards of foreshore and then the ocean as far as the horizon. There is good bathing on the beach here, though it lacks the surf which is considered an attraction further up the coast at Cannanore. This is to all intents and purposes a private bathing beach for the forest rest-house. Occasionally a small party comes out from Calicut to enjoy it, but in frequent visits to Beypore over a period of nearly seven years, I have only once shared the beach with another bathing party. I have never heard of sharks in this locality, but it is well to keep away from the one small reef of rock which breaks the long sandy coastline, since it is apt to harbour sea-snakes, all of which are said to be poisonous. I saw one once, swimming near the rocks, with its head breaking the surface; I swam with all speed in the opposite direction, and luckily it did not choose to follow, for its speed was considerably greater than mine. Bathing here is not the shivery business it is in the British Isles. The water seems scarcely less warm than the air, and the air is warm indeed. It is very refreshing all the same.

A few Indian fisherfolk live on the island, and one can always get freshly caught fish very cheaply. These are of various kinds, the commonest being varieties of flat-fish. Excellent prawns are always obtainable, and fresh prawns curried by a Madras cook make a dish fit for a king. I never ate meat in my Beypore camps, since the fresh fish was such a welcome change to the so-called "mutton" or village fowl of my normal diet. The mutton of South Malabar is goat, and very sinewy goat at that. The climate is too wet for sheep, and besides, the soil lacks lime. The "beef" which is sometimes killed by Moplahs is buffalo, and I have never tried it for even the hardy Moplahs say it is tough. I bet it is.

After about three months of preliminary inspections and study of records, I wrote the reconnaissance report for Nilambur. The recce. report is a necessary preliminary to the preparation of a working plan. It is a detailed discussion of the forests concerned, of the methods employed and their suitability, of markets and prices, etc., etc. It suggests the methods to be adopted in future, and discusses all possibilities for future development, and for improvements in methods and communications. It makes proposals regarding the field work required in preparing the working plan, such as the nature and amount of surveying, mapping, enumeration and description of forests. On completion the report goes to all officers concerned with the district, for their remarks and suggestions. In the early days of the Working Plan Circle there was a somewhat common opinion amongst officers in territorial charge that Working Plan Officers were conceited young idiots, and that everything they said (or wrote) should be contradicted on principle. This attitude sometimes led to voluminous and futile correspondence with the recce. report as the basis for argument. Some years later an excellent standardised procedure for discussion of recce. reports was adopted, which eliminates the possibility of fatuous correspondence.

I had no cause to complain of destructive criticism of my recce. report for Nilambur, but I was embarrassed in a different manner. After the report had passed the other officers concerned, the Chief Conservator approved all my proposals, but he added a number of his own, some of which were contradictory to mine, and some others, while not contradictory, were impossible to fit in without omitting component parts of what I considered to be an ordered scheme, or which had, at any rate, been approved as such. I gave myself a headache trying to reconcile these conflicting orders, but eventually shelved the matter. The working plan was a two year job, and when I came to the final writing of it, a compromise was easily effected, for the Chief Conservator who had approved the recce. report had retired from service.

Problems often solve themselves in Government offices by this "*laissez-faire*" method. There was once a case of an officer who kept on postponing his enquiry into a very complicated charge against a subordinate, which, if proved, would entail dismissal. In due course the subordinate died, which settled the matter simply and finally.

In my recce. report I made some tentative forecasts about the vexed question of the second rotation Teak, but had to leave the problem largely in the air, pending the results of certain experiments which were then in progress, or which were suggested at this stage.

The writing of the recce. report in Ootacamund had saved me from several weeks of the South Nilambur hot weather. I returned to Nilambur - alone this time - in April. The plantations look their worst at this time of year, being leafless, and it is very hot working in them when there is no shade. But there was a much worse sight than parched, leafless plantations to be seen. In the weeks that I had been away, all the plantations above the age of 35 had been burnt, and they made a woeful spectacle with their blackened trunks, and the undergrowth, which had been carefully built up as a soil cover during the preceding (?)20 years, all reduced to ashes. This seemed the last straw - and it had been done deliberately. The tragedy was due to a misunderstanding or a misapplication of orders, I forget which. The idea of a ground fire in the older plantations originated with the Forest Entomologist of the Forest Research Institute in the United Provinces. In the previous year, after local investigation, he had written a note on the insects which eat the Teak leaves over large areas of the plantations each year. The caterpillars, after defoliating the Teak, pupate in the ground and he suggested a ground fire as a possible means of killing the insects in the pupal stage. The Chief Conservator had approved of this being tried in the older plantations but his idea was to have a very light fire early in the dry season, after the style of the "early burning" method of fire protection described in an earlier chapter. There was, however, a delay either in preparing or in getting sanction for the estimate of cost for this and other works suggested by the Entomologist, and there may have been delays for other reasons also, which I have forgotten. In any case, the upshot was that the local staff set fire to the plantations in the middle of the hot weather, when the masses of fallen leaves as well as the grass and woody shrubs of the undergrowth were as dry as tinder, with the result that I have described.

This was no laughing matter, but I remember getting a good laugh out of this same estimate for giving effect to the suggestions of the Entomologist. The latter had discovered that a certain insect - a species of bug as far as I remember - was parasitic on one of the two kinds of caterpillars which cause the defoliation of the Teak. He suggested that it would be a great help if it were possible to "build up a reservoir" of these parasites. When the estimate was sent up for sanction it contained, amongst other items, specifications and estimate of cost of a large masonry tank. The Conservator of Forests happened to be camping at Nilambur when he received the estimate, and as he did not know what the enormous tank could be in aid of, he asked the District Forest Officer what it was all about. "A reservoir for parasites" was the reply. The item was cut out, and the District Forest Officer kindly informed that the flowery language of scientific experts is not meant to be taken literally. The District Forest Officer in question was an Anglo-Indian who had risen from the ranks. He was an officer of great experience, but almost his whole service had been in the scrub jungles of the hot, dry districts, and he was not very happy at Nilambur in the last two years before he retired, since planting and timber operations on a very big scale were outside his experience.

I left Nilambur in disgust after seeing the devastation caused by the fire in the plantations. My recce. report had been submitted, and there was little I could do until I received orders on it, which could not be expected for two months or more. So I decided to make a new working plan for the coconut plantations at Beypore. The previous plan had almost expired, and was, in any case, largely inapplicable owing to the death of a considerable number of the old palms, and to the recent introduction of operations of a new type.

This job gave me a very pleasant seaside camp of about ten days in April. The weather was hot, but the coconut palms gave a good shade. I almost lived on fish, and I bathed twice a day, once after the morning's work, and again shortly before dark.

I knew as little or as much about coconuts as any other forest officer. They are outside our province, and I think this plantation at Beypore is the only coconut property in the possession of the Madras Forest Department. There were palms on the land when it was originally bought to serve as a timber depot. Later Government, on behalf of the South Indian Railway, acquired some adjoining land with the object of bringing the railway on to this island. The latter project was dropped, presumably owing to the high cost of building a very long bridge over the backwater which separates the island from the mainland on the eastern side. But the land had been taken over, so Government wished it on the Forest Department who were already on the spot. Actually it is very useful to the department. It provides land for all possible extensions of the depot which might be contemplated. It assures privacy for the rest-house, and the subordinates' quarters, and the coconut palms, with which it has been planted, bring in a good income.

[Next 9 pages missing.]
[…] practically fool-proof technique. The seedling is trimmed with a sharp knife, leaving about one inch of stem, and about nine inches of root. The root at this stage is like a young carrot. It can be planted in dry soil, and will live without rain for months if need be. In practice, however, there are always showers in April and May, before the monsoon bursts in June, and the stump sprouts at ground level, at the junction of root and stem, as soon as the soil is sufficiently moist. If sprouting is followed by a long, dry spell, the original sprout or sprouts may die, but they are usually replaced by others when more rain has fallen. The method seldom gives less than 90 per cent success from the original planting, and it is a simple matter to replace 10 per cent of failures in the course of the monsoon. It is also very simple to prune off surplus shoots, leaving one to make the tree of the future. The shoots from these stumps grow very fast in the first year, feeding in the early stages on the nourishment stored up in the year old root. Quick early growth soon gets the plants out of reach of weeds, and greatly reduces the cost of weeding. Stump planting is considerably cheaper than pitting and planting small seedlings, and there is no need of continuous rainy weather such as is required for the successful planting of seedlings. This method has now become general in Madras for planting Teak, and has been adopted successfully with several other species. It has enabled us to plant incomparably larger areas than could have been undertaken with our former methods, dependent, as they were on favourable weather and on the employment, during the short periods when the weather conditions are suitable, of a large labour force which in remote localities is often unobtainable. The early growth, also, is much better and more uniform than that obtained either by sowing seed or at stakes or by planting untreated nursery seedlings.

The greater part of my field work in Nilambur was in the Teak plantations, stock-mapping them in three qualities as indicated by the height of the trees, and making the boundaries of areas which had to be treated as failures. These areas were then surveyed by one of the two rangers who assisted me. The plantations are divided up into "compartments" averaging twenty acres each, and bounded by straight cleared lines running roughly north to south and east to west. These compartment boundaries are maintained as fire-lines, to prevent accidental fire spreading from one compartment to another. There were over 300 compartments at the time of my working plan and many more may have been added since. In addition to the stock-mapping, I had to describe each compartment from the point of view of aspect, soil, tree growth, undergrowth etc., and decide what treatment each would require in the next ten years, and the relative urgency of such treatment. As one's range of vision in a Teak plantation is limited, this meant walking back and forth through every single acre of the 6,000 and odd which comprised the plantations, and took a very long time. I was very tired of the work before I finished it. The mornings were all right, but the afternoons were hot and fatiguing, especially when the trees were leafless. I got so bored too with taking my lunch out with me day after day, that in after years I have never viewed my family's clamour for a picnic with any degree of enthusiasm. I broke the monotony of work in the plantations by occasional spells of inspection in the natural forests of the plains and foothills. I rode an elephant for a good deal of the work, both because paths were few and far between, and also because one gets a better view of the jungle from the elevations of an elephant's back. I selected the areas of natural forest to be converted into plantations in the next ten years, and decided on the areas where selection fellings of mature trees should be made. The yield of timber to be expected was estimated from the enumeration and measurements made by my staff in typical sample areas.

The Tamil language in which I had taken my examinations was of little use in Malabar, although some of the words are the same or are closely allied to Malayalam words. I had no time to study Malayalam seriously, but I acquired a smattering of the language, sufficient to give orders, and to get the general meaning of the conversation of others.

The Governor of Madras visits the Nilambur plantations at least once in his five years' tenure of office, and Lord Goschen paid us a visit about February 1927. The Chief Conservator had told him of the deer drives which were a common practice in the good old days, and promised to arrange one for his diversion. Driving deer was prohibited in the shooting rules of some districts, as long ago as 1927, but I cannot remember whether the prohibition - which soon became general - applied at that time to Nilambur. At any rate it was not considered to be good form. In actual fact, if we were not so attached to the deer by sentiment, and especially by the sentiment of preserving him for stalking, he would have been exterminated in Nilambur long ago, for he does a good deal of damage in young plantations. It fell to me to organise the drive and I was far from keen. I did not hold with this method of shooting deer, and I tried to get the show dropped by pointing out that it was the season for the stags to be in velvet, and it would only be by chance that any would be found in hard horn. My protest was unavailing, so I had to seek advice from those who remembered how the drives of the past had been organised.

Two days before His Excellency's shoot, I had a full dress rehearsal. The big herd of chital which I had often stalked in the previous year were still in their old haunts, but they might be anywhere in a stretch of country about three miles long by an average of one and a half miles wide. For the location of the rifles, I chose a cleared compartment boundary which ran in a straight line across the narrowest part of this rough rectangle of old Teak plantations. The Chaliya river was at one end of this line, and an open field of rice stubble at the other. I expected six rifles at the most, and had six "machans" erected along the line at more or less equal intervals. These "machans" or hides were in trees at a height of about eight feet above the ground, not to protect the sportsmen from the deer, but to protect the beaters from the sportsmen, and the sportsmen from each other. Further, a man in a "machan" has a better view than a man on the ground, and is less likely than the latter to be detected by the deer.

On the occasion of the rehearsal the big herd was in the plantation nearest to the Circuit House. I stationed myself in a "machan" near the centre of the line, at the top of a small rise, and the drive commenced. About twenty men were posted at intervals along the edge of the paddy field to act as stops, and prevent the deer breaking cover. The river, with its high bank, acted as a natural stop on the other side. Some forty men took part in the actual driving. They formed a line and drove the deer in front of them by gently tapping on tree trunks with sticks, and keeping themselves well back, and concealed, as far as possible, in the undergrowth. In due course the whole herd came past where I was hiding, several deer passing under my tree. They moved slowly, grazing as they went, and were not at all frightened. I saw one stag of warrantable size in hard horn; all the other stags that I saw were very clearly in velvet, the antlers looking abnormally thick, and covered with dark hair, with soft round blobs at the ends, instead of the sharp white tip of a hard horn. As a drive it could not have been better. But it did not look as if more than one of the shooting party would get the chance of a shot at a stag. Still, there was always the chance of a sounder of pig being picked up by the beaters, and the remote chance of a tiger. In any case, if the second drive proved as successful as the first, the whole party should get a fair view of a big herd of spotted deer in their natural surroundings.

On the day of the gubernatorial shoot I was out at dawn, with scouts in different sectors of the plantation to find the herd. In a short time they came to the rendezvous with their reports. The big herd was in almost the same place that it had been at the start of the practice drive two days before. There were two smaller herds in other parts of the area. So far, all was well, and there seemed little likelihood of failing to produce something for the Governor.

I went to the Circuit House and brought the party out in their cars. There was about a mile to walk from the road to the furthest position. I explained the direction from which the beat would come, and detailed the safety precautions. Since any shots from the "machans" would be directed downwards there was little danger. But to make quite sure, I stipulated that nobody should fire until the game had crossed the line. This ensured the safety of the beaters, and of the line of guns. I also warned the party that practically all the stags would be in velvet.

As the guns took up their positions, a signal was passed to the line of beaters to commence. There were five guns apart from mine. I put His Excellency in the "machan" where I had hidden two days previously, and I stood behind his tree. About twenty minutes after the beat commenced, the deer appeared. The herd was more spread out than on the previous occasion, but several animals passed under the Governor's tree, and he had a fair view of a number of the deer. One big stag in velvet passed close to us. There were three rifle shots from posts between us and the river, a right and left and a single shot. Of course I assumed the worst - that a couple of impetuous A.D.C.s had each shot a stag in velvet. But when the beaters came up the line, and the show was over, I found that all was well. One of the party had bagged a wild boar. Another apologised to me for having missed the stag he had fired at; I was much relieved, for the stag was in velvet. Everybody was pleased with the morning's recreation. I had not held out much hope of anyone getting a stag, so there was no disappointment, for everybody had at least seen the deer. The Governor was not keen on shooting a stag unless it should be a particularly good one, but he was interested in what he saw.

This was the first occasion on which I laid on a jungle show for a Governor, and I was nervous about the chances of success. I was very relieved when it was over, and only began to enjoy the day when we returned to the circuit house, to His Excellency's refreshing ale and a hearty lunch.

The only other beat in which I took part in Nilambur was when a tiger was reported in a fairly narrow strip of plantation between the Calicut road and the river. The Working Plans Conservator was on a visit at the time. It was the same place in which he had shot a tiger some fifteen years previously when he was District Forest Officer. He arranged the beat in exactly the same way as he had done then, and there seemed a very good chance that the tiger would come to one or other of us. But our luck was out. Either the beast broke back unseen through the line of beaters, or else it had moved on before we took up our positions.

There are a number of good snipe swamps near Nilambur, and I occasionally had good fun with the snipe in the cold weather. Apart from snipe, it is a poor district for small game. I got green pigeon sometimes, and an odd jungle fowl. On the last evening of my last camp before going on leave to England, I shot a fine jungle cock, and took the ruff home, to the gratification of my father who used to tie his own salmon flies.

In 1927 the planting of the second rotation Teak was again tried in conjunction with rice cultivation, although in my report on the Travancore work I had suggested that this method was not suitable on level alluvial land. The details as practised in Travancore were faithfully followed, and the results were better than in 1926. But even so the bulk of the area turned out a virtual failure, and in my working plan the association of rice with second rotation Teak was definitely ruled out for the future.

One has to apply for long leave many months in advance of the date when the leave is required. Steamer reservations have also to be made well beforehand, if one proposes to sail in the busy season. When arranging, about November 1927, to go on leave on a certain date in April 1928, I under-estimated the amount of work which remained to complete the working plan. February and March saw me in a flat spin and suffering from writer's cramp, but I just managed to complete the job in time. My main solution of the problem of the second rotation Teak planting was to dig the soil over the entire area at the end of the monsoon in which the Teak was planted, and to repeat the operation after the first showers of the year had fallen in the following April. There were various minor prescriptions with regard to the planting and weeding, and insistence was laid on early planting and timely replacement of failures. There was nothing very original about my proposals. Experiments had shown that soil working improved early growth, and it was obviously better to work the soil twice instead of once only. The first soil working, after the monsoon, was intended to prolong the growing season well into the dry weather, and this is what actually happened. I had had chemical analyses made of soil from second rotation plantations and compared them with samples of similar soil carrying natural jungle growth in the immediate vicinity. No material difference was found in the chemical composition, so it appeared that the first crop of Teak had not deprived the soil of any essential ingredient. I was quite happy about the future, myself, and was very pleased to learn that I would return to Nilambur after my leave to put my plan into operation. I was particularly keen to wrestle with the second rotation Teak, but there were also a number of new developments in other directions, and innovations of method proposed in the plan, which I wanted to see in execution.

We sailed for England early in April. I had then done nearly five and a half years in India, and Elsie well over four, and it was exciting to be home again. We did a lot of fishing in the West of Ireland in the summer and moved around quite a bit in England and Scotland, parking our young daughter as and when necessary. Many people say that they got bored stiff on eight months' leave, and long to be back at work in India before their leave is up. There is nothing like that about us. Although I must say that crawling out of the Mersey in a misty drizzle of rain of a raw November evening, the thought of the sunshine ahead was a pleasant prospect.

Chapter VIII

A PLAINS TIMBER DISTRICT

We returned to India about the middle of December, 1928. I went straight to Nilambur and took charge as District Forest Officer, and my family joined me after Christmas, by which time our furniture and household effects had arrived from Ootacamund where they had been stored during our leave.

The new Teak planting done in the monsoon of 1928 was fairly good. The second rotation area showed nearly 20 per cent of failures, which would have horrified Hugo Wood, but was actually very good as judged by recent Nilambur standards. There had been no rice cultivation to impair the drainage and suppress the young Teak; the soil had been dug after the monsoon, and the plants were still growing vigorously in December, after a month of dry weather. A small clearing in natural forest near Nedungayam had been planted with Teak stumps in conjunction with paddy, according to the Travancore method, and was doing well.

My working plan, which I had left in typescript, had just arrived in print. Owing to my leave I had been spared the job of correcting the printer's proofs for which I was very grateful.

The milk supplied by the local villagers is, like the Nilambur Valley, well watered, so we bought a cow to supply the needs of our young daughter. Malabar cows are notoriously poor milkers, since the abundant rainfall makes for a rank growth of coarse grasses which have little feeding value. The cow yielded rather less than two pints a day, but it was very rich milk, almost all cream. The supply, however, lasted only a few weeks, for the cow met with a fatal accident. She was found dead at the bottom of a disused dry well, some thirty feet deep, about a hundred yards down the hill below the bungalow. Nobody knew of the existence of this old well, which was almost hidden by long grass. I had the death-trap filled up, with the cow at the bottom of it, and was relieved that nothing more valuable had fallen in. We bought another cow, but she also failed us after about a fortnight. The trouble this time was that the calf sickened and died. No Indian cow seems to be able to function without a calf in the offing, and the milk supply dried up. The second mishap put us off dairy farming, and thereafter we had cows driven up to the bungalow and milked under supervision, to prevent dilution. This was not popular with the owners, and we had to pay a considerable premium on the milk to compensate them for the journey up the mile-long drive to the bungalow, and for their loss of profit on added water.

I doubt if our compound would have been a happy place for cows, if we had gone on keeping them. About five acres round the bungalow were cleared, except for scattered trees. Outside the clearing there was dense jungle on all sides. One morning, shortly after our cow-keeping experiments, while I was out working and Elsie was sitting on the verandah, a tiger galloped across the gravel just outside the bungalow. It had come up from the jungle by the river, and went down to the jungle on the east, right through the middle of the compound. There were always deer about, and I suppose it was taking a short-cut to waylay them somewhere. It was interesting for Elsie to see wild life like this on her own doorstep, but neither of us much liked the idea of tigers making themselves so much at home, with our young daughter playing round about the place.

I have mentioned, in the previous chapter, the magnificent view from the District Forest Officer's bungalow. The view and the somewhat cooler air of the hilltop are the only good things that can be said for the house. It was built in the old days when forest officers, if they had families, did not keep them on the spot, and little thought can have gone into its design. Though it looks an imposing pile, its rooms are few and poky. A small dining-room, a small office and a storeroom downstairs; two bedrooms each having a dingy dressing room and bathroom upstairs. The rest is verandah, which surrounds most of the house, both above and below, but it is not nearly wide enough to avoid either the summer sun or the monsoon rain. To keep out the latter, the upper verandah has been glazed in, with narrow window shutters only about one foot wide, so that their number seems to run into hundreds, especially when one has to close them hurriedly, to keep out a sudden downpour with the wind behind it. There is a porch built out in front to accommodate a car. The room above the porch is pleasing in appearance, with a magnificent view from the windows and round three sides of it, but its roof is low, and is an oven by day.

Though the bungalow is deficient in accommodation, it has the tremendous advantage of being right in the middle of most of the work of the district. In almost all other districts we have to go out on tour to get into the forests. Here the forests come right up to the door, and it is possible to visit works in two entirely different parts of the district in a single day. In fact this is what I usually did during my years at Nilambur, and the subordinates hated it, for they never knew when I would turn up, or where.

Being at the top of a high hill, the bungalow has no convenient water supply. There is a good well near the foot of the hill, whence water is carried in a barrel, drawn on a cart by a pair of buffaloes. The same arrangement operates also for the circuit house, when it is occupied, but there is never an adequate supply for both together. In the result, when the circuit house is occupied by the Chief Conservator or a Conservator, the District Forest Officer goes short, and when occupied by lesser officers, the Circuit House goes short. For many years this water supply to the District Forest Officer was free. It was simply drawn by a couple of the buffaloes which are maintained for dragging timber, and nothing was said about it. But one fine day the audit branch discovered it when going into the detailed costs of timber exploitation, and after about two years of correspondence Government decided to charge the District Forest Officer a portion of the cost of keeping two buffaloes. I was in charge when water rent was introduced, and had to pay several months' arrears. But some of my predecessors were even worse off, since they were charged back rent for years.

Our nearest neighbour was a rubber planter who lived about fifteen miles away. A company of a British regiment was stationed some twenty-five miles distant. Calicut, the only town of any size is forty-five miles away. I have, on occasion, been as long as two months alone in Nilambur, without seeing another European. But I was always busy, and the solitude did not worry me. I was very pleased to see a chance visitor, but after long spells of jungle life on my own, I used to find myself very lacking in small talk.

January and February are the lightest months of the year at Nilambur, but there is always plenty to do. I spent a good deal of my time early in 1927 marking for thinning in young plantations between the ages of ten and twenty. It is not a good time of year for this work, since the trees are leafless. But the plantations are of such extent that marking for thinning has to go on throughout the year, except when the monsoon is heaviest, and one's eyes would be deluged with rain while looking up at the crowns. At first I worked all day at the job, but found I got an excessively stiff neck through constantly looking up. Later I knocked off at lunch time, and did something else in the afternoons. The District Forest Officer always has at least one assistant. The latter officer spends almost his entire time marking thinnings. As a respite he checks and measures stocks of timber in depots, a most uninteresting task. I was very well served by my assistants while at Nilambur, and much appreciated their application to the monotonous work which was allotted to them.

There is usually a rush in these last months of the financial year to get the dragging of timber completed, partly to prevent lapse of funds allotted for expenditure within the year, and partly to allow the livestock to have their hot-weather rest in April and May. Elephants drag all the logs, and the bigger sizes of Teak poles. Buffaloes yoked in pairs, drag the smaller Teak poles got by thinning in the younger plantations. Some of these poles are so small that up to about ten of them used to be collected and tied in a bundle to make a load for a pair of buffaloes. I watched this work rather closely one morning, and after a time it struck me that the whole thing was ridiculous. There were two attendants with each pair of buffaloes. On arrival in the plantation they let the animals graze, while they themselves wandered about, collecting one sapling here and another there, and carrying them singly to a central place, in which they eventually tied up a bundle, yoked the buffaloes and proceeded with the bundle to the river bank. In many cases a man walked quite as far in carrying a pole to the central place as if he had carried it direct to the river. I gave the buffaloes a holiday and sent a couple of the men to drive them back to their camp. I then employed all the other men in carrying the poles direct to the river bank, and found at the end of the day that they had done about double the work that they would have done with the help of the buffaloes. There was nothing very clever about this discovery. From time immemorial dragging of poles was the work of buffaloes, and it had just never occurred to anybody to use any other agency. Thereafter these animals were only used for poles which were too heavy to be conveniently dragged or carried by hand. This helped out a heavy dragging programme, and greatly reduced the cost of dragging small poles.

At the end of February we started burning the areas due for planting. There is never much rubbish left to burn after felling the old Teak plantations and the clearings for the second rotation Teak.

But we had good fires in a fifty acre clearing of natural forest seven miles from Nilambur, and in another of about 150 acres in the foothills of the Nilgiris. No rain had fallen after late November, for which I was much relieved, as this was my first attempt at burning clearings since the fiasco at Mt. Stuart in 1925. The original fires spread well over the areas, and it took only two or three weeks to pile and re-burn what remained.

One job which was due to be finished by the end of March was the building of a bungalow for the District Forest Officer's assistant. This however was quite impossible. On my arrival just before Christmas nothing had been done except to prepare some of the timber, and to level the site. The building was to be of laterite stone, and the stone had first to be quarried and then thoroughly dried. I thought that with luck I might complete the job by the end of May, but this also proved impossible, and we had to erect a thatched structure over the unfinished building to keep the rain out of the walls during the monsoon, and leave its completion until October.

As soon as the weather warmed up in early March, I took my family to Ootacamund where we had rented a small house for the hot weather. On my return to Nilambur, after a few days in the hills, I had the very important job of fixing up the two big contracts for the coming year, one for floating the timber of the Nilambur range, and the other for the supply of grain for the livestock of the district. In my working plan I had drawn attention to the excessive cost of many works at Nilambur, and particularly of these two contracts, and I was determined to effect a reduction. Both contracts had been held by one man for several years, and as far as the floating contract was concerned it was difficult to interest anybody else, since we insisted on security owing to the value of the timber handled, and also because the contractor had to make a big initial outlay by way of advances to coolies, hire of elephants, purchase of ropes, etc.

This time I managed to attract a number of tenders from small merchants for grain, by dividing the contract into three parts, one for rice, one for grain, and one for ragi. Here, too, the security deposit we required for the whole of the supply had been more than the small man was prepared to lay down. The tenders for grain were lower than in previous years, but not low enough, and I rejected them all and called for tenders again, before getting quotations which I considered reasonable.

To get the floating rates reduced was not so easy, although I had let it be known for some months beforehand that if there were not a big reduction in tendered rates, we would do the work departmentally. This was bluff. We had not enough elephants to undertake this work in addition to our ordinary dragging, and we could not spare the staff to supervise the work and escort convoys of rafts, without detriment to other work. So while we could have done the work if my bluff had been called, it would have been with the greatest difficulty, and other works would have suffered.

I succeeded in interesting one other tenderer, in addition to the old floating contractor. The rates tendered by both of them showed some reduction on previous years, but not nearly enough. I rejected both tenders, and when advertising for fresh tenders I fixed maximum rates for the different localities in which the timber was lying. This innovation ensured a big reduction, provided I got any tender at all. Both men tendered again, and the old contractor was successful. This was very satisfactory since he knew the work, and I was somewhat doubtful of his competitor's efficiency and ability to carry out a difficult contract.

The saving on these two contracts, by comparison with the previous year's rates, came to about 60,000 rupees, and I was extremely pleased with myself. If only I could make a success of the second rotation Teak, I should soon be able to say "I told you so" - which is a great satisfaction when one is very young.

I had no trouble with these contracts in succeeding years. As far as floating was concerned there was no further competition. The reduced rates allowed a good profit to the contractor, but he had to work for it, and since the contract ceased to be regarded as a means of getting rich quickly, nobody else came into the field. In the next three years, though I had to go through the formality of calling for tenders, I eventually fixed the rates by negotiation - or rather endless arguing - with the old contractor, and the work went smoothly.

One year the lowest tender for one item of the grain contract was submitted by a man of straw. He could not pay the full security deposit in cash, but he offered me his tea shop in Calicut as security. I said I did not want a tea shop, so he then suggested his wife's jewellery. I was not interested in the stones, however beautiful they might appear, but asked him for details of the gold. He gave me the approximate weight of gold, and I made a rough calculation of its value. It was not nearly enough, so I asked him if that was all the gold he could offer. "Oh no, Sahib," he replied. "My wife's mother has much gold in her teeth." We came to some compromise in the end, without the necessity of inflicting forcible dentistry on the mother-in-law in the event of failure of the contract.

In April and May I was chiefly concerned with regeneration work. In the natural forest clearings of the year there was alignment of stakes, followed by planting Teak stumps in the big clearing in the foothills, and sowing seed of rosewood and other species in the smaller clearing where the soil was unfit for Teak. In the clearings for second rotation planting, pits had to be dug before the monsoon, preparatory to planting nursery seedlings. Weeding was in progress in the various plantations of the previous year. This operation, in the case of the second rotation plantations, consisted of digging the entire area with forks constructed for use with the action of a mattock. This was one of the special prescriptions of the working plan, and when it was done in the previous autumn the cost was exorbitant. It was admittedly very hard work, and unpopular with both coolies and subordinates, and when daily wages were paid the progress was miserable. I was assured that no better progress was possible, at any rate in the hot weather, so I took my shirt off and spent a morning digging. I raised a crop of blisters and an almost unquenchable thirst

[NEXT 2 OR 6 PAGES MISSING]

[...] are Indian tea-shops and eating houses here and there along the banks, where the raftsmen tie up for a meal, or spend the night.

I never felt like sparing the time to go the whole way down to the coast on a raft; it would, in any case, be very monotonous after the first day. But the first few miles below Nedungayam, which involved shooting rapids, are good fun when the river is running fairly high, and I did this part of the trip several times.

At the time I was making my working plan, the main obstacles in the way of large-scale exploitation of timber from the natural forests round Nedungayam were the short floating season in the upper reaches, and the difficulty in collecting enough bamboos, within reasonable reach, for floats. To get over these difficulties it was proposed to extract a portion of timber by road, which meant building two big girder bridges, one over a tributary of the Nedungayam river, and one over the latter river itself. The first of these two bridges was commenced before I went on leave, and the second was completed in 1932, some four years later.

During the period of bridge construction I had proposed to divide the exploitation of each year between the Nedungayam river and the other big tributary of the Chaliya some six miles further north. This was actually being done, but even so I found in 1929 that we had more timber at Nedungayam than we could deal with, owing to failure to float the whole stock of the previous year before the water became too low, and also to a bigger yield of Teak from thinnings than had been estimated. In these circumstances the range officer of this range had a brainwave. He got a few strong dug-out boats of about thirty feet length, and tied two big logs to each. The logs lay in the water parallel to the boat, and the latter gave the buoyancy necessary to float them. The first trip was made without difficulty, and we developed this method to such an extent during the next few years that the problem of floating completely disappeared. The method was subsidiary to that of floating with bamboos, since it was slightly more expensive. The boat rafts were much more manageable than bamboo rafts, and made the journey to the coast very quickly. It was fortunate that nobody had thought of this means of floating before the bridge construction was well under way, otherwise the bridges might never have been sanctioned. As it is, they have been a great boon in providing facilities for touring and inspection at all times of year, and they will, eventually, carry their share of timber, when development proceeds beyond the capacity of the river.

[Here followed a page on auctions]

I liked the monsoon season at Nilambur better than any other. It is the coolest time of the whole year, and there is any amount of interesting work going on. When the original planting is over there is a good deal to be done by way of replacing failures. There is also weeding, and it is a rush to get this done before the weeds suppress the young plants. Growth is so fast at this time that one can almost see things growing, and the difference that even a week makes in a young Teak plantation is most noticeable. Felling, dragging and floating are interesting enough, but I found it required an effort to devote sufficient of my time to them, in the face of the superior attraction of the young plantations during the marvellous growing weather of the monsoon. At this time, too, there is always the possible excitement of a flood, though this can hardly be reckoned as an attraction in view of the worry it involves, and the damage it may bring in its train. I was spared this worry in my first year as District Forest Officer, but I was to know all about it a year later.

I never found a raincoat which could keep me dry for more than a few hours when the monsoon was at its heaviest. A sailor's oilskins might do, but they would be uncomfortably warm to walk in. I very soon gave up the idea of trying to keep completely dry, and simply wore a shirt and shorts, and carried a cheap umbrella which kept my head and shoulders dry, and enabled me to light and smoke a cigarette, or a pipe, in comfort. For the rest of me, I was wet all day, but constant movement kept out the cold. A hot bath at night was very comforting, after which I had dinner and settled down to the day's office work. In the monsoon the indolent Malabar cooly excels himself as a late starter, so I could sit up till 1 a.m. and still have time for plenty of sleep before next morning's work.

The monsoon season has one final advantage in that the District Forest Officer is left in peace. Nilambur is the most important timber district in Madras, and as such it comes in for a great deal of inspection by superior officers of the department, and sometimes of the Government. It is also a show place, with its continuous record of one hundred years of Teak planting, and attracts visiting officers from other provinces of India, and occasionally from the Colonies. But with a rainfall of 120 inches, of which the greater part falls between early June and late August, the monsoon weather is considered to be much too foul except for the man on the spot, and he is left as undisputed monarch of all he surveys.

I spent the last fortnight of September 1929 in Ootacamund with my family, thus finishing my month's "recess" of which I had taken the first half in May. September is a good month in Ootacamund. The monsoon is over, and the trout are in fine condition and usually very lively. There are also the festivities of "Hunt Week", ending up with the point-to-point races of the Ootacamund Hunt. For followers of the royal and ancient game there are golf competitions. The rolling downs, after three months of rain, are a vivid green, and the whole country looks delightful when the sun comes out again.

We moved down to Nilambur at the beginning of October, with a much larger family this time, with two children and two "ayahs". Keeping children in India is like keeping horses - one horse one "syce" (groom), one child one "ayah". But there is a limit, and we reached it once when we had three children and three ayahs, and one of the latter was a dud. We dispensed with her services, and never again employed more than two "ayahs", even when our family increased to four.

The final weeding of the year in the new plantations is done as soon after the monsoon as possible, to allow the young plants to take full advantage of the good growing weather which continues until the end of November. Some pruning is necessary at this stage, to remove surplus shoots, subsidiary leaders and stout side branches.

Floating continues until November. Felling, of some kind or another, goes on throughout the year, and dragging is always in progress except during two months in the hot weather when the livestock get a rest.

Above Nedungayam the river is too rocky for floating, so that all timber from the forests higher up has to be carted to Nedungayam during the dry season before floating. A cart-road continued up the valley for about five miles, and has since been extended. Temporary cart-tracks are taken into the forest from the main cart-road, to reduce the lead for dragging by elephants from stump-site. Buffaloes are employed for carting. When the logs are too heavy for one pair of buffaloes, a second pair is added, and occasionally a third. In this way logs up to about 3 (?) tons in weight can be removed; but such heavy loads are pretty severe on the road when carried on a single pair of wheels.

Living in the bosom of my family again, I modified my bachelor habits to the extent of coming home to lunch several days a week, instead of staying out all day and every day. The latest arrival was not of an age to take much interest in the countryside, but our elder daughter was now three and a bit and had quite definite views on what she liked, which was to go out in the car and to bathe in the river, and to see the elephants. We managed to supply all these requirements. We often went there of an evening and practically always on Sundays, for I usually inspected the elephants in their camps on Sundays, this being their day of rest. Near home we had a fine bathing beach for a child, about two miles from our bungalow, which we often visited. It was at the confluence of the two main tributaries with Chaliya, and there in the dry weather the water was scarcely two feet deep and there was a large expanse of sand. Our little daughter preferred this to Nedungayam, where the water is deep, and the beach mainly stones and pebbles.

The dry season of 1929-30 brought the usual spate of fair-weather visitors. The Chief Conservator came about November to see how the "new broom" had been sweeping. He thought I was talking big when I said I had over 98% success in the new plantations of the second rotation. So we had a bet on it. He was to count one hundred plant spaces in any rows he liked to choose, and if he found more than one failure in any series of 100, I would lose five rupees. There were none missing in either of the first two lots of a hundred that he counted, so he gave me best. All the young plantations were in a flourishing condition at this time. The response to two soil-working operations in the 1928 plantation of the second rotation was very marked, and we had made good the failures of the previous year. I think this was the first time that general opinion began to sway in favour of optimism for the future of the second rotation. I had, by now, no doubts about it myself, but it required another two years to eliminate argument.

The Inspector General of Forests, India, was with the Chief Conservator on this tour. He had spent most of his service in Burma, which is the real home of the Teak, and I found his comparisons very interesting.

My chief new interest in 1930 (apart from a third daughter born later in the year) was the shifting of the second clearing and planting in natural forests, from the foothills beyond Nedungayam to a place called Nellicutta, close to the foot of the ghaut road leading up to the Nilgiris.

Two small Teak plantations had been made here in the years 1872 and 1873, after which the locality had been abandoned, owing to the anxiety of malaria. There is a "serambi" here, but it was scarcely used at all since the place was considered to be a death trap. The soil, however, was the best which remained unplanted in the whole valley, and there were about (?) thousand acres suitable for Teak. The Teak of 1872 and 1873, though very badly damaged in the early years by wild elephants, showed many individual trees of magnificent growth. The Nellicutta reserve is bounded on the east and south by the northernmost of the two big tributaries of the Chaliya, so it contains a good deal of the river alluvium which has proved to be the ideal soil for planting Teak at Nilambur. Away from the river there are several low hills with gentle gradients and good deep soil except at the very top. Between the hills there are grass swamps and swampy forest at the lowest levels, which have to be carefully avoided in planting, since Teak does not tolerate bad drainage. Nellicutta was attractive enough as a planting proposition to make it worth while spending extra money on the work, and in the working plan I had proposed to buy a lorry to transport coolies daily to the spot, in case the place were found to live up to its unsavoury reputation for fever.

The locality proved to be feverish, but no worse, in my opinion, than many other parts of the foothills. We built huts for coolies, but they were not very much used. Most of the men preferred to walk as much as eight miles from their homes in the morning, and the same back at night. My idea of bringing coolies from Nilambur, some fourteen miles away, was not feasible, since the work at

Nilambur employed all the available labour, so we were saved the expense of buying a lorry. I frequently camped at Nellicutta during the next two years, and was fortunate enough to avoid malaria, myself. Most of the subordinates and coolies suffered from fever off and on, but not more often than in the forests round Nedungayam where they normally worked. The only real anxiety I had on the score of health was once when we were particularly busy, and had a lot of coolies camping on the spot. Without any warning a cooly was stricken with cholera, and was dead within an hour. We burnt the body promptly, and disinfected the huts and surroundings. I was fearful of an epidemic which, apart from the toll it would take of life, would mean good-bye to planting at Nellicutta for that year. Luckily it turned out to be a sporadic case, which was not repeated.

Quintus with his wife and son.

There was a minor scare during another of my camps at Nellicutta. About nine o'clock one night a cooly came running to the "serambi" to say that there was a very big snake in their hut, which had chased out all the coolies. I went to investigate with a petrol lamp, and a rifle not having my shotgun in camp. The snake was there all right, a python about twelve feet long. I collected the scattered coolies behind me so that they could not get in the line of fire, and I shot the snake in the head with the rifle. The python, though a big snake which will kill and eat a small dear, does not attack men, nor are its fangs poisonous. The white-tanned skin is very pretty and can be made into attractive knickknacks for ladies such as handbags, shoes, belts, writing cases, etc. I shot several other pythons in the foothills during my years in Nilambur. They are fairly common, though one does not often come across them.

The first clearing at Nellicutta was about 250 acres, and we burnt it at the end of February. In these forests the original burning of a clearing is done at night, because there is less chance of strong winds than by day, and therefore less likelihood of fire escaping into the surrounding forest. As a further safeguard we used to clear a fire-line all round the area to be burnt, and about fifty yards outside it. Fire escaping into this fifty yard belt of standing forest could be put out before it reached dangerous dimensions, and the cleared line prevented it creeping out unnoticed. A large gang of men was distributed all round the perimeter of the clearing, armed with leafy branches, to watch for escaping fires and to beat them out. We set light to the clearing just after dark, firstly in a few places in the middle, and then all round the perimeter. It was a fine blaze, and went on burning all night. It is common to see animals of various kinds escaping from the fire when big clearings such as these are burnt, and I had a rifle with me, hoping to have a pot at a pig. I saw a few deer breaking away, but nothing else in the animal line. Towards morning, however, I shot a python as it was making its way down the river bank in the south of the area. Burning is hot and thirsty work and I drank several bottles of beer in the course of the night. About 7 a.m. when the fire was dying down, I went back to the "serambi" where I was camping, and had a much-needed bath followed by breakfast, after which I went to bed for a few hours.

As far as I remember this 1930 plantation at Nellicutta was the first big one that we planted completely by the new method of Teak stumps, and it was most successful. Being a remote locality, there was not much enthusiasm for rice cultivation, but a few cultivators tried their luck in about 50 (?80) acres and got quite a good harvest; though they had to do quite a lot [...]

[...] healthy but the rain is too severe [....] out of doors. The air, too, is so saturated with moisture that even in a house it is impossible to keep clothing dry and it goes mouldy and grows whiskers in the damp almost immediately.

In my first inspection I had ranted at my predecessor for his excessive caution in siting depots on the tops of hills for storing the timber of the final fellings prior to floating. This almost doubled the distance for dragging, for he had dragged them up the hill and then I had to drag them down again, to get them down to the river. In my second year I placed all such depots on the top of the river bank, leaving trees standing in the depot sites, partly for shade and partly to secure the logs in case of flood.

Shortly before the monsoon we roped the timber in the depots and anchored the ropes to the standing trees. In a normal year the river does not come above the bank at all, except in places where the latter is unusually low, and such places are avoided as storage depots. We got some of the timber away in the first few weeks of the monsoon. Then came a very heavy period of rain, so we closed down on floating for the time being, and prayed for fine weather. I fear my own prayers were half hearted, for I was still child enough to think that a flood would be good fun. Anyway, the flood came. We did further roping of timber as the river rose. Eventually the water overtopped the bank by six feet or more in most places. For three days the high ground on which my bungalow stood was an island. Many of the houses in the Nilambur village, a mile away, were under water, and the less substantial of them collapsed. The middle of the village is on high ground, which saved my office, the range office and the quarters of the subordinates. I had to use a boat across half a mile of water to get to my office, instead of going down the road.

I spent most of the three days of flood visiting the various places where timber was stored on the river banks. We had a good many boats out, and poled them about in the plantations, securing the logs that had broken adrift from the depots. Fortunately most of the Teak, both from final fellings and thinnings, was on the Nilambur side of the Chaliya, for it was impossible to cross the roaring flood that was coming down the main channel.

Teak logs are too heavy to float to the coast without bamboos. They are buoyant enough to move about in the water almost submerged, for some days, until they become so water-logged that they sink. The timber in the depots was stacked in two tiers, the logs of the upper tier lying at right angles to those of the lower. Since the roping had been done after stacking, it had not been possible to get at every log in the bottom row to tie it. Thus, when the flood came, and the stacks rose up in the water, odd logs from the lower tiers were washed out of the stacks, and floated off, if not spotted and roped by the parties working from boats.

Stacks of logs are well known as hiding places for snakes, and when checking depots one has to be on the look out for them. During this flood I realised how very numerous are the snakes which make their homes amongst the logs, for they could be seen everywhere, marooned on the top rows of the stacks, or on single logs floating down the river. Most of them were harmless rat snakes, or grass snakes, but we killed a number of cobras.

The timber depots of Nedungayam and Nellicutta were not affected by the flood. These places are a good deal higher up the valley than Nilambur, and there is sufficient fall below them to carry the flood water away without breaking the banks to any extent.

In the vicinity of Nilambur parts of the young plantations of the year and of previous years were submerged, but of course nothing could be done about it while the flood lasted.

When the water subsided I made a hasty survey of the damage as far as young plantations were concerned. Small Teak plants which had been under water for some days were dead, and we replaced them as soon as the deposit of mud dried sufficiently.

It was impossible to discover our loss in timber without a complete check. I had two assistants at this time, and they and I, as well as several rangers, were occupied for nearly a fortnight in taking stock. In the end we discovered that the flood had left us with more timber than we had before it. But when we had got half-buried logs out of the mud, and verified all marks, it became clear that we had salved a lot of timber belonging to private forest owners, which had to be returned to them. I sent a ranger down to the coast by boat. He identified several dozen Government logs and poles which had been salved along the river by locals, and he paid the usual salvage fee of, I think, a rupee each. There must have been upwards of 30,000 logs and poles in the riverside depots which were affected by the flood, so I felt I had come out of the business very luckily. As a result of this experience I continued my practice of roping timber on the top of the bank during the next two years. I did not have the worry of another serious flood, and there was a great saving of money and of elephant power, as compared with the former practice of stacking on high ground away from the river.

There is a good deal of rather poor natural forest near Nilambur where the soil - a disintegrated laterite - is not deep enough to grow good Teak. In the working plan I had proposed to plant fifty acres of this type of forest each year, by way of large-scale experiment, leaving the choice of species and of method to the District Forest Officer. I tried various species and methods myself, between 1929 and 1932. I was very keen on rosewood, which is more valuable than Teak, when it reaches large size, and is a beautiful wood for furniture, veneers etc. It is found, here and there, growing quite well on soil of this kind, but it seems to have some aversion to being concentrated. I got good results in the first year both by direct sowing of seed, and by planting stumps. But many of the plants died in the hot weather, even though I planted them in some places under standing jungle trees, and in others under the shade of a kind of lentil specially sown as a nurse.

I had considerable success with a tree called Xylia, one of several species known as "iron-wood" for obvious reasons. Its timber is used for railway sleepers, and is therefore valuable. But there is not much point in spending money on raising this tree artificially in Nilambur, since it comes in naturally in large quantity, on the type of soil with which we were dealing.

Timber being floated down the river from Nilambur to Calicut.

The two species with which I had complete success were the West Indian mahogany, and the cashew nut. Mahogany had been grown experimentally in Nilambur in the eighteen nineties. In thirty years it had attained a girth of six to eight feet on the shallowest of soils. It almost invariably forked low, but in view of the rapid growth in girth, a bole of even twenty feet long yielded a very good volume for its age. The only trouble was that the timber merchants would not work at it. They are very conservative, and suspicious of anything new. In time they may come to appreciate mahogany, but while there was so little prospect of selling the timber, it did not seem worth while growing this tree on any considerable scale, so I tried something else, after making a couple of small plantations.

The Cashew is a tree of South America which came to the West Coast of South India centuries ago, with the Portuguese. It is very common as an occasional tree in native gardens along the western seaboard, but its commercial possibilities have been very tardily recognised. About 1925 a European firm on the west coast of Madras started to buy the nuts and prepare them for export. America, where they know a good edible nut when they see it, has been the chief importer, but recently the cashew nut has been finding its way to England and other European countries, and the supply is not nearly equal to the demand. There has been some private planting of the nut in recent years, but when I tried about fifteen acres in 1930(?), a plantation of even this modest size was unknown. We sowed the seed direct in a clearing, and the experiment was an immediate success. The area had to be closely watched during the few days which elapsed between sowing and germination, since the nuts are so tasty that not only do monkeys go for them, but we found the small boys of the village grubbing about at the stakes and collecting the nuts we had sown. The tree grows fast, and starts to bear fruit in four to five years. When in full bearing a plantation cashew should be extremely profitable. But I do not think much has been done in this line since I left Nilambur. The forest department plants for timber, not for nuts, and my cashew nut venture, though successful, found no great favour. The financial aspect of my profession has, however, always had a strong appeal for me. I would not advocate planting forest land with cashew nuts or any other nuts or fruits, in competition with private enterprise. But where private interests are not involved, I see nothing whatever against it, and I would even grow trees for their flowers if I thought there were money in it.

I spent about a week in Ootacamund in the middle of the monsoon of 1930, when our third daughter was born, but took the greater part of my "recess" in the hills in September. We had a memorable Christening party during Hunt Week. Another "abandoned" wife had been spending the hot weather with my family in Ootacamund, and had had a baby about a week before ours. Our second daughter had not been Christened at the normal time in the previous year. We either forgot or postponed it, and eventually went down to Nilambur for the cold weather with the child still in a state of original sin. In September 1930, with three infants in the house unbaptised, we decided to do the right thing in style. As a preliminary I went to the registrar of births and other vital statistics, to register our two, for I had forgotten the matter of registration also in the previous year. I registered the later birth first, which was quite in order, but when I came to our second daughter who was by then fifteen months old, the Indian clerk was very doubtful. He spent a long time consulting books of rules, and finally came to me and said, "I am very sorry, sir, but the child is time-barred." Apparently births have to be registered within six months. He suggested that if I moved in the matter of getting permission for late registration, I might be prosecuted for having evaded the law, so "time-barred" the child remains, so far as Indian registration is concerned.

At the triple baptism the two new-born infants were dealt with first, and slept peacefully through the ceremony. Our second daughter meanwhile had been running round the font - she was very precocious on her feet - taking a great interest in the proceedings, laughing at what was happening to the babies, making faces and noises at her friends in the congregation, and generally being the life and soul of the party. Then her turn came. The parson grabbed her, lifted her into his arms, and proceeded to baptise her, and he did not spare the water. This did not appeal to her at all and she disgraced us by howling the house down.

From the church we repaired to the Club, where we had reserved the ladies' section for the afternoon. Ootacamund was unusually full, with visitors up for Hunt Week in addition to residents, and as both families had invited all our friends, we had a large representative gathering. Champagne flowed freely, and I think a good time was had by all. Elsie and I certainly enjoyed our multiple Christening party - much more so, I am sure, than if two or more of our daughters should ever decide to leave us by way of a multiple wedding.

Early in October we returned to Nilambur, this time with three children. We had only two "ayahs", but we had two cars by then, since the family when together was rather a crowd for one, and besides we needed one car in Ootacamund and one in Nilambur for the greater part of the year. The inconvenience of the bungalow became more apparent as our family grew in size. Catering for children, too, was very difficult. The milk problem grew no easier. The bazaar chickens were usually tough. We used to get fish sent from Calicut on ice, but the bus service was unreliable. The journey of forty-five miles took anything from four to eight hours, and the fish often arrived bad. To put the finishing touch to these domestic trials, all three children were stricken with an obscure fever round about Christmas, and we spent the holidays nursing them, usually two at a time. Nilambur has no doctor of standing. We consulted both the Indian sub-assistant surgeon, and also the vet. employed to look after the Government elephants, but neither was helpful. They said it was just fever. We knew that, without having recourse to experts. But temperatures ran very high, and the youngsters were much pulled down after two bouts of two days each, with a day's respite in between. We were so concerned by this visitation that we decided to take the children to Ootacamund as soon as they were better, and not to bring them down to Nilambur again. We had a house in Ooty on an indefinite lease, so there was no difficulty in giving effect to this decision. We made the move in February 1931, and I spent my last fifteen months in Nilambur alone.

Except during the monsoon it is usual to hold auctions of timber at Beypore about once a month. This made a pleasant break of a couple of days by the sea. When living alone at Nilambur, I sometimes spent a night in Calicut following an auction, to see something of my fellow man. They had a custom of long standing in the Malabar Club which I believe has since died out. This was the sociable (or unsociable) bachelors' weekly dinner held every Saturday night. The description of bachelor was applied in its widest sense, and included all adult males. Any visitors who turned up were the guests of the residents, or it may have been the other way round. I do not remember, and it does not greatly matter, for they used to be cheery gatherings, and I sometimes timed an auction so as to coincide with this stag-party. As far as I remember dinner was never before ten p.m., and often later. Team games on billiard tables and other frivolities prolonged the evening until the small hours. Eventually most of the revellers slept in the Club whether they had homes of their own in the town or not. I unfortunately missed the memorable occasion when a rubber planter from Borneo thought the Malabar idea of a cheerful evening much too dull, and proceeded to shoot the place up light-heartedly with a revolver.

We planted another big natural forest clearing in Nellicutta with Teak in 1931. Both this and the area planted in the previous year made most vigorous growth, and fully justified the small extra cost of planting in this remote and feverish locality. I was very proud of these two plantations but the apple of my eye was the second rotation Teak planted in 1931. There were three compartments, totalling about seventy acres. The nearest of the three was only about 400 yards from my bungalow, and even before the old Teak was felled I guessed this compartment was going to be something out of the common. The soil was all deep river alluvium, and the drainage was perfect. The area was triangular in shape, with the Chaliya draining one long side from the base to the apex, and a small tributary draining the other long side. Many of the old trees were magnificent specimens of nine or ten feet girth and about 150 feet total height. When clear-felled and cut into logs the timber lay so thick on the ground that it looked as if nearly half the area would be required for storage space prior to floating. But luckily there was some spare land outside the compartment, to which we dragged all the timber, thus leaving the whole of the felled area free for replanting. We had not, at that time, adopted stump-planting in second rotation areas, otherwise the results might have been even more spectacular than they were. To give the plantation a flying start I had the pits sown direct with Teak seed in April. Two months of occasional showers produced germination in over 60 per cent of the pits, and many of these seedlings were a foot high and growing vigorously when the monsoon started in June. We planted seedlings straight away in the pits which showed no germination and replaced the odd casualties as they occurred. Weeding and soil working were carried out well, and at the appointed times, and there was no stopping the Teak growing. I was so fascinated by this area that I used to visit it practically every evening that I spent in Head Quarters, for six months after planting. During the monsoon I would plant seedlings in the odd blanks I found, but there were never many of these, and by the cold weather I would have offered heavy odds against anybody finding one plant missing in an acre, which is a tall order at the spacing of six feet by six feet, giving 1210 plants to the acre. Before it was one year old this plantation was well above my head, and I am a generous two-yard measure in my boots. Though a second rotation area, it was streets ahead of the highest quality Teak of the first rotation at the same age. Taken as an isolated example it would have been unwise to consider this compartment as other than a freak. But by this time all the second rotation Teak, which had been planted from 1928 to 1931 inclusive, was up to the original standard of the first rotation crops. The bogey of the second rotation had been laid.

Chapter IX

ELEPHANTS

Wild elephants are common throughout the moister forests of the Western Ghats, and their subjacent valleys from the Bombay Presidency to Travancore. East of the Ghats proper, they are also found in well-watered parts of the Mysore State, and of the districts of Coimbatore and Salem.

They are protected under the Wild Elephant Protection Act, and may not ordinarily be shot except in self-defence, or when they invade private property. Individual animals are proscribed as "rogues" when proved to be a danger to human life, and, in the Madras Presidency, they may then be shot by holders of game licences covering the forests concerned. It is unfortunate that the proscription of a rogue can seldom be effected until he has taken one or more lives, since the first warning of danger is usually that a man has been killed. Of recent years we have notified all solitary male elephants as rogues. This has probably resulted in a small saving of life. It has undoubtedly resulted in the shooting of a number of innocent animals, since though a solitary elephant is always to be suspected, he is not always a rogue, and sometimes goes back to the herd after a short spell of solitude. The destruction of a few innocents with the guilty is not, however, a matter of moment, since we have elephants enough, and to spare. I am not aware of any attempt to obtain rough statistics of wild elephants in Madras, but the general impression is that they are on the increase.

The only use of the wild elephant is to keep up a supply of animals suitable for capture and training, either for work or for ceremonial such as temple service or adding to the magnificence of a Rajah's retinue. For these purposes the supply is much more than adequate, and some judicious thinning out would do no harm. It would, on the other hand, reduce the very considerable annual loss for which elephants are responsible. They cause much damage to the crops of villagers who cultivate fields near the forests. Tea, coffee and rubber estates, similarly situated, also suffer considerably. Within the forests, damage is not usually noticeable since the area of the forests is vast. Young plantations, however, are very susceptible to injury, especially if made in small clearings in the jungle.

Loss of life due to attack by wild elephants in Madras is inconsiderable. I am unable to remember figures, but these are published annually by the Government. Most of my service has been in districts inhabited by elephants, but I have only twice been near the spot when people have been killed. The first

Catching elephants for training, Kargoodie.

time was at Nilambur when one of a gang of women cutting grass for the Government buffaloes was the victim. The elephant was never heard of again. It was in the hot weather, and he left no tracks which could be followed. The other was in the lower plateau of the Nilgiri district. One night a man was watching a rice crop in an enclosure in the forest. He was (presumably) sitting in one of the roofed shelters, raised about five feet off the ground, which are made by the cultivators to accommodate watchers engaged in scaring away pig, deer, etc. His body was found a few feet away from the hut, so he must either have been pulled out of it by the elephant, or else been caught while trying to run away. An elephant, when he kills, is very vindictive about it. He pounds his wretched victim to pulp with his feet, as well as goring him with his tusks. High explosive does not make a sorrier mess of a man. I followed the elephant until I lost his tracks, and I lay in wait for him the next night in the hope that he would return to the rice field. But he had gone right away from the locality. He had, however, been seen about the place before the accident. We had a fair description of him and I got him proscribed at once. He was shot several weeks later by a game licence holder, some ten miles from the scene of his crime.

The only accident involving a forest officer during my service occurred in the Ganjam district in the north-east of Madras before its transfer to the province of Orissa. There were, I believe, only four or five elephants in the whole district, so it was unusual to come in contact with them. The officer in question was, however, chased by a tusker. He had no rifle, so had to trust his legs, ineffective though they are, for an elephant can move faster than a man, and nothing is an obstacle to him. In making his escape the officer took a bad toss - amongst rocks as far as I can remember - but luckily the elephant left him to follow one of his subordinates. The elephant caught none of the party, but the officer had broken his leg so badly that he was never again fit for the active outdoor life of the forest department. Still, it is an ill wind that blows nobody good. For the next fifteen years or so he worked in the head office in Madras, as assistant to the Chief Conservator of Forests, thus saving one of the rest of us from having to take turns at a job which was very distasteful to those who like the jungle. I relieved him on his retirement in 1938, and had more than enough of the office desk during the six months in which I was chained to it.

A herd of elephants moving through the jungle is an impressive sight. A tusker goes ahead as a scout, and the rest follow some distance behind, usually in some sort of file, or single file. Calves keep close to their mothers, often beneath their bellies. A herd may be as small as half a dozen. The biggest I have seen was about thirty-five, but herds may run up to fifty or even more. For all their vast bulk, a herd of elephants can move very quietly, and it is often their smell, and not the noise they make, which warns one of their proximity. I cannot describe the smell of a herd of wild elephants, but it is characteristic, and strong, and hangs about a spot which they have been frequenting for some time after they have left it. If they are not suspicious of the presence of man they make plenty of noise as they browse, breaking bamboos, branches of trees, etc. In appearance they are very different to the tame elephant as one ordinarily sees him. The latter has his two baths a day and only gets the chance to look disreputable at night, when nobody is about. He looks black shortly after his bath, and dark grey when thoroughly dry. The wild elephant, however, unless he is actually in water, keeps his body covered with mud, or with dry earth which he throws over himself, presumably to keep away the flies and other insects. As a result he suffers all over from what might be called a muddy complexion.

Herds of elephants avoid man as far as possible, and are therefore almost always harmless. I would not, however, trust any elephant if I met him close up, and face to face, on a narrow path. There is, too, the rather remote chance of getting in the way of a stampeding herd, in which case the advantage would be with the elephants. I once had an uncomfortable few minutes in the middle of a herd of them. I was walking along a cart-road with a couple of subordinates, on my way home from a day in the Nellicutta plantations. When I reached a sharp bend, I saw elephants crossing the road in single file about twenty yards ahead. They did not seem to be aware of our presence, but they were a bit too close for one's peace of mind, and my reaction - as well as that of my companions - was to drop back quietly, round the corner until the herd had cleared off. But when we had gone a short distance or so we saw more elephants behind us, crossing the road from the opposite side and about thirty yards away. It seemed an extraordinary coincidence to bump into two herds of elephants at the same time, moving so close to each other, and in opposite directions. The explanation was not long in coming. It was a single herd, and they were simply cutting off the corner in the road by following their own course through the jungle. There was nothing to be done except to stand motionless at the bend and watch until they had all crossed and re-crossed. I had a rifle in my hands, but had no intention of using it except in extreme emergency, for the last thing we wanted to do was to scare the elephants and possibly cause a stampede. If the elephants were aware of our presence they showed no signs of it. They just went on their leisurely way; much too leisurely it seemed to us, though the whole performance can only have taken a few minutes.

Two methods are employed in India for capturing wild elephants. By the "Keddah" method, which is used in the Mysore State and by the forest department in Assam, whole herds, and usually several herds together, are captured at one time. The Madras forest department uses only the pitfall method, by which elephants are caught singly. I shall not attempt a detailed description of the Keddah method [... ... ...] Although I have seen various stages in the operations in Mysore, firstly during a drive when the film "Elephant Boy" was being prepared, and later when a Keddah was synchronised with the Viceroy's visit to the State. The principle is to start on a wide front, and drive along a valley, collecting all or most of the elephants which may be in the valley. The frontage is shortened as the drive nears its end, and finally the elephants are herded into an enclosure from which they cannot escape. The enclosure which I saw was bounded mainly by an elephant trench, too wide for an elephant to step across, and fortunately they either cannot jump or else never think of doing so. The entrance was a wooden stockade which was closed when all the elephants were inside the enclosure. The actual drive may take several weeks. There is no panic about it. The elephants move along at their own pace, keeping well ahead of the long line of beaters which stretches across the valley. There are "stops" along the sides of the valley to prevent elephants breaking out on the flanks.

A keddah is a slow and elaborate operation, and is a very costly business. [...] in these circumstances it is difficult to cover the costs of the operations by sales. Except for young tuskers of the strongest build, the prices offered are very low when a hundred or more elephants are put up for auction at one time. Keddah operations in Mysore are therefore conducted much less frequently now than formerly. They are still necessary at intervals, to replace wastage amongst the large herds maintained for forest work and for palace service.

The pit-fall method, as used by the Madras forest department, has been described in an earlier chapter. It is simple and cheap, and has the further advantage that only a few tame elephants are required to assist in capturing. Operations are undertaken periodically every year in the four timber districts where most of the departmental elephants are employed.

The biggest "catch" I have seen was about the year 1936, in the lower plateau of the Nilgiri district, where we had twelve (?) falls at the same time in pits within a radius of about 100 yards. This was undoubtedly due to the herd stampeding after the first elephant had fallen, and the system working out in accordance with the book. This rich harvest was an embarrassment. We did not want so many for we had already had several single falls that season, and the market was dull. We captured the best eight animals and released the other four.

[.....] kraals, and were obliged to [... ....] speed. It took us 2 ? days to complete [... ... .] was unusually slow, for [..... ....] field a brace of elephants, and one pit [... ....] was the record number of four. Luckily [... ... .] much of a size, otherwise the big [....... ....] the smaller or feebler, or tramp [.... ....] sometimes happens to feed and water the elephants which had to be left [... ... .] more nights but it was not easy. A bucket of water on a rope was smashed flat by the angry recipient [... ....] By throwing large quantities of water [.... ....] elephants we kept them fairly cool [... ....] water with their trunks from the bottom of [.... ....] it when offered clean [... ....] politely but for [... ....] pits, but the poor beasts were too upset to [........]

[.......] route and was close to the main road to Mysore. Crowds of sightseers came down from Ootacamund by car, for it is very rarely that the public gets a chance of seeing a wild elephant, much less seeing a bunch of them being forced into domestic service. Elsie brought our three young daughters to see a bit of the fun; it gave them something to talk about when they went home to school in England shortly afterwards. The spectators made our work no easier. My responsibility was to capture the elephants safely. But in allowing the public to come on the scene, I felt I was responsible for their safety also, and some of them showed little circumspection in the way they moved about around the pits. We did our releasing of unwanted elephants late in the evening after the crowd had been sent home with the assurance that work was over for the day.

It is impossible to prevent elephants receiving minor bruises and abrasions while capturing them; and after they are put into the "kraal" they cause a lot of minor injuries to themselves by butting and kicking the wooden bars of their prison. Severe injuries in capturing by the pit-fall method are very rare. I have never seen any myself, and the only serious damage I can remember having heard of was a case which occurred some years before I first went to India. A young cow elephant fell in a pit when she was well advanced in pregnancy. When put in the "kraal" she was seen to be suffering great pain. The local forest veterinary inspector was in no doubt as to the trouble, but a wild elephant is not amenable to treatment of any kind. The vet however was as brave as he was humane. He had the elephant roped to restrict her movements as much as possible, and then got into the "kraal" along with his wild patient, and performed a Caesarian operation which was completely successful as far as the mother was concerned. The calf was too premature to survive. This veterinary inspector, an Indian Christian, was a splendid man with elephants. He later became Inspector of Livestock for the forest department, with gazetted rank. This operation, performed on a wild elephant, constitutes a feat of skill and daring which is probably unique.

The elephant concerned was never much good for work. She was a big animal, and perfectly healthy, but when given heavy loads to drag she always lost condition. I had her at Nilambur for all my time as District Forest Officer, except for short spells when I succeeded in getting her transferred to other districts - from which she always came back like a bad penny. In learning to recognise one's elephants, one usually looks for points of individuality about the head end. But with Kali one went to the tail end when in doubt, to identify her by the scar left by the operation. For some fifteen years after her unique experience she avoided maternity, either intentionally or by chance. But she produced a calf while I was in Nilambur about 1930. The birth was natural and there were no complications though it probably took longer than usual. In the ordinary way the calf is born when the elephant is out grazing at night, but Kali chose to have hers by day and labour lasted for several hours. I had a young European assistant at the time, ("Griff" Griffiths) who happened to be passing the spot in the Teak plantations which the elephant had selected for her confinement. He remained throughout the proceedings, and, with the "mahout" and one or two others, was able to render the elephant some assistance. He was a very junior officer at the time, full of enthusiasm, and no doubt intending to do something big in India. But he can hardly have expected to do anything so big in his early service as midwife to an elephant.

The training of an elephant commences the day after his capture. He is trained by the man who will be his first "mahout", and they very soon get to know each other. Until he has got the confidence of the animal, the trainer must stand outside the bars to give the earliest lessons. But it is usually safe for him to get inside the "kraal", with his pupil, within a week. Teaching is done by kindness rather than severity. A stick is necessary to indicate to the animal the action required of him, but it is seldom needed for punishment. Sugar cane plays a large part in the elephant's education. He is rewarded with a piece when he obeys the word of command correctly. Each order is a single word. It is repeated endlessly in a loud and authoritative manner, and at the same time the elephant is induced to adopt the attitude required, by prodding with the stick, or by use of the "mahout's" hands. When the movement is correctly carried out, the "mahout" says "aisa" (meaning "thus" or "so") in a soothing voice, at the same time patting him and giving him a tasty tit-bit to eat. Both in the early training in the "kraal", and the advanced training when the elephants are instructed for riding and for work with timber, all orders are given by word of mouth. This involves the use of a very considerable vocabulary, and is an indication of the extreme intelligence of the elephant. Starting as a wild animal he is taught within a few months to perform more numerous and more complicated movements than are ever required of other domesticated animals with centuries of servitude in their blood. And all this in response to the spoken word, whereas the horse requires considerable aid by way of the reins, the rider's legs, etc., and even a gun dog requires signals as well as oral orders.

The language used to the elephants is Urdu, but being a North India language it has become so corrupted in the foreign jungles of the South as often to be scarcely recognisable in the mouths of our elephantmen. The latter belong mostly to the jungle tribes of the districts in which they are employed, such as the Paniyas, Naickens, Kurumbas, Irulas, Mulus, Kaders, etc. Most of them are uneducated. According to the locality, they speak Malayalam, Kanarese or Tamil or local dialects of these languages. I once asked a working mahout in Nilambur what language he used in giving orders to his elephant. He replied that it was "elephant language", and this is probably the opinion of most of the attendants, although the few Moplahs employed on elephants in Malabar may know better, (Moplahs are Moslems) and, even in the South, a Moslem of any education usually has a nodding acquaintance with Urdu.

Our departmental elephants are named shortly after capture, or, in the case of calves born in captivity, soon after birth. In the old days of the forest department little discretion was used in selecting names. It was common practice to name tuskers after forest officers, and cows by the names of their wives, sweethearts or other female appendages. As a result we still have a number of elephants bearing such inappropriate names as "Frank", "Donald", "Kitty", "Phyllis", "Lou", etc. Some years ago English names were wisely prohibited. But apparently even this restriction did not go far enough, for there is the story of the ranger who wished to honour a senior Parsee officer, and consulted a junior European officer who was something of a wit. The ranger asked whether the latter thought the senior officer would like the honour. The reply was "No, he is too modest. But perhaps he would like the elephant named after his famous relative." The ranger inquired who the famous relative was, and the wit gave the first Parsee name that came into his head - "Readymoneywallah". This somewhat unusual name was duly proposed by the ranger, but was stopped somewhere in its upward passage through the usual channels. Higher authority, however, got to hear of it and saw fit to issue an order that none but Indian names be used in future. We have a number of elephants with the dignified, stately names that I consider suitable for the lordly elephant. In this class I would put the tuskers "Akbar", "Bahadur", "Maharajah", "Sirdar", "Sultan" and the cows "Nurmahal", "Muntazmahal", "Ranee" etc. We have other good names too, which I have forgotten. But we have discarded many of the finicky, futile variety which would be apt enough on a pet poodle, but are ludicrous when applied to the stately elephant.

As soon as he enters the forest department, whether by capture or by birth to a tame cow, a service register is opened for each elephant as for any other Government servant. This register is maintained throughout the elephant's service, and goes with him on transfer from one district to another. The following are some of the headings under which entries are recorded: [... ....] and sex [... ....] if born in captivity name of father if known; estimated age when captured [.... ....] on; temperament; height; dragging capacity [.... ....]; health; domestic occupation; [...... ....]; record of work done; notes of inspection by veterinary officer. The registers are kept by the Forest Officer and are produced at the elephant coup on every inspection by the District Forest Officer, Conservator or Chief Conservator of Forests, or by the [..... ......] of the Directory of Veterinary Services. With the exception of [..............s], all these headings require frequent additions so the registers make an interesting record. [... ... ...] occurrences, in the case of cows, deal mostly with their experiences of maternity. Their amorous dalliances are recorded if observed or suspected. But frequently the first indication of their condition is when they

give birth. In fact so capricious is the frame of an elephant that at times the staff has been unaware [...... ....] actual [..... ....
....
....] is usually blank which confirms the bleakness of their love life in captivity. On very rare occasions they have been observed to have intercourse with tame cow elephants, but the practice of hobbling the elephants when turned loose greatly cramps their style; and during the "musth" period, when tuskers are most likely to seek female society, we tie them up, since they are dangerous at such times.

In the wild state the elephant spends most of the 24 hours feeding his vast bulk. In captivity they are turned out in the jungle to graze, after the day's work. But to make up for the time spent at work instead of grazing, and to restore the energy used in working they are fed on concentrated [...]

[4 pages missing]

[...] them is their due, but I am fairly convinced that they can count, at least up to seven. Sunday is a holiday in the forest department and the elephants know when Sunday comes round just as well as does the staff. I used to make a regular inspection of the elephant camps in Nilambur most Sundays, doing one camp at the time of the morning meal and the other at supper time. I made a habit of inspecting harness when work was in progress, since this is the best way of testing the fitting. But on one occasion I had the elephants harnessed up after breakfast on a Sunday to check the fitting and condition of the harness before turning the animals loose for their holiday. Never again. They were much too unhappy about it, restive, trumpeting, grumbling, and obviously nursing a grievance. They would have gone to work if forced to do so, being well-disciplined, but they would have gone reluctantly, and would not have put their backs into it, on the Sabbath.

Where water and grazing are abundant and good, and when the camps are not kept too long in one place, tame elephants usually enjoy good health. They live entirely in the open. The camp is simply a place where their food and stores are kept, and where they are brought for feeding and medical attention. At Mt. Stuart, during my early service, there was a great deal of sickness amongst the elephants, chiefly stomach and liver troubles, due to internal parasites. Timber work had been going on year after year in the same locality. Water in the dry weather was scanty and bad. The surroundings of the camp and the grazing grounds were breeding places for disease owing to [... ....
....] Sickness, and mortality was relatively high. In Nilambur, the Nilgiris and South Kanara, where I had later experience of elephants, I saw very little sickness of a serious nature; in all

these districts, good water and grazing are available throughout the year, and deaths amongst the departmental elephants are rare.

Except when anthrax is suspected, a post-mortem examination is made when a departmental elephant dies. (With anthrax there is the risk of the surgeon becoming infected during the autopsy.) I attended one such post-mortem on an elephant which had become weak and anaemic and just pined away. A post-mortem on the carcass of an elephant is a big business. All the preliminary work of opening up the huge body was done by strong coolies, mostly armed with felling axes. Then the veterinary inspector got busy. How he found the organs he wanted, amongst the mess, was something of a mystery to me. It was also a mystery how the wretched elephant had lived so long, considering the large numbers of internal parasites of two or three different kinds which the vet. showed me, and the degree to which some of the organs, including the heart, had become atrophied.

Minor digestive disorders are common, although some elephants seldom or never suffer trouble of this sort. Three days' indigestion associated with constipation, followed by three days' diarrhoea constitute a frequent entry in the health pages of the service registers. As far as I remember, the elephants never worked during the periods of indigestion, and rested when suffering from diarrhoea which, incidentally, is probably caused by the treatment for constipation, although a surfeit of such things as fresh young bamboo shoots is sometimes responsible.

A good deal of working time is lost through these minor ailments, but it is maternity amongst the cows that is the bane of the busy forest officer's life, where elephants are concerned. I always used to groan when the vet. came to me - as pleased as if he himself had been instrumental - to report that one of the cows was pregnant. This meant about six months off work, since expectant mothers are rested for a short time before the event, and for several months afterwards.

Many of our cows never calve in captivity, but some make rather a habit of it, either for the sake of the holiday or just to satisfy their maternal instincts. We had a lot of this nonsense when I was at Nilambur. Kitty, Nurthahal and Kuttipaal - all habitual offenders - again qualified for the maternity benefit, and Kali got herself into trouble for the first time since her Caesarean operation many years before.

In the last thirty years or so I think only one of our elephants born in captivity is definitely known to have been sired by a tame tusker. All the rest are the result of love affairs with wild tuskers, which the tame cows have met while turned out to graze at night. These affairs are occasionally observed by the mahouts when they go out in the mornings to fetch the elephants in for the day's work. Tell-tale marks on the cow elephant in the mornings sometimes give rise to suspicion, but usually the approach of a domestic event is not suspected until pregnancy is well advanced.

The theory is very widely held that elephants live to a great age. One hundred and fifty or even two hundred years is suggested. The usual reason in support of this theory is that one never finds dead elephants in the jungle. This might be used as an argument to show that elephants live for ever, but really it proves nothing. It is very rare to find the body of any wild animal which had died from old age. When an elephant becomes too old and decrepit to lead the wandering life of the herd, I believe he takes himself to the remotest part of the forest that he can find; to hide when ill is a natural instinct. Water would be the greatest need of a dying elephant, so he would stick very close to a river in his last days. The river in due course would break up, disperse and conceal such bones as remained after carrion eaters of all kinds, from the hyena to the ant, had dealt with the carcass. If elephants lived to a vast age, we would sometimes catch some very old animals in pits, but I have not heard of any which were estimated to be more than about sixty. I remember, some years ago, reading a scientific article in which it was stated that man is the longest lived mammal. As between man and elephant our experience with tame elephants in the Madras forest department would seem to corroborate this statement. While I was at Nilambur a tusker, which had been a splendid working elephant, died at the age of about 65. He had slight dropsy, but his main trouble was simply old age, and it was very apparent. I have not heard of any passing the age of seventy. It is, of course, possible that captivity and work tend to shorten the normal life of an elephant. On the other hand we put them into honourable retirement when too old for work, and continue to feed them on concentrates, which keep them going for years longer than if they were cast adrift, and had to collect for themselves the vast amount of bulky food which an elephant needs to eat in order to extract the minimum nourishment which his system requires.

I should like to think that the stately elephant lives for a couple of centuries; there is something romantic in the thought. But I greatly doubt whether the centenarian is proportionately as common amongst the elephants as amongst the human inhabitants of countries like New Zealand and England which stand high in order of longevity.

Chapter X

AMERICANISATION

Between 1922 and 1929 the more important timber forests of the Western Ghats underwent a change in the management which it is convenient - if not wholly accurate - to describe as Americanisation. The introduction of American methods was unpopular with most forest officers in Madras at the time, and since most of the new ideas ended in costly failure, the general attitude of recent [...

....

....]

on, but looking back [....]
subsequent progress [....]
Emphasise the good points and [....]
gives credit wherever it is due [...
...] Madras did little to introduce [...]
during the first Great War partly because...
sufficiently recovered from central [...]
the forest department had neither [... ....] ties necessary for a sudden expansion, and [... ....] contractors were difficult to buy in a hurry [.... ....] sowed the seed of mechanisation in men's minds [... ....] became available the seed germinated [....] Americanisation was upon us. Other provinces of India [.... ....] probably none so [....]

The first step was the appointment of an engineer to inspect the important [.... ....] development. As a result of his rapport he was given a contract as Chief Forest Engineer and was allowed to import another American engineer to assist him, with the title of Logging Engineer. Machinery and plant were bought and installed, and in quite a short time we had one large and up-to-date sawmill running, three other sawmills designated "portable" and tractors humming in the forests, and a babel of new words such as "projects", "timber-cruising", "yarding", "skidding", "bumming", etc. together with some choice epithets which we were assured were terms of endearment amongst lumberjacks on the Pacific Slope, but which were definitely offensive to our civilised Indian personnel.

The superior staff, on the engineering side, was further increased by the appointment on short contracts of two British engineers by the employment obtaining from the Government of India Office [...]

[4 pages missing]

Transport of the sleepers from the Silent Valley was the most difficult and costly part of the work. When operations started, a few years before my visit, the locality of felling was just inside the crest of the outer slope. The lead for dragging the sleepers, from the sawing scaffolds to the depot near the foot of the hill, was only about three miles, and it was practically all down the steep slope to which I have already referred, where the main work of the dragging coolies was to guide and control the sleepers in their descent. At the time I saw the operations, all the more accessible parts of the valley had been worked over, and felling had proceeded so far into the interior of the forest that they had almost reached the stage of taking two days to drag the sleepers out. The drag could still be completed in one day, but it was extremely hard work. The dragging coolies left their homes in the plains in the early hours of the morning, climbed the hill before daylight as we had done, and walked about six miles in from the crest, to collect their sleepers. These they dragged to the edge, in their own time. It was mostly downhill, but the slope was gentle and gave little help. The air, however, was cool in the shade of the forest and at an altitude of 3,000 feet. At 5 p.m. or later, when the sun had lost its heat, they took the sleepers down the steep face of the hill, delivering them at the depot about dark. For this long day's work, the coolies received one rupee each. This was nearly three times the wage of an ordinary field labourer at that time, but they earned it. Two men dragged each broad gauge sleeper, while the metre gauge size was a one-man load. The broad gauge specification is nine feet long, ten inches wide, and five inches deep. The volume of such a sleeper is just over three cubic feet, and the weight in a heavy wood such as Mesua Ferrea [Indian rose-chestnut or Ironwood] is about 175lbs(?). The metre gauge sleeper is 6 feet by 8 inches by 4½ inches, and its volume and weight are half those of the broad gauge. To cover the wear and tear in dragging, the sleepers were given about half an inch extra in thickness at the time of sawing. An extra half foot in length was also allowed, to give room to cut a drag-hole at the forward end; besides, the leading end became so worn by friction over ten miles of earth and gravel and rock, that it ended up with an edge almost as sharp as a razor, instead of being five inches thick. So even if there had been no drag-hole, the end would still have to be cut off and discarded as being below specification in thickness. The drag ropes used were lengths of cane, one for each cooly. On the level, and down gentle slopes, the coolies walked in front, dragging the sleeper behind them. On slopes steep enough for the sleeper to slide of its own weight, they trotted in front, and a bit to the sides of the path, keeping the nose of the sleeper pointed down the slope.

Their progress down the almost precipitous outer face of the hill was an amazing sight. They ran and jumped from rock to rock, dodging out of its way when it seemed likely to hurl them down the mountainside, but always holding the cane ropes in their hands, and keeping the sleeper nose on to the slope. How they escaped serious injury I cannot think. It made me breathless just to watch their headlong rush down the slope in a cloud of dust, with the heavy sleeper crashing and bumping and bouncing along behind, between and before them. Accidents, however, were very rare. In several years' work, I heard of no broken limbs, but one man was killed through getting in the way of a sleeper which had broken loose from a pair of his companions higher up the hillside.

Examination of the sleepers in the forest was very important. The sawyers were not paid for defective sleepers, and if any such were passed in the forest, not only were the felling and sawing charges lost, but also the still heavier cost of transport, since a sleeper rejected by the railway is only worth its small firewood value. Even with the strictest passing in the forest one had to expect at least five per cent rejections from cracking and splitting between the time of conversion and that of delivery to the railway, sometimes as much as three or more months later. The profit on accepted broad-gauge sleepers from the Silent Valley at this time was about four rupees each. The railways paid eight rupees. Felling and sawing cost one rupee, dragging two rupees, and sundry charges including overheads about one rupee, making a total cost of production of about four rupees. This is very good business, out of timber which could not be transported from the hills in any size greater than a sleeper. The metre gauge sleepers fetched three rupees each, but they cost about two rupees to produce, so their number was restricted as far as possible, in favour of the production of the more profitable broad gauge.

The Nilambur district remained largely outside the influence of the new lumbering methods, although it was, in fact, about the only district in Madras where these methods could have shown a clear profit in all phases. No other district could compare with it from the point of view of concentration of valuable timber species over a very large area of fairly easy country. Certainly no other district could have guaranteed a permanent supply of millable timber of readily saleable species to the big sawmill, which had been unprofitably installed in the next-door district, to saw the unfashionable evergreens. But Nilambur had been a going concern for three-quarters of a century. Its time-honoured methods of elephant haulage and cheap river transport were working satisfactorily. It had its own market on the coast for both timber in the round, and for poles and was making better profits, as far as could be seen, than would be possible if the existing methods were radically altered. Its annual output of timber could be largely increased without· appreciable change of method, and was, in fact, almost doubled before I left the district. In these circumstances the district did not undergo any revolutionary changes, although one big lumber "project" was contemplated and the preliminary work undertaken, and we also had some experience of tractor haulage, and of sleeper operations at high altitudes. Further, we gained two excellent girder bridges, largely on the strength of the "project" which did not materialise.

In 1929 I was somewhat short of elephant power to deal with an increased out-turn of timber, and applied to my Conservator for the transfer of two or three elephants from another district. None could be spared. But before I knew where I was, a tractor rolled up, complete with crew, under the management of the engineering branch.

It is not quite correct to say that the tractor rolled up. It did roll most of the way, but it became bogged in the last lap, when trying to negotiate a small stream where the road bridge was not strong enough to take its weight. I had to send elephants to pull it out. They must have smiled at having to rescue the machine which was coming to do their work for them. It was an inauspicious start.

I had no responsibility for the tractor in the first year. All I had to do was show it the work. Its own crew did the rest, and were supervised by the forest engineer in charge of sawmills and extraction, who paid occasional visits. But my district had to pay the costs of working, which made me dislike it intensely, for it fairly ate petrol, and was constantly losing working time by breaking down. I turned it loose in Nellicutta to drag the timber off parts of the area which was being felled for planting Teak in the following year. The locality was about a mile and a half from the river, to which the logs had to be carted along a temporary cart-track which we made from the river to the clearing. What I wanted was to have the logs collected into a number of small dumps to which the carts could be taken. But the tractor's method was different. It was equipped with what I think they called "skidding" - apparatus - or it may have been "yarding". Anyway the principle was to anchor the tractor to a stout standing tree, and to run out a long wire rope from the tractor to the logs which had to be collected, and to drag them in by winding up the rope on a drum. There were pulleys tied to standing trees, and blocks and tackles and other infernal machines involved. The whole thing made a hideous noise, and I was never too happy watching it after hearing of the sad fate of a man who was winding up the rope on one occasion when it snapped and cut him neatly in two. There was nothing much wrong with the business if the logs could have been collected into small dumps. But the experts said that the cost of making frequent moves, then re-setting the apparatus would be prohibitive. So the tractor just sat, and pulled in all the timber within the radius of its rope, and piled the logs pell-mell in a huge, crazy heap about thirty feet high. The cost was more than if elephants had been used for the same work. But this was not the worst. We still had to dismantle the two or three crazy piles into which the logs were collected, in order to load the timber on to carts. This was difficult and dangerous work, and could only be done by elephants. Great care had to be taken so as to avoid injury to men and elephants from the tumbling logs. The work was therefore slow, and the dismantling of the heaps used about as much elephant power as would have been required to drag the logs off the area in the first instance, without working the elephants overtime.

After this experience I never used the tractor again. But I was told that I had to keep it for use in the following year. I was still rather short of elephants, so could not argue. The tractor work was extremely expensive, but even after it had done its worst, the value of the timber was high enough to give a margin over and above the total cost of production. At this time the era of mechanisation was drawing to a close. Various unprofitable "projects" were closing down and the special engineering staff was being reduced. So the tractor was handed over to me, lock, stock and barrel and my only hope of ever getting rid of it rested on what I thought was the unlikely possibility of its sale, towards which I was told that efforts would be made. It was, in fact, bought in the following year, for a paltry sum, as scrap iron, I imagine, though the story at the time was that a Malabar man of means thought it would increase his prestige to keep it outside his front door as an ornament, besides being handy for the children to play with.

We continued for a short time to haul the logs in to a number of small dumps. The range officer, who was frequently at Nellicutta in connection with planting, kept an eagle eye on the petrol, which had been unaccountably getting mixed with water between the time of issue from store, and use in the engine. Intelligent locals, on much lower wages, replaced the less skilled members of the original tractor crew. A material reduction in cost of dragging was effected, but it was still too expensive. Then the range officer, whose brain coupled the job of dragging with elephants, had the idea of using the tractor as an elephant. As many logs as it could drag were chained to its tail, and it was made to drag them from the stump site to the river, over a distance of about one and a half miles. This was the most economical way we found of employing the tractor. It was still more expensive than the elephant plus the buffalo cart, but the difference was not great. The tractor in question was very old, and far from efficient. It was also a very heavy model, being a ten tonner, and with its huge caterpillar tracks it cost a lot to run even when unladen. A light and efficient tractor, used in this way, might be quite a reasonable proposition over leads that are too long for the elephant, and too short for the economical use of the country cart, which takes a long time to load.

In 1927, while I was engaged in making the working plan for the Nilambur Valley forests, the Americans took a fancy to the forests of the steep slopes above the valley which are mostly evergreen. The Logging Engineer reported on the timber of these hills in most glowing terms; it was the best thing he had seen in the way of a stand, since leaving the "Pacific Slope". The opinion of most forest officers was that the hills are much too steep for any but the most conservative of selection fellings; the function of these forest-clad slopes is to conserve and regulate water supply, and to prevent erosion and floods, and in the working plan for the valley I had prescribed that no felling should be undertaken in the hills. The Logging Engineer was, however, allowed to get busy on what he called "timber cruising", which involved a topographical survey, and a computation of the stand of timber. A large gang of "cruisers" was employed in the hills during 1927 and 1928. In 1929 when the special engineering branch was closing down and the Logging Engineer had already gone back to the States, I was given the "cruise" data, and told to make a working plan for the hills, in addition to my work as District Forest Officer.

This was the most distasteful task which has fallen to my lot in the forest department. I was not prepared to propose anything in the nature of concentrated fellings on these steep slopes which receive the full blast of the south-west monsoon, with an annual rainfall which is probably over two hundred inches. (Rain gauges just over the crest of the hills, and about 3,000 feet above the forests in question read over 300 inches in the year.) Selection fellings, cautiously carried out, could do no harm from the point of view of erosion. But I could see no point in it. The hill forests are mainly evergreen. Very few species are sufficiently valuable to be worked at a profit, since the locality is remote, and the country too difficult for extraction of anything bigger than a railway sleeper. A profit of a few thousand rupees a year might be made, with a great deal of trouble, but there was no reason to go to these difficult hills to make more money. We were expanding our output in the deciduous forests of the plains and lower foothills, where there was an abundance of valuable timber, and ample scope for still further expansion should the market require more wood.

The preparation of a working plan for the hills involved little outdoor work, since all this was supposed to have been done by the "cruising" party. Such touring as I did, in order to get a general idea of the forests, was very pleasant, though the going was steep and rough. The real work was to extract useful information out of the "cruise" data, which were a regular Chinese puzzle, whose perpetrators were by then scattered to the four winds of heaven. I managed to get the assistance of one of the rangers who had taken part in the "cruise", but he was not helpful. It seemed to me that the volume of timber had been overestimated, and I wanted to find how the "cruisers" had arrived at the volumes of trees which appeared in their cruise-sheets, since their only measurement was that of the diameter at breast height. This ranger told me in all seriousness that the Logging Engineer had given them a form factor, and that the last form factor used was greater than unity. If this were true it would mean that the trees were of greater diameter at the top than at ground level, rather like inverted pyramids. It was obvious that the Logging Engineer could not have been responsible for such folly, but it caused grave doubt as to the reliability of the figures computed by his subordinates.

I was not pressed to produce the working plan quickly and I never could spare much time from my ordinary work as a District Forest Officer. I puzzled away at the "cruise sheets" in any spare time I had for several years and in the end could make very little use of them. Most of the analysis of figures and preparation of maps was done in the Nilgiris after I had left the Nilambur district. I had a great deal of assistance from my wife in this laborious work; without her help I doubt if the working plan would ever have been finished. Not that that would have much mattered, for the plan, when completed, was so unambitious and unconvincing that we would have been as well without it. It was not a work that I liked putting my name to, and the best that could be said about it was that it would not do the forest any harm.

The evergreen forests of the Nilambur Hills were very much an unknown quantity, until the Americans drew attention to them. From an altitude of about 500 feet above sea-level (which was roughly the limit of timber working in the foothills) up to the tops of the Nilgiris at an average elevation of about 7,500 feet, was virgin forest, surmounted by the steep grass and rock slopes of the summit. No felling of any kind had been done since the Government had come into possession of the forest about the year 1880 (?). And in view of the remoteness of the locality and the difficulty of the country, it is doubtful if any timber worth mentioning had ever come out of this tract, though it is probable that small quantities of Poonspar [Calophyllum tomentosum, formerly selected by Moors for their dhows] poles had been extracted from the lower evergreens to make masts for ships, at a time when the former owners had no regard for the cost of employing elephants to drag timber over a lead of ten miles or more. We regarded these high-elevation forests as a most important water catchment area, and an insurance against disastrous floods, erosion and the silting of the rivers in the lower valley.

Protection of the forest presents no problem. Theft of timber is impossible owing to the difficulty of the country. The only practicable outlet is down the valley by way of Nedungayam, past the headquarters of the range officer and the homes of all his subordinates, so there is practically no chance for outsiders to get up to mischief. The only human inhabitants of the forest are a jungle tribe called the "Shola Naickens", of whom there were thought to be about seventy souls, in my time. Nobody knew exactly how many there were. They are extremely shy, and never came down even as near civilisation as Nedungayam. Our subordinates can make contact with them if need be, but they avoid the outside world as far as possible. In about a dozen tours in the hills I only came across them on two occasions. Most of them ran away at sight of me, but I managed to have some converse with a few of the bolder men through the medium of a forest watcher of a more civilised jungle tribe from lower down the valley. Their language appears to be a dialect of Malayalam. It was completely unintelligible to me. They are of very small stature, the adults being little over 4 (?) feet in height. In other respects they resemble the other hillmen of South India, whose chief characteristic is an unruly mop of thick, curly black hair on men and women alike. They live in and on the forest, within which they are nomadic. In the dry weather they live in caves and under the shelter of overhanging rocks in the beds of the mountain streams. In the monsoon when the rain is terrific, and the streams are roaring torrents, they live in crude shelters of leaves and grass which they build high up in the trees. Their food consists of roots, fruits, honey, etc.. The only time they get a variation from this primitive diet, is when they collect minor forest produce for the contractor to whom we sell the lease annually. The procedure when they work for the contractor is for them to collect and dump the produce (such as honey, beeswax, ginger and Dammar) in a recognised spot near the foot of the hills, and take away the barter of low value, which he leaves for them in the shape of rice and cheap cotton cloth. Loin cloths of the latter form the only covering of the men and women. The youngsters I saw were dressed in their birthday suits.

There were no paths other than game tracks in these hill forests until the "timber cruisers" set to work. They made about thirty miles of footpaths, which enabled one to do a round tour through the upper deciduous forest and the lower part of the evergreen zone, that is up to 2,500 feet or so. Paths were not made in the higher evergreens but there was little obstacle, beyond the steepness of the slope, to climbing up to about 5,000 feet, if one kept to the cols on which the biggest forest grows. Here the canopy of the trees is so dense that there is little undergrowth except the seedlings of forest trees, which are not an impediment to walking. The "Nullahs" between the cols make very heavy going, and are often impassable. They are sometimes blocked by landslides, and usually contain a thick tangle of reeds or almost impenetrable cane brakes, covering a rugged bed of rock and boulders. The cane is the Nilgiri (or "Neilgherry") cane which one knows as a light walking stick. In the rough it is a really nasty bit of work. It straggles over the ground, in a dense mass, as a creeper of twenty yards or more in length. The cane is the core of the creeper, and is surrounded by a thick green outer covering armed with cruel [...]

[Rest of chapter - 20 pages - missing]

WORKING DRAFT
Chapter XI

Henry Tireman's Plan. Wanted to do it when warned for transfer. Last chance. Discussed with Peter. Recce camp. Dan Cave's appearance on scene. Party at Nedungayam. First day hot and thirsty. Cold night. Camp fire. Own cooking. Second day. Two sticky places... Describe whole trip including coolies in culvert. Returned to Nilambur and spent last few weeks mostly on elephant, mapping areas for planting.

Chapter XI

A MOUNTAIN CLIMB (1932)

[FIRST ? PAGES OF CHAPTER XI MISSING]
We worked out a plan for tackling Nilgiri Peak, about 8,200 feet high, and the most imposing of the crests in the horseshoe, though actually about a hundred feet less than the highest. This was the route said to have been taken by the Survey of India officer forty odd years before.

Our preparations were thorough, for we did not want to go to all the sweat of climbing most of the way, and then having to turn back. I had a couple of rough grass huts built at an elevation of about 3,000 feet, which would be our first base. At the same time a forest watcher of the jungle tribe near Nedungayam[...] (knew the whereabouts of) [...] the ancient who had climbed the mountain in his youth, and set out to explore the route with a couple of companions. They made the complete ascent at the first attempt, and made their way across the Nilgiri plateau to the main road from Ootacamund to Calicut, and back to Nilambur by motor bus. This was very encouraging. But these jungle men are as surefooted as goats, and their success did not necessarily ensure ours. They said there were two bad places on the route they had followed, but they thought "even the Sahibs" could make it, especially if they took off their boots.

Before Peter [A.S. 'Peter' Dawson was the Forest Engineer. He learnt forest engineering in Canada, served in the first World War and then came to north India making log slides before moving to the Madras Presidency. He was responsible for building the bridge over the Karumpuzha river at Nedungayam near Nilambur in 1931, which still stands] had returned to his headquarters we had decided to make a preliminary reconnaissance ourselves, and we kept to this plan despite the success of the watcher and his friends. The route to the camp at 3,000 feet lay up a long valley. For more than half the way there was a footpath made by the "timber cruisers", and above it there was a fairly well-defined game track close to the main stream that drains the valley. It was a steady uphill pull, steeper in some places than in others, but offering no difficulty anywhere. In fact we took baggage elephants all the way to the camp, which enabled us to take enough kit to be comfortable.

We spent a very pleasant couple of days at this camp, inspecting some of the higher evergreens, and trying out the Nilgiri Peak route. We climbed up to about 6,000 feet, including one of the bad places, and took the rest on trust, since the watcher assured us that the second danger point was no worse than the first. Having got so far we were sorry that we could not go straight on, but having made no arrangements in this direction, we had to keep to our original plan of making the climb a fortnight later.

During this fortnight there was a chance addition to the climbing party. Elsie was down at Nilambur for a few days to see about packing the furniture, and we were having a drink before dinner one night, when a car drove up to the bungalow - a most unusual occurrence in a place where we had no neighbours, and where visitors from a distance either gave notice of their coming, or arrived earlier in the day. A very apologetic youth got out, and explained that he had lost his way. I don't know what he was so apologetic about, unless he thought he had blundered into an illicit love nest in the jungle. He was an officer [Lt. Dan Cave] of the detachment of the British regiment (Somerset Light Infantry) stationed twenty-four miles away at Malappuram, and had been trying to find his way to the river for a bathe. But as it was then long after dark, he did not need much persuasion to give up the idea and have dinner instead. In the course of conversation one of us mentioned that I was proposing to climb the Nilgiris the next week. Our chance guest became very excited at the idea, and asked if he might join the party. He looked strong and well-built, and was at least six feet tall and younger than either of us, so I could see no reason why he should not join us, and so it was arranged.

Nedungayam was the rendezvous for the expedition, and we all met on the appointed evening, in time for a swim before dark. There was a slight complication through the arrival, that day, of the Forest Utilisation Officer, to pass a batch of my sleepers, on behalf of the railways. In the normal way he would have spent the night with me at Nilambur, but as it was he had to sleep on the train in the Nilambur station. However, we took him out to Nedungayam for dinner, and eventually sent him back to the station on a push-bike, since he was too considerate and independent to let me take him in my car, which was to remain at Nedungayam while we were up the hills. He was also very considerate and independent in the matter of a bottle of whisky which he had in his grip. He knew that we were travelling light up the hills, and was alarmed by the rapid disappearance of whisky before dinner, lest we should be stranded without a drink on the mountain. I assured him that we had enough. It was a pleasure party on my home ground, so I had insisted on provisioning the expedition, and had taken adequate steps. But I found that the other two had also slipped in a bottle of whisky each in case of emergencies. Now I had a third bottle forced on me. We were limited as to the kit that the party could carry, and I had planned out all the loads beforehand. There was no place for surplus bottles, so as there was a holiday feeling in the air, the only obvious solution was to drink them. This solution was pleasant at the time, but the liquor took a bit of walking off the next morning.

The distance from Nedungayam to the first camp was about eighteen miles of which the first six miles were by cart road along which we rode on elephants, to lighten the subsequent exertion. At the end of the road we left the elephants and started climbing with our coolies, of whom there were, I think, ten. Each had a load of about twenty pounds, including his own blanket and his rice for the journey, all carried on his head. Peter, Dan and I each carried a pack and a water-bottle. They did not seem to weigh much the first day, but they felt as heavy as lead the second, when we got near the top.

We had not been very quick off the mark in leaving Nedungayam, and it took the elephants two hours to cover the first six miles, so the sun was well up when we started climbing. The month was April, and the deciduous forest of the lower slopes was leafless, so we had a very hot and sweaty climb of over an hour before we got into the welcome shade of the evergreens. From then on, the first day was plain sailing. We reached the camp at the 3,000 feet level at about 4 p.m. which gave us plenty of time to make our dispositions for the night. This would present no difficulty to an English hiker, but in India one gets into the habit of relying on servants, and we had none with us, so we had to think things out for ourselves.

We had tea going in good time, since we had plenty of help to collect wood, make a fire and carry water from the stream hard by. Then we had our evening bath. The stream bed was a mass of huge, rounded boulders, but between them there was anything up to six feet depth of water, crystal clear and cold as ice. To restore ourselves after the chill of our ablutions, we made a brew of hot whisky toddy, which went down very well.

Quintus (second left) with climbing companion Peter Dawson (centre) and fellow FOs Griff Griffiths (left) and Robbie Robinson (right).

For dinner we did nothing more ambitious in the way of cooking than to heat up tins of various kinds of food, and fry potato chips. After a large meal we all set to and collected masses of dry fallen wood from the forest, and driftwood from the stream bed, and made two big fires, one for ourselves and one for our retainers. The fires served several purposes. They gave cheerful warmth to sit by, for the night was cold. They also kept off the mosquitoes. And as we were carrying no firearms they were an insurance against any wild elephant that might feel playful towards our flimsy huts. There was a small herd in the vicinity when we arrived, but they had sheered off from the noise we made in preparing the camp.

The camp fire was so warm and cheerful compared with our cold hut, that we sat up late, swapping yarns. The coolies scorned their hut and slept close to their fire, and spent a warmer night than we did, for our beds consisted of a ground sheet, one blanket and a mosquito net each. The ground is hard to sleep on, until one gets used to it, and we were up early in the morning, feeling stiff and chilly.

We cooked an elaborate breakfast and took our time over eating it, for we seemed unlikely to have another comfortable meal that day. It was about 9 a.m. when we loaded up and set off. The sun was well up, but in the dark evergreen forest we could neither see nor feel it, and we had to step out briskly to keep warm.   There was no mistaking our route, for our watcher had taken the precaution of blazing trees along his line the first time he went up. We continued close to the stream for about two miles to a place where the valley bore off to the east, whereas our direction was almost due north.

Following the valley it had been a steady climb, steeper than the previous day, but still easy enough to keep up a fair pace. Now we were starting up a long ridge of much steeper gradient which slowed us up considerably. The next two miles or so took us well over an hour. We were still in evergreen forest, but the height and density of the trees kept decreasing as we climbed. There was little indication [... …….. ……… …… ……… …… .]

All this time we were unable to see our objective, owing to the jungle that had become dense. At last we had our first view of the hilltops. Here we stopped to have a rest. We had filled up our water bottles a mile further back and the coolies had filled the hollow sections of bamboos which they always carried from a small stream which was the last water we should find till we were over the top. Over this question of water for the slow and difficult final stages of the climb, I had had what I considered a brain wave [... ……… ……. ….] to carry a liberal amount of water, so why […… …….. …….. …….. …] Accordingly we had half a dozen of beer in addition to […… ….] bottles of water. We split a bottle amongst the three of us […… …..] now on to the top and set up the empties in conspicuous places along the route for the guidance of any other fools who might try to follow in our footsteps in the future.

Nilgiri Peak was […… ……. ….] us. For the last few hundred feet of its height it consists of […. ……] broken occasionally by "chimneys". It looks an impossibility for anyone other than an expert. Luckily the summit of the peak did […. …….. ….]

We removed our hobnailed boots for the last stage. I put on rope-soled canvas boots, and I think the others used shoes with rubber soles. The real rough stuff then started.   The sparse jungle gave place to occasional stunted rhododendrons and a sparse scrub of bushes. The surface consisted of rock in various stages of disintegration, from the firmly bedded rock of the mountain to a detritus of small pebbles. The slope was extremely steep, but not really dangerous, since there were usually enough bushes and roots to give a firm handhold if one's feet slipped. Where the surface was reasonably firm we climbed with our feet and sticks only. Over loose patches we pulled ourselves up from bush to bush. The only two dangerous places were big sheets of smooth rock with a slope of about forty-five degrees at the crossing, and a vertical drop below. But even here there were sufficient handholds either on roots or rock projections on the uphill side.

[4 pages missing]

[…] even though the last five miles were all by road with a good surface, and mostly downhill. We therefore broke up the party again. Peter stayed with the coolies while Dan and I walked on, and I was to come straight back in my wife's car to fetch them.

We dumped our packs and everything we carried. This made such a difference that we felt almost fresh again. Being very lightly clad we felt the cold night air of the hill-tops very keenly, and had to walk fast to keep warm. We did the five miles in about an hour and a half, mostly in silence, for we were much too tired to talk. Once we had a heated argument. We came to a place where the road divided. Both of us knew this road slightly. I insisted that our way lay to the right. Dan was equally sure that we should go left. Finally we parted, each going his own way. In about a hundred yards we met. Our two roads had joined up again. One of the branches was just a diversion to allow cars going in opposite directions to pass, where the original road was narrow. We were not too angry to laugh, and we had no more arguments. Dan thought he could take a shortcut, for we were in country where he had hunted a few times in the previous season. However, as he did not seem too sure of himself and I was certain of the road, we kept to it.

Shortly after midnight we reached Ootacamund. We were not expected till the next day, and my household was asleep. But Elsie did not take much waking, and we soon had some whisky inside us, and arrangements in hand for a meal. Dan went to sleep by the fire, while Elsie and I drove out to fetch in the rearguard. We found Peter and the coolies sitting in the ditch over the remains of a fire. Peter was in uproarious spirits. His one regret was that he too had not walked the last five miles. But he was not quite so keen as to refuse a lift, and walk in on his own, when I suggested this very practical means of getting even with Dan and me. He said he had had some trouble with the coolies. He had asked them to go with him and collect wood for a fire, as they had lain down exhausted, and were likely to get pneumonia at the least, as it was a cold of which they as plainsmen had no experience. But they feared he would try to make them walk on to Ootacamund, and they were not having any. So to escape him they had gone to ground by crawling into a culvert under the road. He collected wood himself, made a fire, and prepared tea for the party. Even when he called them out for tea, they were suspicious and continued to lie doggo under the road. He then lit a fire at the windward end of the culvert and smoked them out of it. Or so he told us, and the remains of the fire were there to bear him out.

Ten minutes took us all home. The coolies were fed, and left to sleep by the kitchen fire. We had a warm meal, but were too tired to be very hungry. However we did full justice to a reviving drink - hot rum toddy, I think it was. Steaming hot baths, with bundles of fragrant fresh eucalyptus leaves soaked in them, removed much of the stiffness from our aching limbs. We needed no rocking to sleep that night.

We reckoned that our second day's journey had been roughly thirty miles, starting with a continuous climb of about 4,500 feet. From our camp in the evergreen forest, up to the crest of the hills, was about five miles - a negligible distance, but much the hardest work of the day. The circuitous route which we took from Nilgiri Peak to the Mukerti ford must have been a good ten miles for we discovered later, that we had been well over half way up Mukerti peak before we hit the bridle path. From the Mukerti ford to Ootacamund by the route we followed was fourteen miles. Our failure to find the Mukerti fishing hut was because it lay in a valley tributary to the main stream, and could not have been seen from the ford even in daylight. The obvious place for a fishing hut is right on the fishing water, so none of us had suspected a pitfall of this sort.

When I came to, in the morning after the climb, I arranged for some of the local forest people to guide in the coolies we had left near Mukerti Peak. They turned up in good shape about mid-day, and went home by bus the following day, well pleased with their unusual expedition, and with the remuneration they received for it.

On my return to Nilambur I spent most of my last fortnight riding about the forest on an elephant. I had been lucky in my choice of the natural forest areas which had been planted with Teak in my time as District Forest Officer, and before I left the district I was ordered to select and map the areas which should be planted in the five years following my departure. I was not keen on the job because I thought the exact selection of sites was best left to the officer who was going to do the planting. However, orders are orders, and I trailed back and forth on an elephant in the Nellicutta area and in the foothills east of Nedungayam, examining the forest, and mapping what I considered to be the most suitable area. In this, and indeed in all work in the Nedungayam range I was very ably assisted by the local ranger. [Ranger Kunhirayan. The full story is told in Browne's 1929 Revised Working Plan for the Nilambur Valley] He was one of only two Moplah rangers in the department, and was an absolutely first-class man in the country and at the work he knew. He had been ranger at Nedungayam since about 1920, and had rendered distinguished and dangerous service during the Rebellion of 1921-22, in which he saved the lives of the District Forest Officer and his family. He also got all the Government elephants away when the Moplahs attacked and burnt the forest stations at Nilambur and Nedungayam. He had them turned out in remote parts of the jungle with their hobbles on and kept in touch with them throughout the Rebellion by surreptitiously sending out [......... ....] The elephants [...... ....] brought in after 18 months of [........ ....] required considerable [..... ....] as far as I remember only one or two were missing. The hobbles had eaten into the legs of many and they still bear the scars so caused. For his service [.... ....] he was awarded the title of Khan Sahib. After [..... ....] Nedungayam where he handled a very heavy charge with the greatest efficiency, and was so successful that he was never transferred elsewhere. He retired as a pensioner a few years after I left Nilambur.

In the Nilambur district I had been very well served during most of my time by this excellent ranger. Although I was pleased enough to be going to the Nilgiris, it was a real wrench to be parting with these fine subordinates, and with the two Indian officers who were my assistants for over two years, and whose kindness and consideration I had greatly appreciated.

Chapter XII

THE NILGIRI FOREST DISTRICT

The Nilgiri forest district to which I was posted in May, 1932, is a small, fairly compact charge, of four ranges, two on the upper plateau and two on the lower (or "Mysore") plateau. If the work were confined to the normal type of forest operations, the district would be the easiest in Madras, but as things are (or were) it was the heaviest district of which I had held charge.

The difficulty of the Nilgiris, from the forest officer's point of view, is that the district is too small, too homogeneous and too healthy. In most districts it is the broad plains which are considered habitable, and in them reside the agricultural and industrial population which have pushed the forest back until it is more or less confined to the hills and to other remote tracts, which by reason of inhospitable soil or lack of communications are not in demand for cultivation. In such circumstances forest management is comparatively unhampered by outside human influence except in those forests which border on the cultivated land. In the Nilgiris, however, much of the land is equally suited for forestry and for such agriculture as is practised, and in the more accessible parts of the upper plateau, forests, tea gardens and potato patches are all jumbled up together. The cool and healthy climate of the hills has also attracted large numbers of settlers of some means and much leisure (many of them being Europeans and Anglo-Indians) for whose recreation, facilities have to be provided in the reserved forest areas. To reconcile all these varied interests with forest management is a constant problem; to please everybody is impossible. The work, as I have said is hard, but there are magnificent compensations. The climate must be one of the best in the world. The food is the best I have come across in India, chiefly because all the ordinary English vegetables flourish throughout the year, and because the climate is cold enough to hang meat until it is tender. There is sport to suit all tastes, including both big and small game shooting, hunting and fishing. In the main residential centres there are the usual social amenities.

The forests of the Nilgiris are not commercially valuable. The district just about pays its way, but no more. In fact the difference between the annual revenue and the annual expenditure has often shown a small deficit. Indirectly, however, these forests are of the highest value in that they protect a water catchment area of very great importance, and greatly reduce the incidence of soil erosion and the severity of floods.

Avalanche

Ootacamund is the headquarters of the district. It is also the summer headquarters of the Government of Madras. As a hill station it dates back to about 1820. At an altitude of 7,000 to 7,500 feet it is cool throughout the year, with light frosts in winter, but it never experiences snow or severe cold. There is an excellent road and also a railway up from the plains in the south-east of the Nilgiris, and to the west of Ootacamund another road descends to the lower plateau, and branches off to Calicut and the west coast, to Coorg and Mysore. From Ootacamund - or "Ooty" as it is more generally named by Europeans and Indians alike - roads radiate out all over the upper plateau except in the remoter parts, of which one has been described in the preceding chapter.

"Nilgiri" is a Tamil name meaning "blue mountain" and is descriptive of these hills when a local species of Strobilanthes is in flower. This is a low shrub which grows amongst the grass of the hillsides. It is inconspicuous at ordinary times, but when it flowers, as it does once in seven years, the hills are clothed in blue and present a picture of unusual beauty.

In the upper plateau, that is in the Nilgiris proper, the biggest forest work is the production of firewood, of which very large quantities are required in Ootacamund, Coonoor and Wellington. The indigenous forest is a stunted, slow-growing evergreen type, and when most of it has been used up in the vicinity of these townships, it had to be replaced by something which would give much greater bulk in a much shorter time. Various species from Australia were introduced, and success was soon obtained with two kinds of Acacia, and with one kind of Eucalyptus.

[11 pages missing]

[...] can guess the severity of the downpour on a really wet day in the Kundahs. The wind, in exposed places, is strong enough to lean against. Sometimes the wind leans too heavily, and on occasion I have been blown back in trying to cross very exposed ridges, and have had to make a detour at a lower level. I have never found any means of keeping dry in this fierce, driving rain. It is therefore necessary to keep moving, otherwise one becomes chilled to the bone. Rain, mist and low cloud obliterate all landmarks, so it is unwise, at this season, to move about in country that one does not know really well. Shortly before I went to the Nilgiris, two Indians lost their way one bad day in the monsoon. They were working in connection with the rain gauges I have mentioned, and had gone out without a guide. Search parties failed to find them, and it was not until after the monsoon that their skeletons were discovered.

All this sounds very unpleasant, but I enjoyed even the wildest weather, in the outer Kundahs. There is something grand about the fury of the elements in a wild, mountainous country. Most enjoyable of all, probably, is getting back to camp, wet through and shivering with cold, after hours of being buffeted by the weather. First there is the sanctuary of a roof and walls, as an escape from the wind and the rain. Then a hot bath, dry clothes, a good fire, and a hot drink. Simple things, all of them, but very highly valued by contrast with what one has left outside. The more fiercely the wind rages then, the better one is pleased with life.

My first camp in the Kundahs was in wild, wet weather in July. I had been ordered to re-commence the experiments in afforestation of the grasslands which had been abandoned some seven years before. The month of June had been spent in planting Teak on the lower plateau, and Bluegum in the vicinity of Ootacamund. This left me no time to make any sort of plan for the experiments in the Kundahs. I had, however, collected some seedlings, and had them done up in balls of moss, several weeks before planting. There was little choice as regards the kind of plant to be used. Eucalyptus were the only seedlings we had in nurseries, and these were not in the least likely to succeed in the severe climate of the outer hills, besides being aesthetically unsuitable to that type of country. Self-sown seedlings of a species of cypress were available near Ooty, and also seedlings of a somewhat similar tree called Frenella. I had a couple of thousand of these two collected and mossed, together with a small number of seedlings of an attractive small tree called Hakea, which is sometimes used for shelter and shade in high elevation tea gardens.

With two pony-loads of plants I set off for the Kundahs, in very wet weather early in July. My first camp was at Avalanche, about 16 miles by road from Ooty, where there is a trout-stream, and a good rest-house. A range of hills rises steeply to the south and west of Avalanche, from which a bridle-path takes off, crosses the hills through a saddle about 1500 feet above the Avalanche river, and then winds its way across a very exposed, undulating plan for about twelve miles, before commencing the descent to the Silent Valley in Malabar. A subsidiary bridle-path branches off, from the saddle, to the east of the main path, and leads to the Nilgiri Game Association's hut on the Billithadahulla river.

With a Forester and a few coolies I spent a couple of days planting Frenella and cypress seedlings along one side of the bridle-path for about two miles above Avalanche. I chose the path not because I expected such success as to produce a shady avenue, but because plants in such a position would be easy to find, and easy to maintain, if they survived. I also planted about a quarter acre of Hakea in a re-entrant near the path, which offered a certain amount of shelter from the elements. It rained all the time, but being on the lee side of the range of hills, the wind was not much of a trial. I was able to catch a few small trout each evening for my dinner, though the weather was too cold at the end of the day to attract bigger and more self-respecting fish.

From Avalanche I crossed the saddle and went on eight miles to the forest rest-house at Bangitappal. This is in wild, remote country, with no human habitation within fifteen miles, excepting Avalanche, which scarcely ranks as a human habitation since it is only the headquarters of a few unwilling subordinates of the forest department and of the game association, who spend most of their time seeking a transfer to more sociable surroundings.

The rest-house lies in a long, narrow valley, with a low range of hills on either side. The south-west end of the valley is more or less open, and the monsoon whistles up it. Most of the "shola" in this valley has been burnt out in the past, leaving grass and rock on the slopes and a level grass plain in the valley bottom, with a fair-sized stream running through it.

I was accompanied on this tour by a Forester who knew a bit of English, and was very keen to air his knowledge. On the way up from Avalanche he told me that some of the previous attempts at afforestation had been made "near the watershed". I was very surprised that he should be familiar with this somewhat unusual expression, and asked him what he meant by the watershed. He explained that it was a shed built near the saddle as a shelter for the hydro-electric people when they went up to measure the water in the rain gauges. There was such a shed too, and by a coincidence it was directly situated between the slope down to Avalanche and the drainage in the opposite direction towards Malabar.

We planted the remainder of our seedlings on the reverse slope of a low hill at the back of the rest-house, in a re-entrant which got a bit of shelter from the biting blast of the monsoon. This work took several days, as we had only a few coolies, and pits had to be dug before planting. After selecting and lining out the area, I left the Forester to get the pits dug while I went off with a forest guard to see what I could of the country, which was not very much, for the weather was very wet and misty, and visibility was negligible. What we did find - though with difficulty for we were not following beaten tracks - were two streams which had been stocked with trout two years before, and had just been opened to fishing for the first time. I got a few beautiful trout in one of them. We struck only the upper waters of the other, where the fish were very small. But there were lots of them, and I got a dozen inside an hour.

Under the cover of some of the surviving "sholas" we found self-sown seedlings of Rhododendron, and transplanted a few dozen of them in the experimental plot. This, being an indigenous tree of the countryside, was one that I would have liked to plant in large numbers, but it is extremely slow growing, and slow to spread itself naturally. It was to the Frenella and Cypress that I pinned my faith. Both are fast growers in the milder climate round Ooty, and they seed profusely and extend rapidly, at a very early age. My idea of afforestation in the Kundahs was to establish small centres of tree growth which would gradually spread outwards by natural reproduction. With this object in view, my experimental plots were located well up the slopes of hills, so that the fairly heavy cones would be distributed downhill during rain. The upper slopes too are less subject to frost damage than the lower levels.

For four more monsoons I persevered with these experimental areas, and with a few fresh ones in other parts of the Kundahs. I added two kinds of Acacia to the species with which I started. Nothing did well. The plants lived through the monsoon all right, but made scarcely any growth either of root or shoot, owing to the extreme cold in this season. After the monsoon these grass slopes dry up very quickly, and large numbers of the plants died of drought. Then came the frost [... ....] coverings as used [..... ....] Eucalyptus plants near Ooty. After five seasons only a few hundred plants survived out of perhaps five or six thousand which had been planted during these years. But a number of [.... ....] When 4 years old, and strongly established and showed every sign of going ahead.

I was very interested in this work and was not disheartened by the small measure of success. The very difficulty of raising trees in these adverse climatic conditions had its own attraction. In my last two years I tried introducing hardy shrubs along with the tree seedlings to serve as nurses, and by the time I left it was apparent that this method would ensure success and that the shrubs should be well established before the trees are planted. This is what I should have done in the first instance but I was impatient to get on with the trees.

Two of the ranges in the Nilgiri forest district lie on the "Mysore plateau" to the west [….. …..] of Ootacamund at an elevation of 2,500 to 4 [……] feet above sea level. An occasional change of…

[…….. ……….. ……….. …………. …………. ……….. ……….. …….]

Tours in these lower ranges were very pleasant.

One of these ranges, with its headquarters some 40 miles from Ooty, is worked for timber. The annual rainfall - about 45 inches as far as I remember - is insufficient to grow timber of large size and good quality. But there is a good proportion of teak in these forests, and it is bought at fair prices by the Mysore timber merchants. Timber of a few other deciduous species is also worked when prices are good. There are large quantities of fine, big bamboos, which would find a ready market in Mysore or Ooty, could they be transported at a reasonable cost. But Mysore is some sixty miles away, and Ooty, though only forty miles, involves an ascent of 4,000 feet, so in both cases the cost of transport is prohibitive except for produce of fairly high value. About a dozen departmental elephants are kept in this range for dragging the timber. Frequent capturing operations are undertaken, sometimes with great success, as I have mentioned in an earlier chapter, when I referred to the capture of eight elephants out of twelve that had fallen in pits at the same time.

The timber operations in this range being on a small scale, there is not a great deal of artificial regeneration to be done. About thirty acres are planted with Teak every year, so coming from Nilambur this seemed to me a mere flea-bite. But the plantations are doing quite well and should, in time, add considerably to the value of the rather poor forests. In my time we did all the planting by means of teak stumps along with grain cultivation. There was little demand from the small local population for the use of the land, so we did most of the cultivation departmentally, threshed the grain and fed it to the elephants. A crop of hill rice, which we tried in my first year, gave only a light harvest, so thereafter we grew Ragi, which did very well.

The other range on the lower plateau contains forest of a much poorer type. In the space of a few miles, going east, the rainfall decreases from about 45 to about 20 inches. The jungle could be worked for fuel, but there is no local demand, since the population in the vicinity of the forests is very small. The only produce of value is sandalwood, of which about ten to fifteen tons are extracted annually. Thus, after eight years, I got back to the "bloody parasite" and found that the sandalwood rules, owing to thefts and swindles in the meantime, had been considerably tightened up. Having no assistant, I was my

Ooty Downs.

own "double-lock officer" for the final clearing depot. I had to make frequent visits to this range while sandalwood work was in progress, but as the quantity was small the operations did not take very long. We sent the wood to North Coimbatore (my first district) for sale.

Since the bulk of the forests of the upper plateau and outer slopes are maintained as a water catchment area, and for the prevention of soil erosion, it follows that a good deal of the District Forest Officer's time is spent on general inspection, to see that the subordinate staff is carrying out its protective duties. In the heat of the plains this job of looking for trouble is apt to become irksome, but in the cool, bracing air of the hill-tops it is a very pleasant exercise. As far as I remember there are over 400 separate forest reserves in the Nilgiri district. It has therefore been necessary to relax the usual rule whereby the District Forest Officer must inspect each reserve in his district at least once in two years. If the rule were enforced he would have little time left for supervising works such as timber and sandalwood operations, planting, repairs to roads and buildings, and all the rest of it. He is however expected to get all round the district as often as he can.

In the more recent assignments of land for cultivation of tea and field crops, some thought was given to the matter of conservation of water, and an attempt was made to protect the sources of streams. In some places, however, the protection provided was so meagre that nothing was retained except the absolute head of the stream, with an acre or so of jungle around it. Better than nothing - but not much better. Approaching one such diminutive reserve on one occasion, I saw from a distance that no attempt had been made to keep the usual boundary line around it clear, so I started to curse the forest guard for his negligence. He excused himself by saying that if he were to clear a boundary of even ten feet, there would be no reserve left! This I found to be almost literally true, for the reserve tapered into a strip of tree growth about four yards wide on either side of a small stream which issued from a wider patch of "shola" higher up the hillside.

Forest offences such as theft of firewood and small timber pieces, and grazing without permits are very common in the vicinity of the towns and villages, and near the tea estates. Elsewhere there are encroachments, by cultivation over the forest boundary, and much illicit hunting and shooting of game. To the best of my recollection an average of at least thirty forest offences were reported to the District Forest Officer every day from the two ranges of the upper plateau, and the number of offences detected is but a small fraction of those committed, since the staff cannot be everywhere at the same time.

Where forest crime is common it is inevitable that frequent attempts should be made to bribe the subordinate staff and thus obtain their connivance. Extortion by the subordinates is also a possibility, but both offences are extremely difficult of detection. In all my service I have only proved one case of extortion, and it happened during my first month in the Nilgiris. It started from an almost ridiculous incident, but in the end it resulted in the dismissal of the range officer, his two clerks, two foresters, and three forest guards. My enquiry, examination of witnesses and recording of evidence took over a week. Preparation of charge-sheets against each individual, further enquiry and examination of witness on receipt of his reply, and finally putting up the case against each subordinate took up a great deal of my time for the best part of six months. The documents, all written in my own hand in the first instance, ran to hundreds of pages of foolscap. Finally, after the dismissal of the culprits, I had to report at length on all the arguments they used in their appeals against the sentence. The first appeals lay to the Chief Conservator of Forests, and were rejected. Most of the appellants then appealed to the Government. These appeals also were dismissed. Finally some of them appealed to the Governor of Madras. This attempt also was fruitless, but the consideration of all these appeals took up a great deal of everybody's time, and it was three years before I heard the last of this case.

The case occurred at a time when the question of illicit shooting of game was receiving serious attention by the forest department and the Nilgiri Game

Association. An old Mahommedan gentleman was driving in a car to Mysore and stopped at a roadside tea-shop near the headquarters of the timber range on the lower plateau. There were some doves on the road, and to please his little son who was with him, he shot one of them. One of the forest subordinates spotted this, and arrested him. Others joined the party while the old man was being taken to the range officer, and they convinced him that he had committed a very serious offence. Actually a dove is not game, and as far as I remember the actual road surface where he shot the dove is not included within the reserved forest through which the road runs. Anyway they parted with fifty rupees as hush money. When he got back home his friends persuaded him that he had been swindled, and he made a complaint to me, in writing. He did not mention the range officer, or in fact, more than two of those I eventually found to be implicated. I sent the complaint to the range officer for enquiry, and he reported that it was a false complaint. The enquiry, however, was sketchy and not very convincing, so I took the matter up personally, and found that he was in it himself, as well as several others who had not figured in the complaint. I was sincerely sorry for the ranger, whom I liked. He had only a year left before retiring with a pension, which of course he lost on his dismissal. He had a very good record of work in the department, and I believe he was little more than a dupe in this case. The real extortioners were a clever couple of his subordinates, who took the lion's share and only brought in the ranger, by means of a small present, to ensure his silence.

While this case was still going on I caught out the range officer on the neighbouring range on the lower plateau, tampering with his cash accounts and helping himself to Government money. He was also dismissed.

The dismissal of a ranger is comparatively rare for [....... ....] same district, and [............... ....] same time caused a great sensation in the forest department. They left me with a very bad taste in my mouth, for it was all very unpleasant.   But they have helped [...... ....] any subsequent relations with subordinates [...... ....… ....] reputation for smelling out secrets, and [....... ....] cannot bear the light of day fight shy of [...... ....] district.   It used to be told as a joke [........ ....] got orders to transfer to a

new post, the bad lots [...... ....] Jurisdiction apply for long leave or transfer [....... ....]

A sad duty [....... ....] my second year in the Nilgiris in connection with the death of Hugo Wood, the pioneer of Teak planting in Mt. Stuart. We had returned [......... ....

....] to me the previous year, on taking charge of the district his instructions regarding the action to be taken on his death [..... ....] in failing health and had expressed [...... ....] Mt. Stuart [......]

[.........]

[.........]

that before his death he had himself made a number of funeral arrangements as was possible for a man to make while still living. He had selected the exact location of his grave; amongst his earliest Teak on the Mt. Stuart hill which looks out to the west over the later plantations. He had obtained permission of Government to be buried there, and had either purchased the necessary plot, or taken it on perpetual lease, I forget which. His grave was dug about a year before he died, under his instruction, and at his cost, and he even went so far as to have his coffin made, and kept in a spare room in his house many months before his decease. His solicitors in Ooty had the necessary instructions regarding undertaking, and the conveyance of his remains to Mt. Stuart. All I had to do was to fix the date and time of burial, and notify as many forest officers as I thought could attend.

[8 pages missing]

Chapter XIII

THE NILGIRI GAME ASSOCIATION
D R A F T

Discuss its origin. How DFO is concerned - adds 25% to his work. The committee-mindedness of retired people and futility, of fishing, voting on shooting, etc.

Cliques and factions. Selfish proposals - persevered with until passed. Monthly meetings good fun. V's case of jungle fowl in close season and committee ramp.. Despite irresponsibility of some and selfishness of others, NGA still does a lot of good.

[This Chapter is missing completely]

Chapter XIV

SHOOTING IN THE NILGIRIS
D R A F T

Great variety of game owing to division into two plateaus of different altitude, climate and vegetation. Lists of game to be found. Bison viewing from elephants. Paragraph to most other species or groups, and describe stalking my Ibex, Sambhur, etc.. Sambhur hinds. Small game shooting. Poaching and catching poachers.

[Several pages missing]

[…] elephants in the low country of the Nilgiris that there are usually a few rogues at large, and in my time two or more were shot most years. The tusks belong to Government, but are almost invariably given to the person who shoots the rogue. I have heard the odd case in which Government gave only one tusk, on the grounds that the gentleman concerned had shot a number of elephants previously, and had always been given the tusks, which are of considerable value, and that if he wanted both he should pay for one of them.

Bison are found in large numbers in the low country, and their heads are greatly prized, especially by young army officers, who spend their annual leave in the Nilgiris. They are beautiful big beasts, and even in the days when I still thought it fun to shoot Chital stags, I had no desire to shoot one of these fine cattle, unless it should be an unusually big bull. I have occasionally gone looking for a big fellow both in the Nilgiris and in other districts, but I cannot say I was ever disappointed in failing to find what I sought.

I saw a great deal of the bison of the lower plateau during my years in the Nilgiris. When important official visitors, from His Excellency the Governor downwards, came to see the forests, it became a popular diversion to take them for a ride on elephants to view the wild life of the jungle. On these rides we looked for bison in particular, and almost always got up with a herd of them. If one keeps very quiet it is possible to ride an elephant close up to wild animals, without disturbing them. They take the riding elephants for the wild ones which share their jungle home, and are not alarmed. On several occasions I have ridden close to a herd of bison for nearly an hour before they discovered something unusual about our party, and bolted. It is fascinating to watch these magnificent wild cattle in their natural surroundings.

After I left the district the opportunity of viewing wild life from elephant back was extended to the public, mainly with the idea of awakening public interest in the jungle fauna, and in the question of wild life preservation. When elephants could be spared from forest work, members of the public could book them for a jungle ride, on payment of a fee of ten rupees for an elephant to carry two visitors. This innovation was very popular, and one particular herd, which could usually be found without going very far into the interior of the forest, must have been very frequently photographed. I have seen several excellent reels of film showing bison in these forests, taken by amateur photographers from the backs of riding elephants. My predecessor in the Nilgiris was very successful at this sort of thing, and got good moving pictures of several other kinds of animals as well, including wild elephants, and a tiger.

Chital, a spotted deer, are very common on the lower plateau, and include heads which are very good for South India. In the north-west of the area our forests adjoin a game preserve in the Mysore State forests, which helps to maintain our stock of game, especially bison and chital. This game preserve is not a complete sanctuary, but the shooting is reserved for the family and guests of His Highness the Maharajah, and the prevention of poaching is fairly successful.

There are black buck in the dry jungles of the eastern of the two ranges on the lower plateau, but they are not very plentiful, and I never saw a head big enough to attract me, even though I had not shot a black buck elsewhere.

In my opinion the Nilgiri ibex (or Tahr) represents the cream of the big game shooting in these hills. As a trophy his head cannot be compared with those of the Himalayan ibex and the other big goats and sheep of the Tibetan borders, and elsewhere in the upper Himalayas. But I believe he is quite as difficult to stalk as the latter, and although one has not the rarefied air of the higher Himalayas to contend with, the habitat of the Nilgiri ibex is also very difficult country, and one has usually to work very hard to stalk and shoot a mature buck. They live amongst the cliffs and crags of the highest hills, along the southern and western edge of the upper plateau. In very wild, wet weather they sometimes come in a few miles towards the interior of the plateau, but visibility is then so bad that stalking is impossible; and there is little chance of bumping into these wild goats in a mist, since their sense of smell is very acute, and usually gives them more than enough warning of the approach of their enemies.

Horns measuring 14½ inches represent a good head for this ibex. The accepted standard of maturity is the grey "saddle" which the bucks develop with advancing years, and it is only these "saddlebacks" which may be shot. The quality of the trophy lies in the whiteness, and clearness of contrast between the saddle and the rest of the skin, and it is usual to mount the entire skin with head attached, as is generally done with tiger.

Although there are many hundreds of ibex along these outer hills, the saddlebacks are not at all common, and they are extremely wary. Very often one does not find them at all amongst the herds of does and kids and "brown bucks". They frequently feed apart from the herds, accompanied, as a rule, by two brown bucks, which act as sentinels while the saddleback grazes or rests. On an average about six saddlebacks were shot each year while I was in the Nilgiris. I went after them myself in any time I could spare, whenever I was near the ibex country during the shooting season, but it was not until my fourth year in the district that I was successful.

It was during the grass-burning season, and I was burning in the game country south-west of Bangitappal. I was beginning to despair of shooting an ibex, and had taken out a native "Shikari" to look for saddleback in the country round about, while I was working. It was a lazy way of doing things, but I could not spare the time to scour the hills myself. The "Shikari" stayed out all day and every day, searching in all directions, but with nothing to report in the evenings except brown backs or doubtful saddles. About the fifth day, however, he came to me where I was working, at about noon, and said that he had found a herd with three saddlebacks in it, one of them being a very big one.

I ate my lunch hastily and set off with the "Shikari". He had left the herd about four miles away, on the edge of the hills looking down towards the Silent Valley. They had moved on when we reached the spot, but we sighted them through binoculars, after going another couple of miles. Then began a long stalk, after making a big detour in dead ground, so as to approach them up-wind. There were about thirty in the herd, and they were grazing amongst a lot of rocks on top of a low ridge. We got on a level with them, and within about 100 yards, by means of painful crawling, and hiding behind rocks and clumps of grass when any of the animals looked up. There was, however, no sign of saddleback, so we lay down behind cover, and watched the goats as they grazed, and moved in and out amongst the rocks.

After about twenty minutes, since no saddleback had come into view, we retraced our steps - in other words crawled out of sight - and made a bit of a circuit, so as to approach from another angle. In doing so we must have made a noise, or given them a touch of our wind, for when we got to a place from which we ought to have seen them, the herd had disappeared.

We searched the country with glasses from several view-points, and finally spotted them on a hillside a further two miles away. A second stalk followed, similar to the first but much harder work, for a steep rocky ridge intervened between us and our quarry, and had to be crossed without attracting the attention of the ibex. Finally, when we emerged from dead ground, and expected to see the herd within two hundred yards, the brutes had moved on. Actually they were not far away, for we soon found them. But this time they were very watchful and suspicious, and it did not look as if they would allow us within range. We crept up a narrow rocky "nullah", keeping out of sight as far as possible. When we reached a spot from which we should have got a good view, the ibex had moved on, round a shoulder of the hill. We followed, and found them on another hill, facing us, with a small valley in between.

There were no less than four saddlebacks, and one of them was a grand old buck. He stood out as the patriarch of the herd, much bigger in body than any of the other bucks, with a white saddle showing up most distinctly against a background of what appeared to be black hair instead of the usual drab ginger, or so-called brown. I was out of breath, my heart was pounding after the climb and I was in no shape for a steady shot. Besides, I was using a magazine rifle with a rather clumsy backsight, which made it slow to get on the mark. But the ibex could now see us clearly, and started to stampede, so there was not a moment to spare. The old buck was broadside on, and I aimed amidships and loosed off as quickly as I could. The bullet struck the rock just below his belly. The sound of the shot reverberated round the cup of the hills, and seemed to puzzle him, for he stood still, instead of bolting. I felt too shaky to aim up so I raised my sights from 100 to 300 and fired again, but could not see the strike of the bullet. To my amazement the ibex remained quite still. The "Shikari" whispered that my second shot was high, so I lowered the sights to 200, aimed behind the shoulder, and fired. This time, to my great relief, the old buck toppled over, and rolled down the steep hill towards the valley which separated us. He was dead when we reached him. The second shot had hit him in the spine, and must have paralysed him, which explained why he had waited for a third. The actual range was about 150 yards.

He was a very fine specimen of the Nilgiri saddleback, and worth waiting four years to secure. His horns were not big. One was 13½ inches, and the other still less owing to having its tip broken, probably in combat for leadership of the herd. But the saddle was the best I have seen, and the rest of the skin was unusually dark in colour, making an effective background for the grey saddle.

There was less than an hour of daylight left, and we were some ten miles from camp. I lay in the grass and rested, while the "Shikari" removed the skin. As time was short, he skinned the carcass up to the head, then cut through the neck, and took off the head complete. We were very weary when we got back to camp, in the moonlight, about 10 p.m. I wanted to soak the skin and head in a bath of brine for the night, but the "Shikari" was not one for taking any chances with such a good skin, and he set off with it for Ootacamund about midnight. Even by taking all short-cuts, this meant a walk of at least twenty miles, but this at the end of a long day did not deter him, and he delivered the goods to the taxidermist after breakfast the next morning, having first visited my house and proudly shown the skin and head to my family.

The Sambhur is found at all altitudes in the Nilgiris, but in the thickly wooded country of the lower plateau he is difficult to locate. In the rolling grasslands to the west of Ooty, and in the lower hills and valleys before one reaches the rocky fastnesses of the ibex, there is magnificent stalking of sambhur to be had. They take to the cover of the "sholas" by day, but before 10 o'clock in the morning and after about 4.30 in the evening, they are out in the grass. The country is beautiful, the air exhilarating, and the going is pretty good if one's wind is sound enough for the hill-climbing which is often involved.

I shot only one sambhur stag in the Nilgiris, and I got him easily, and quite early in my time in the hills. It was in the course of a tour all round the outer rim of the plateau, which I made with Peter Dawson, looking for sites for inspection huts. There was considerable poaching of ibex going on, mostly by coolies from tea estates. On their off days they used to hunt the ibex with dogs, and many does and kids were killed in this way. We had no camping places in the ibex country, so it was difficult for the forest staff to look out for poachers, unless they had previous information of a hunt. Peter had worked out a design for a cheap inspection hut, and I had got permission to build two of them.

Our first camp was at the fishing hut on the Mukerti river. From this camp we walked westwards to Nilgiri Peak - the scene of our arduous climb a year before - and examined the country eastwards, back to Mukerti Peak, choosing two possible, sheltered sites, close to perennial water. I was looking out for a saddleback during the whole of this tour, but although we were continually seeing ibex, we saw only one saddleback in the course of more than a week, and we did not see him for long enough to get a shot.

The second day we sent our kit by pack ponies eastwards to the hut on the Krurmund river, about three miles away, while we planned to get up on the hill-tops, and work round until we were due south of this hut, to which we would make our way across about six miles of hill and valley in the evening. But we had hardly gone more than half a mile up the first hillside in the morning, when we sighted a sambhur stag and a few hinds on a level with us, and about 400 yards away. The stag looked a good one, and the wind was favourable, so we crawled in his direction, and got up within about 150 yards without being seen. The rest was easy. The stag had massive antlers, of no great length. They measured 34 inches, but as they had the very wide span of 38 inches and were perfectly balanced, the head made an impressive trophy. I had the complete head and neck mounted, and was so satisfied that I did not try to shoot any more sambhur stags, although later on I had several easy chances of a considerably bigger head.

I sent the head and skin in to Ooty, and we continued our tour of the hilltops, coming down each night to camps in the valleys to which our kit had gone by the shortest route. It was a very happy trip. Peter was a great hill climber, and made his way up a number of steep eminences while I skirted the bases. Wandering here and there amongst the hills from daylight till dark, we must have walked at least 25 miles a day. I don't think I have ever felt so fit, and we had the most enormous appetites when we reached camp in the evenings. It was the cold weather, and the air was particularly keen and bracing. The cold, eventually, was Peter's undoing, for it brought on a very violent attack of fever. He gave me a bad fright, for the symptoms looked very like blackwater, which is often fatal. We cut short our tour by several days, and I took him on a pony for about twenty miles to the nearest road, where there was a camping shed of sorts, and where I had prepared to spend the night. But he was so ill that I decided not to risk staying. I managed to borrow the only car in the village. Its owner could not drive, and his driver was away, so I drove it myself, and sent it back the next day. The car was strange, the lamps bad, and the road narrow, winding and very rough. It was a miserable journey of about 24 miles, and I was very relieved when I fetched up at the hospital at Ooty about midnight, with my then unconscious passenger. Fortunately my fears about blackwater fever were unfounded, and Peter was up and about within a week, but in no condition to walk the hilltops for some weeks to come.

Although I gave up the pursuit of sambhur stags after shooting one good head, I did a lot of stalking of hinds during my last two years in the Nilgiris. The game association had decided that it would improve the breed if old, barren hinds were destroyed. A few licence-holders helped, but nobody was particularly keen on doing the destruction, since there was no trophy to be had out of it, and it meant getting in immediate touch with the nearest fish watcher so as to get the meat transported for feeding trout in the hatcheries and stewponds, and in selected stretches of the streams. I therefore did most of the shooting myself, and shot something like fifteen in two seasons. When I had overcome my dislike of the idea of shooting females, I enjoyed the stalking. I made up my mind not to let any animals get away wounded if I could possibly avoid it. This made the stalking more difficult, for I did not shoot until I was so close that I felt pretty confident of killing. I do not think I fired at any range longer than sixty yards.

Using a 450-400 double-barrelled rifle, I seldom required the second barrel. A lighter rifle would have sufficed, but the 400, with a soft-nosed bullet, was more effective. Barring one hind that I missed completely, when I was short of breath after puffing up a steep hill, nothing that I fired at got away. But I had many fruitless stalks through endeavouring to get really close before shooting. There was one exceptionally big stag in part of the country where I frequently shot old hinds. Licence-holders were always out after him, and some people bought licences specially, in the hope of bagging this one stag. But he was very crafty, and always eluded his pursuers. Three times, while out after hinds, I came on him by chance, and at close quarters. Each time I drew a steady bead on him, to assure myself that he was easy meat. Then I lowered my rifle, feeling very virtuous, and showed myself, and let him take himself off. He was bringing in good money to the game association by attracting licence fees, and I had got one good stag already, though not nearly so big as this fellow. He was about the place during my last two years in the district, and had not been shot, up to the time I left.

We had a number of the sambhur skins tanned, and made up into boots and shoes, suitcases and so on. The skin gives a soft suede leather which makes comfortable footwear, but it is not recommended for boots for rough work which involves frequent wetting. A tannery firm in Madras dyed some of the leather in attractive colours such as blue, dove-grey and maroon, and we had smart, coloured jerkins made for the children, before taking them home to England in the late winter. The jerkins were soft, warm and windproof, and looked very attractive.

Tiger are fairly plentiful in the Nilgiris, especially in the low country. More are killed by beating than by sitting up. A really sporting method of tiger shooting is sometimes possible on the upper plateau, when an animal is located in a small "shola" surrounded by grassy downland. The sportsman places himself suitably, outside the covert, which is then driven by a few beaters. The tiger emerges, to be shot (or missed) by his adversary, who is sitting or lying in the grass on much more equal [...]

[Three pages missing]

[...] since there was only one eye-witness, and he had already pinned the crime on the wrong man, if this story were true. These two brothers were prominent on our black list of undetected poachers. No more was heard of their poaching activities after this case. Presumably they were thoroughly frightened by the narrow escape of one of them. This was satisfactory from the point of view of game protection, but was no consolation to the unfortunate family of the subordinate who had been wantonly killed while doing his duty.

Chapter XV

THE NILGIRI TROUT

The upper plateau of the Nilgiris is well watered, and contains a number of really big streams, but strangely enough, until man intervened, these waters held no fish above the size of a minnow.

The first attempt at artificial stocking was made in the early days of European settlement on the hills, when a species of carp was brought up from the plains and turned into the Pykara river, some ten miles west of Ooty.

The carp grew and multiplied, and no doubt provided acceptable sport when no other fishing was available. But in the later years, when trout were introduced, the carp became a pest, eating trout fry and ova. Raking the spawning beds of the carp and destroying as much of their ova as possible, have been a regular part of the work of the Nilgiri Game Association for years past. In my time we went a step further by leasing the right of netting the carp to some professional fishermen of the plains. Large numbers of the carp were caught in the nets. But even if the water were poisoned, it is doubtful if all the carp could be exterminated. It is probably sufficient to keep their numbers down as far as possible. Fortunately they have not spread to any other waters on the plateau, though I believe their spawn can be carried on the feet of birds.

I cannot remember when the first attempts were made to acclimatise trout in the Nilgiri waters. At a guess I should say it was somewhere around 1900. Brown trout, brought from England as eyed ova, were first tried. A small hatchery was started, and a number of the trout were eventually turned out in one or two of the rivers. They did not succeed in breeding, however, either in the hatchery, or in the streams. It is on record that the time of spawning of the cock and hen fish did not coincide - thus giving rise to the phrase "poor fish", which has since become a common expression of pity, tinged with contempt. The brown trout likes very cold water for spawning, and it is possible that the water of the Nilgiris never becomes cold enough for its successful reproduction.

The next attempt was with the rainbow trout, imported, I think, from New Zealand. For some years there was little success, but the authorities wisely persevered. Finally, by getting eyed ova from Ceylon, where the rainbow had been successfully established, it became possible to get going on a big scale, and nowadays all suitable waters of any size are stocked with rainbow trout.

The man who carried this project, through many disappointments, was the late "Fish" Wilson, a pisciculturist trained in Britain, who was specially employed by Government for this work. A memorial pillar is erected in his honour at Pykara, and every trout fisher in the Nilgiris owes him a debt of gratitude.

Practically all the waters are reserved for fly-fishing, for which a season licence costs one hundred rupees. A daily licence can be had for five rupees, and there are also licences for periods of one month, one week, and the week-end. The usual limit of fish allowed on a daily licence is ten, with a minimum length of eight inches. But in certain waters that tend to become overstocked, the association sometimes finds it desirable to remove the size limit, and to let people kill as many fish as they can. There is no reservation of streams or of beats. A licence-holder may fish wherever he pleases.

The trout do not run so big as in Kashmir. In the best stream the average weight of all fish caught in one season, during my time, was between 8 and 9 ounces. In most streams, however, the average is more like 6 ounces. Fish of one pound are common in the streams, but those weighing two pounds and over do not often fall to the average angler.

The best fishing water, while I was in the Nilgiris, was the Mukerti Lake. This water used to be one of the best trout streams, rather like a small salmon river in size. In connection with a hydro-electric project, a big masonry dam was built across it, some eight miles below its source, which converted the river into a lake about five miles long, and about a mile across at its widest part. As the dam rose, the water crept slowly over the grassland of the valley, submerging worms and insects of all kinds, and providing so rich a banquet for the trout that, within a year, fingerlings had grown to a pound or more in weight, and the bigger fish had prospered in proportion.

The seasons of 1935 and 1936 saw magnificent sport on the lake. The game association provided a boat, but it was little used, for the trout were feeding close to shore, all round the lake, and one got better results by fishing from the bank.

The fish rose freely most days when there was a fresh wind, and those anglers who braved the wildest of the monsoon weather got the best baskets. It was very unusual to catch a fish that was less than a pound in weight. The smallest fish taken was usually nearly 1½ pounds, and trout from 2 to 2½ pounds were very common. They were fat and strong and full of fight, and unless one could turn a fish that made for the centre of the lake, he simply took out all the line, until something broke.

I do not remember anything over 3 pounds being caught in these two years, although there must have been bigger fish in the lake, for the old leviathans of the former river must also have profited by the rich feeding. My best was 2¾

Bill Courtney, a friend, trout fishing in the Pykara river.

pounds, and I had a number around 2½. Elsie and I gave ourselves something of a fright one day on the lake. To avoid long walks up the subsidiary valleys in the course of fishing the shore, we had borrowed a tiny rubber boat, which one made buoyant by inflating a sort of bolster at either end. We decided to cross the lake to try a special bay on the other side, and foolishly embarked about the widest crossing we could have chosen. Half way across, my end of the boat started to deflate alarmingly, and I spent the rest of the trip pumping like mad to keep some air pressure up, and baling out the water we were shipping, while Elsie paddled for all she was worth. When we made the shore we found a puncture, which we patched. But thereafter we only used the boat for crossing creeks and narrow bays.

The lake trout were not very fussy about what flies they took, but they liked a bit of colour, and were very partial to flies with silver bodies. In later years they have risen less freely, and many have turned into bottom feeders. The fine condition of the early years has not been maintained, but I believe one can still get very good fish on the fly.

One can camp by the fishing water, either in the game association's hut near the head of the lake, or in the Government inspection bungalow at the dam. But as the dam is only about 24 miles by motor road from Ooty, most people fish the lake by the day, without camping.

The headwaters of the Bhavani river, and other small water, both in the remote parts of the Kundahs, were stocked with trout for the first time in 1930. As usually happens when there is no indigenous fish bigger than the minnow, the trout had a great time until the natural supply of food ran short. In 1932, when the streams were opened to fishing, the fingerlings of 1930 were nearly two pounds in weight. I caught a few beautiful fish of about 1½ pounds in 1932, and more in the next two seasons, including one of 1¾ pounds. But within five years of the original stocking, the trout had so increased in number that the bigger ones could not get enough to eat. I had ample evidence to show that many of them turned cannibal, but this did not help them much, since thousands of small fry kept to the tiny tributaries where the big ones could not get them, and where they ate up all the food that should have found its way into the main stream. The big fish ranged downstream, as rainbows do, in search of better feeding, until they finally disappeared. The Bhavani descends by huge waterfalls to the plains of Coimbatore, and the other stream falls in two or three steps of about a thousand feet each, into the evergreen forests of Nilambur. Trout would not be likely to survive such falls, and even if they did they could not live in the warm waters of the plains.

Since the Mukerti has been converted into a lake, the Krurmund is undoubtedly the best trout stream in the Nilgiris. It is about 11 miles from Ooty by road and bridlepath, and can also be reached by motoring 24 miles to the Mukerti dam, and walking a couple of miles across country. The Nilgiri Game Association maintains a two-roomed fishing hut right on the river bank, where the bridle path crosses a ford, on its way to Mukerti.

There are upwards of six miles of fishing water on the Krurmund, and there is considerable variety, from rocky gorges, falls, and swift runs, to deep lazy stretches where a dry fly, skilfully used, should do better than the wet fly which is generally used in the Nilgiris.

The game association spends a good deal of money on the Krurmund, and is fairly successful in keeping up a [...]

[4 pages missing]

[...] I was always interested to see the work going on at Avalanche, where there is a hatchery, with the usual stockponds and fryponds. It was fascinating to watch the head fish watcher - who is an expert - stripping the big breeding fish at spawning time. The breeding stock is usually taken from the Nilgiri waters, but occasionally some new blood is imported from New Zealand.

If all the trout which breed in the streams would distribute themselves uniformly, there would be no need for artificial re-stocking. But what happens is that the top waters are usually overstocked, while the lower waters, which are heavily fished, require some replenishment every year or two.

In addition to re-stocking with trout bred in the hatchery, we used to catch a lot of the surplus fish in the upper waters of several of the streams, for introduction lower down. I often helped the Fishing Superintendent and the head watcher in this work. We found that netting was too expensive, and that the cheapest way of collecting the fish was to catch them on a small fly. This was excellent practice in the close season. There were always plenty of trout, but the water was extremely low and clear during the cold weather when this work was done, and one had to fish fine, and fish carefully. I reckoned a hundred was a good day's work for me. The Superintendent, being lighter of hand, used to catch more, and the head watcher usually got most of all. He not only threw a beautiful light line, but he had the eyes of a hawk, and could see exactly where nearly every little fish in the river was lying. These small trout, when taken on the fly, are lifted in a landing net, and the hook very gently removed without handling the fish. It is necessary to hold the fish steady while disengaging the hook, and this is done by keeping several folds of cold, wet net between the fish and one's hot hand. A man with a large tin carrier, covered with wetted blanket material, accompanies each rod, and receives the live fish from the angler. The water in the carriers is changed frequently. The mortality in catching these fish for restocking was well under 5 per cent. Most of them were lightly hooked and came off easily, and it was only the very few that were severely pricked which succumbed. The disgorger was required for less than 20 per cent of the fish caught.

During the latter part of my time in the district, a fishing sub-committee was formed to make plans for permanent stream improvements, before all the reserve funds of the game association were spent on the employment of a European superintendent of fishing whom they could not really afford. As one of this sub-committee, I made a survey of the Emerald Valley stream and of its tributaries, and prepared a plan and estimate for works of improvement which seemed possible and desirable. The main line followed was to make small dams in suitable places in feeder streamlets, thus forming ponds for the propagation of various kinds of water insects, and for the introduction of a breeding stock of fresh-water shrimps and snails. Most of the dams were made before I left the Nilgiris, but I doubt if much interest was shown thereafter - as often happens when the originator of a scheme goes away. The idea of the sub-committee at that time was to take up the improvement of one or two fishing waters every year, and I think it is a pity that the policy was not continued. The details of the method proposed were experimental in the first instance, and some of them were probably unsuitable, but I feel sure that the general idea was on sound lines, and would be much preferable to the costly business of "handfeeding" and tying up meat in order to increase the food supply of the trout.

The rainbows of the Nilgiris provide excellent sport, in a good climate, and amongst the most attractive surroundings. For those who like to live at the waterside, there are the three furnished huts maintained by the association. Those who prefer to live amongst the social amenities of Ooty can fish all but the most remote waters by the day. The dates of opening and closing the various fly-fishing waters vary slightly from one season to another, in accordance with the stocking, and the condition of the water and of the fish. But generally there is fly-fishing to be had from the beginning of April to the end of October, and there are the "coarse-fishing" waters open throughout the year.

Chapter XVI

THE OOTACAMUND HUNT

It is easy to understand why shooting and fishing in the Nilgiris are very much the concern of the District Forest Officer, through his official connection with the Nilgiri Game Association. But his relations with the Ootacamund Hunt are less obvious, and require some explanation.

The country hunted by the Ooty hounds lies almost entirely in reserved forest. It is mostly grassland, but it is none the less forest reserve, and as such it is controlled and managed by the forest department. In connection with the game association, I have indicated that game management and forestry do not always see eye to eye. Divergence of interest as between hunting and forestry also requires reconciliation at times. Further, the hunt employs a good deal of labour every year on the upkeep and extension of rides through woodlands, and the paved crossings through the swamps and treacherous stream beds which are very common in the hunting country. Friction between this labour and the lower subordinates of the forest department would be inevitable, if the labour were solely responsible to an outside body, unconnected with forest management. The hunt constantly requires the permission of the forest department to carry out this and that improvement in the hunting country. It therefore suits both the hunt and the forest department that the District Forest Officer should be an official of the hunt, and for many years it has been the practice of the hunt committee to make him their honorary secretary, if he is willing to undertake the onerous duties involved. In these circumstances I was intimately concerned with the affairs of the Ooty Hunt during my years in the Nilgiris.

Supervision of work on rides and crossings I was often able to combine with forest inspections, but the correspondence, finance, supplies to kennels, and all the other multifarious duties of an honorary secretary had to be done in my spare time. However, I considered that five seasons' hunting with the best pack in India was ample compensation for my labours.

The Ootacamund Hunt is, for India, an old institution, dating back, as far as I remember, to about 1840. Hunting was spasmodic at first, and was dropped for some years, until about 1845 (?) when the hunt was re-started on a regular footing by Captain (later Colonel) Robert Jago, a former officer of the old Madras Army, who had become a forest officer for the Nilgiris and the adjacent forests of the Coimbatore and North Malabar districts.

Ooty Hunt, flat racing

Since Jago's time the hunt has gone from strength to strength. There are now some 50 couple of foxhounds, partly imported from England, and partly bred in Ooty. Hounds meet three days a week. A European kennel superintendent is employed. Reserve funds have been built up sufficient to tide the hunt over possible lean years, or to cope with an emergency such as the destruction of the whole pack by an epidemic.

Unlike the hunts in Northern India which are run by and for the military, the Ootacamund Hunt is primarily intended for the civilian residents of the Nilgiris living in, or within reach of Ootacamund. Amongst the residents one must include the Governor and his staff, and the officials of the Madras Government, since Ooty is their summer headquarters, and since their support of the hunt is both generous and regular. Casual visitors to the hills help with the finances, and so do the officers of the small British garrison at Wellington, while several Indian princes and noblemen subscribe with great generosity. But the number of regular followers is small, as compared with big cantonments in the north, and subscriptions are therefore high, by comparison. Hunting is expensive in other ways as well. Oats and other imported feed are very dear by the time they have been transported to the hills. Carriage of horses is an expensive item for visitors from Madras, Secunderabad and other distant places. Even stabling is costly for those without premises of their own.

In view of the small number of regular members it is impossible to maintain the hunt at a high standard, out of subscriptions alone. There was no difficulty in the spacious days shortly after the first Great War, when Ooty seemed to be full of money. But in recent years it has been necessary to rely more and more on the proceeds of racing in order to finance the hunt. In my time we used to raise over 15,000 rupees annually, that is well over a thousand pounds, from this source. This involved a great deal of work and worry. There was usually one day's gymkhana racing on the flat in May, and always one day's flat racing for hunters, and one day of point-to-point races in September. The hunt takes a percentage from the totalizators and sweepstakes, and realises various other moneys from entrance fees, lotteries, car park fees, and so on. This racing is not a very reliable source of revenue since it depends largely on the availability of money amongst the Indian community, and their willingness to risk it in betting. The weather, too, plays an important part, and one year we went so far as to insure against rain on the day fixed for the point-to-points, or rather to insure a minimum profit, which amounted to much the same thing.

The hunting country covers about eighty square miles, and lies immediately to the west and south-west of Ootacamund. It consists of rolling grass downs, interspersed with swamps and patches of woodland, both of which, though frequent, are usually of small extent. Some of the hills are steep, and it takes a horse some time to get used to them, so as to get up with the least waste of energy, and to come down with speed and safety. On the grass the going is firm and good. The swamps are dangerous, and have to be negotiated by the paved crossings maintained by the hunt. Stream banks, too, are usually unsafe, so the smaller streams have to be crossed by paved or otherwise sound fords, instead of jumping them. Despite these obstacles, which have to be crossed by obligatory routes, the faster horses and the better riders are able to keep up with hounds. The English thoroughbred has come much into favour of recent years, in preference to the waler (horse imported from NSW) and the countrybred, so most people have fast horses nowadays. Many criticise the country for its lack of fences and banks. It has, however, the attraction of wildness, there is plenty of fast galloping country, and so far as thrills are concerned I personally got quite as much thrill as I wanted, coming down steep hills with my heart in my mouth, and my mouth somewhere about the horse's ears.

The jackal is hunted, and usually gives a good run. There is seldom any difficulty in finding a jack, though they are sometimes scarce in the smaller coverts close to civilisation. It is very common to pick up a line that has been taken during the night or early morning, and to follow it for a considerable distance before the jack is viewed.

Cubbing starts in late March or early April. The hunting season opens early in May, and closes usually some time in October. There is some showery weather in April and May, but until the monsoon starts early in June, the downs are too dry to carry a good scent, and on the hard side for horses. From June until the end of the season, hunting is of a very high order. The Master of Foxhounds (M.F.H.) almost invariably hunts hounds himself. Two or three members of the hunt assist him by whipping in, and there are usually two Indian whips amongst the Hunt servants.

The meets are usually at 6.30 in the morning, which means getting up well before daylight. This is rather a trial until one gets accustomed to it, but there is always the consolation that one is better off than the horses and the "syces" (grooms), who have to set out very much earlier. Most of the meets are on or near a road, and can be reached by car in half an hour or less. Some are so close to Ooty that one can hack out in twenty minutes or so.

During my first two seasons the hunting days were Tuesday, Thursday and Saturday. Then Sunday was made a hunting day instead of Saturday, so as to suit tea planters and others with whose work the hunting interfered. Apparently the London directors of some of the tea companies got fussy when they heard that tea planting near Ooty was in progress only for three days a week, since there were three days' hunting, and Sunday was a holiday in any case. To overcome this objection the planters agreed to hunt on Sundays and plant on Saturdays, thus making four days' planting per week.

At the time this change was made, I unwittingly gave the opportunity for a jest at the expense of the forest department. At that time three forest officers in addition to myself were stationed in Ooty, and all hunted fairly regularly. One of the Governor's A.D.C.s, who had a pretty wit on occasion, asked me how I liked the Sunday hunting. I said it did not suit me, as I had been in the habit of fishing most Sundays. He said nothing to me about it, but went round telling his friends how sorry he was for the forest department - "Poor overworked forest officers. They can't go fishin' for the huntin'."

Hunt week, in the third week of September, is a popular annual gathering in Ooty. There is an afternoon's flat racing, for hunters, to start with, and the week ends with the point-to-point races on the downs. There is a puppy show which does not attract many spectators other than the Hunt committee and members who have walked puppies. A "lawn meet" - more popularly described as a "coffee house" meet - is, however, a great attraction. Held on the edge of the downs, usually in perfect weather, and at a slightly later hour than the normal meets, this meet is attended by large crowds on foot, in addition to everybody in Ooty who can raise a horse. There is an undoubted attraction in the colourful spectacle of hounds and horses and pink coats, against the vivid green of the downs, in the brightest morning sunlight. An additional attraction is provided in the form of such untimely refreshments as sweet cakes and sticky liqueurs, in addition to coffee, and stimulants such as "horses' necks" and other revivers

Quintus with Countess, his horse used for hunting.

based on brandy, which are quite legitimate fare even at this early hour, in view of the Hunt Ball the night before, which has limited the night's sleep to an hour or two. Various other junketings during the week culminate in the hunt dinner in the evening of the point-to-point races. This is a stag-party, and just as well.

One of my last and most pleasant memories of Ooty is in connection with the Hunt, when Elsie and I were their guests at a dinner they gave for us just before we left for England on leave at the beginning of 1937. The hunting season was over, but it was round about Christmas, and the resident members of the hunt club were reinforced by others from the plains, who were up for the holidays. We greatly appreciated this honour, for the Ooty Hunt is not given to demonstrations of this kind. We had made many very good friends in the Nilgiris, and left the district with very real regret.

Chapter XVII

THE FOREST COLLEGE

I always succeeded in avoiding the jobs that were going in the Madras Forest College, so I have not much call to write about it. Furthermore it does not exist any longer, for it was closed down in 1939 by the Congress Government, as a measure of economy. Nevertheless it served a very useful purpose for twenty-five years, and it deserves some notice in passing.

The college was located about two miles out of Coimbatore, in five spacious buildings, on its own estate of several hundred acres. Its purpose was the training of young Indians for appointment as forest rangers in the Madras Presidency. But several other provinces such as Bombay, Central Provinces, Bihar and Orissa were quick to realise its value, and used to send their prospective rangers to Coimbatore for training. Several Indian States and the Government of Ceylon did the same, and the fees paid in respect of these outside students were of great help in meeting the cost of running the institution.

The college course lasted two years, and during my service there was usually an intake of 25 to 35 students each year, so that there were usually upwards of 50 in the senior and junior classes together. About three-fifths of the college year were spent on lectures in Coimbatore, and the remainder on practical tours in the most important of the chief types of forest in the Presidency.

The staff consisted of a Principal and two instructors of the Indian Forest Service on the Madras establishment, and two instructors from the Madras Provincial Forest Service. This appears a large staff for the number of students concerned, but each class had a large range of subjects and required two instructors to cover them adequately. The Principal had heavy administrative duties, which, with the general supervision of instruction, left him little time for lecturing. Few forest officers have either the gift or the inclination for teaching, but we were usually able to find enough with both the ability and the wish to instruct in the different subjects. There were few misfits, and the standard of instruction was very high, as proved by the attainment of the students at the final examinations held by external examiners.

For those who could put up with the academic life, the Forest College was a very pleasant job. (Coimbatore is an excellent headquarters station, with a good climate.) The officers had unlimited opportunities for recreation with the students for whom there were facilities for playing hockey, football, cricket and

Madras Forest College, Coimbatore, 1938 Front row (left to right): G. Virwanathan, E.S. Dawson, H.P. Ward, J.A. Wilson, R.S. Browne, V.G. Darrington, F.R. Madan, P.W.F. Walpole, A.A.F. Minchin, J.H. Longrigg, C.C. Wilson, A.A. Khan, T. Clear, V.N. Sergariri Rao, D.L. Sathe, W.G. Dyson, P.W. Davis, E.V. Podman-abha Pillai, A.L. Griffith.

tennis. For over two months in the year the students were on vacation, and while the staff were not allowed to leave Coimbatore at such times, they had extremely little work to do at headquarters. Their touring was all in very interesting forests, and they had their own permanent hutted camps, in which they were able to settle down for weeks on end, and to make themselves really comfortable.

My only relations with the students were to give them an odd informal lecture on local topics when they toured in my district, and to examine them at the final examinations which were held at the end of June each year. [The Principal, J.H. Longrigg, is in the centre of the photograph above. He was present when the first batch of students were given their awards in 1914. Later hw joined the staff as O.C Junior Division 1919-1921, and returned to the College as Principal at the end of 1936. He saw the last batch of students pass out in July 1939 before the College closed for the duration of the war. The Prospectus signed by him and 2-year Syllabus approved by the Chief Conservator are shown in Appendices D and E. They fully support Sir Harry Champion's description of the Forest Rangers.]

About ten officers were required for these examinations, one for each subject. It meant a considerable sweat, first to set a question paper, then to mark the answers, and finally to hold an oral examination. In some subjects there was a practical examination as well. We used to get an examiner's fee of a hundred rupees, which was small enough remuneration for the work involved, but even this was cut out during the world slump, in 1930 or 1931, and was never restored.

The only advantage in being an examiner was that it gave one nearly a week in Coimbatore, on duty, at the time of the annual gathering known as "forest week". The occasion was the conclusion of the college year, starting with the oral examinations, and ending with speech day and the distribution of prizes and certificates. With the assembly of some ten outside examiners, added to the college staff and the two District Forest Officers stationed in Coimbatore, there was the nucleus of a good party. Close on the heels of the examiners arrived the Chief Conservator and the six Conservators of Forests. They constituted the "board of visitors" for the consideration of the examination results, and in addition they spent two or three days in conference discussing matters of forest policy, administration and management.

In addition to the forest officers who were officially required to be present, as many others as could make it used to come to Coimbatore for the last couple of days of forest week. Every officer who had a wife brought her, but children were not encouraged - unless they happened to be grown-up daughters.

The accommodation of this large gathering might appear to be a problem, but the hospitable bungalows of the local forest officers seemed to have elastic properties, and when strained to the uttermost, they were supplemented by tents as sleeping quarters. Not that sleeping entered into the question very much, for there was a late party, somewhere or other, every night.

On the athletic side there were tennis competitions, both at the Forest College and against the Coimbatore Club, hockey matches between college sides, and a cricket match between the officers and the college, which the college almost invariably won. There was usually some kind of a silly sports meeting, which included such highly dangerous pastimes as obstacle races in motor cars, tent pegging from ditto, and so on. One year we had a treasure hunt in cars by moonlight, with all the youth and beauty of Coimbatore joining in. Competition, however, was not very keen, for after the scramble for the first clue, a number of couples forgot what they were supposed to be out for, and remained lost until the hue and cry had subsided, when they stole back to the rendezvous for the refreshments which formed such an important part of all competitive meetings during forest week. The Chief Conservator returned long after the treasure had been found. While looking for a clue he had put his hand on a snake - or so he said. It sounded a lame excuse for being late, but nobody was so tactless as to ask his fair partner to corroborate.

There were luncheon parties most days during the week, and dinner parties every night. When the latter broke up early, that is before about 2 a.m., the younger element and many who were old enough to know better, used to adjourn to the Club, and dance to a gramophone, and keep the bartenders busy for the rest of the night. The bar servants of the Coimbatore Club enjoyed forest week as much as the rest of us, for they reaped a rich harvest in late fees.

In one of the slump years it was suggested that the usual lavish entertaining should be restricted, and people said that this was done, but I cannot say I noticed much difference. The only change I remember was that instead of entertaining the members of the Coimbatore Club to a dinner and dance on the final Saturday, we gave what I think was called a "cocktail dance". To this our guests arrived about 6.30 p.m. instead of 8.30, which is the usual time of assembling for dinner. There was a buffet meal running the whole time, and a bar conveniently placed in a corner of the ballroom, at which dancers helped themselves as they passed. The show ended about midnight, instead of 3 a.m. or so, but what with the early start at a thirsty time of day, and the simplicity and convenience of obtaining refreshments, the entertainment proved considerably more expensive than the dinner and dance which it was replacing in the interests of economy. However, the innovation was so popular with the residents of Coimbatore that we never reverted to the more formal entertainment of former years.

In forest week of the same slump year, Peter Dawson, the Forest Engineer, invented an economy cocktail. He had a bungalow and an office on the Forest College estate, and he and his wife were most generous and popular hosts. The cocktail which was to save such a lot of money, without reduction of the party spirit, was called "forester's rummy". It was made from liquors distilled in India, which were considerably cheaper than imported spirits, and, if anything, more potent. I give the recipe verbatim, as nearly as I can remember it. "For a cocktail before dinner for a party of eight, mix two quarts of rum with one quart of gin and one of whiskey. Add a dash a lime juice, if there are ladies present. Shake lightly and serve in tumblers. Crushed ice may be added if desired by individuals, but not more than a teaspoonful to the tumbler, otherwise the cocktail loses body."

I argued with Peter that this cocktail, which was made entirely of "hard liquor", could not possibly be cheap. He agreed that as far as drink was concerned it was no economy, but if people did justice to his forester's rummy they were practically incapable of eating after it; in fact they were quite likely to forget that they had not had dinner, and just call for their cars and roll off home before dinner was served!

Actually the forester's rummy was not as fierce as all that. I saw it drunk in large quantities in his house, and his guests managed to eat quite a lot afterwards. Perhaps they cheated on the crushed ice. Whether they did or not, the exhilarating effect of the mixture was very marked, and I can seldom remember a more lively party. The whiskey used was good Scotch, only the rum and gin being country-bred. In the experimental stages Peter had used a whiskey distilled in India which he called "squirrel brand", but it was not a success. He said this whiskey tasted of turpentine and was so strong that two drinks of it would make a chap climb walls. Hence the name of "squirrel".

Speeches and prize-giving on the last Saturday of forest week occupied about two hours, which was a bit of a trial, for although Coimbatore is cool enough in June, it is none too comfortable indoors at 2 o'clock in the afternoon, dressed in a "store suit". Some hundreds of the European and Indian residents of Coimbatore used to be invited to the prize distribution, and to the garden party which followed it.

The latter was a very pleasant function. Tea was served at small tables under the trees in the attractive college grounds, to the accompaniment of a band - usually the band of His Excellency the Governor, from Ootacamund, which is only some fifty miles away. To digest their tea, the visitors were led slowly round the college premises, and shown the sights, prominent among which was the well-stocked forest museum. As the sun went down they needed no leading back to the tables, from which tea had been removed to make way for something stronger.

About once in three years the Governor honoured the final function at the College in person, and gave away the prizes. In other years some high official of the Madras Government presided. In 1938 it was the Congress Premier of Madras. His presidential speech must have cost him a good deal of thought, for he had "come to bury Caesar, not to praise him". It was the swan-song of the Madras Forest College, for its abolition had just been decided on, to have effect twelve months later. The Premier was the man who had ordered its abolition. He therefore could not, and did not, expect a very hearty reception at an institution which was extremely proud of itself and of its record, and which had done a great deal, during a quarter of a century, to foster that "esprit de corps" which is so strongly established amongst all ranks of the Madras forest department. I forget the gist of his speech, but remember that he skated round thin ice with tact and decorum.

The final prize-day in 1939 was a family party. Not a happy one, but one in which the chair and the meeting were in complete harmony. Our president for the occasion was a very popular ex-Chief Conservator, who had been knighted in his retirement a few years earlier. [This should say 'honoured'. It was Thomas Whitehead who received the C.I.E. (Companion of the Indian Empire) in 1938] He had been the finest administrator the Madras forest department had known, and commanded the greatest respect both within the department and outside it. He had remained in Madras after his retirement as a forest officer, in order to hold a post of the greatest importance, under the Government, in quite a different line. His heart, however, remained with his old service, and in inviting him to preside at this final ceremony at the college, no more fitting choice could have been made. His address was simple, but straight from the heart, and made a profound impression even on the casual visitors from the town.

Whether or not the Governor's band was available for the garden party, by His Excellency's courtesy we always had his dance band of recent years for our final entertainment at the Club. The last of these, in 1939, was declared to be the best of all. The band were dressed as forest guards, and dispensed lively music for hour after hour, and the more beer that was pressed upon them, the livelier became the music. Fun was fast and furious, and was kept up till a late hour. But for the first time I was one of the few who went home early. I was recovering from an illness, and in any case my heart was not in it. The passing of the college, and the ending of those very happy annual gatherings of comrades could not but cast a shadow. And during the previous year the Reaper had thinned our ranks of two who for years had been amongst the brightest spirits at these forest week activities, one of them being my greatest friend. [Peter Dawson. See p213. His obituary was printed in the Indian Forester for 1938]

(The other death was that of Gilbert "Robbie" Robinson, a Silviculturist who died of acute appendicitis.)

Chapter XVIII

THE FAR WEST

At the end of the last chapter I have skipped a couple of years ahead of my general sequence, so must now return to 1937, when I went on leave, after nearly five years in the Nilgiris.

I was long overdue for leave, not having been home since 1928. While in Nilambur I had intended taking leave in 1933, but when the chance of the Nilgiris came in 1932 I had snapped at it, since such opportunities do not come every day. So well did our family thrive in the splendid climate and bracing air of Ootacamund that we decided to make the most of it, and live as a united family for as long as possible. A small kindergarten school [Miss Mucklows, where many children of Forest Officers went] supplied the necessary education for our three daughters. Our small boy, born in 1933, required no schooling. In these circumstances we postponed our leave until January 1937, by which time our eldest daughter was over ten and getting a bit old-fashioned for the kindergarten.

Having been so long without leave, I light-heartedly took a whole year, instead of the more usual eight months. The only trouble about such long leave is that after the first eight months, one automatically goes on to half pay. A trifle like this caused us no concern at the outset, but by the time we had bought and furnished a house in England, and got the girls started at school, we were so broke that we could only put up with about two months on half pay, and I was obliged to ask for permission to return to duty, late in October, before my leave expired.

The Madras Government made no difficulty about my returning early, and I was told that I would be posted to the southern of the two forest districts in South Kanara. I was far from pleased. Of the thirty odd districts in the Presidency this was almost the last I should have chosen for myself, had I any say in the matter.

Elsie stayed in England with the children, and I returned to India alone. I sent off my furniture and household effects from Ootacamund by train, and then bought a car and took myself by road to Mangalore, which was to be my new headquarters.

The South Mangalore district, to which I was posted, was a failed "gold mine" of the American era. It was to have been one of the biggest shows in the development of the forests of the Western Ghats, but it had never got anywhere.

Quintus with his daughters (from left to right), Penelope, Chloë and Kathleen.

Its beautiful forests are full of beautiful trees, which nobody wants. Where fire and other malpractices of "homo sapiens" have destroyed the original virgin forest, there is a rather inferior jungle of semi-deciduous type. But the bulk of the forests are the big, tropical evergreen type which flourishes in a rainfall of 150 to 200 inches, and, as I have already mentioned, most of our evergreen timbers are of such low value that it seldom pays to extract them.

This, then, was my new district. There was next to no work to do, and I was bored stiff. Had the shooting been good I should not have grumbled at this enforced rest-cure, but these dense evergreen forests are not attractive to game, and apart from a very occasional "Battue" of green pigeon, I never used gun or rifle.

Mangalore, the headquarters, struck one as being the end of all things. I was as far west as I could go, for it is right on the Indian Ocean. Nor could I go much farther north, for the railway, which creeps up the coast from Calicut, comes to an end at Mangalore. Like many towns in Madras, Mangalore strikes one as a place with a past, but no future, and very little present. It was an important trading station in the days of the Portuguese. Tippoo Sultan thought it worth fighting for. But to-day it is a decrepit port, whose only claim to distinction is the "Mangalore tile" to which it gives its name, and which is made in large quantities from the clay which has so silted up the mouths of the two rivers which meet at Mangalore, as to ruin the place from the point of view of shipping. Even small steamers have to stand out a mile or so, beyond the sand bar, and all loading and unloading is done by lighter.

The most important business in Mangalore is the curing and shipping of the coffee which is grown in the hills of Mysore and Coorg. Coffee prices were very low when I was there in 1937 and 1938, and both planters and curers were depressed. Tile and brick manufacture probably comes next, and the tile and brick makers seemed pretty depressed too. I was not feeling particularly bright myself, having left all my family in England, and altogether I thought very little of Mangalore. There were, however, a few cheery bachelors who were good company.

When in headquarters I went to my office religiously every morning, but try as I might I could never find more than an hour's work to do. Incidentally, the office was three miles away from my bungalow, so my daily hour was quite expensive in petrol. The mail was delivered in the evening, after office hours, and was sent to my bungalow. I usually dealt with the letters immediately, but this seldom took more than half an hour or so. Office work had been the bane of my existence in all my other districts, but when I got to about the only district in Madras where there was practically no office work, I found life extremely boring.

I spent a great deal of my time on tour. There were three forest ranges in the district, and all of them had sleeper operations going on. But this work was not on a very big scale, and there was little else.

In the most southern of the three ranges there was also some working of timber in the log, and about ten elephants were employed. Small plantations of Teak were being made here, on rather shallow laterite soil which would never be considered for Teak at Nilambur. As far as I remember, I got this planting stopped, since I considered that if there were money to spare, it would be far better spent on further increasing the plantations in either North or South Malabar, where Teak flourishes.

The forests of South Mangalore run up from sea level to 4,000 feet or more. But in my time both sleeper-working and production of round timber were confined to the plains. There was nothing doing in the hills, nor were there any facilities for camping except on the plains, where the climate is warm and exceptionally humid.

South Kanara is a very backward part of Madras. There are few roads, and fewer bridges. There are, however, many rivers. These are crossed in the dry

Quintus with his driver, Govinde (and dogs Bunty & Baloo) and 'the floating car'.

season by means of boat ferries, capable of carrying a car. In the monsoon one just does not use the roads which have unbridged rivers.

On some of the roads there are rivers with neither bridges nor ferries across them. If the bottom is fairly firm, and the depth not more than about 18 inches, such rivers can be forded fairly easily, by cars. But even in the dry weather, occasional local rain may be so heavy as to make the crossing difficult - or impossible. About forty miles out from headquarters, on my way to camp, I once ran into a heavy rainstorm, which had apparently been going on for some hours. About two miles short of my destination there was a wide ford, about two hundred yards across. The river was rising rapidly, and I had either to make a dash for it, or return ignominiously home. There were a few locals about, who said it was still possible for a car, and two of them said they would walk in front, and show me the shallowest crossing. Night was falling, and so was the rain, in sheets. My camp two miles away seemed very attractive, so I decided to take a chance. I got across all right, but not without some very bad moments. The bottom was hard enough, but consisted mostly of small, rounded boulders which tended to roll from under the driving wheels. The water was deeper than I expected, and half-way over I struck a particularly deep patch in which my car actually floated. It was a station wagon with a light, plywood body. The water was nearly a foot above the running boards in the deepest part, and it seemed to lift the car up in the water, so that the back wheels only struck a rock here and there. I was carried downstream, out of my course, but soon struck some shallower water where the wheels were able to grip again, and I made my way to the far shore. I was extremely relieved to be across. Such of my kit as was on the floor of the car was soaking wet, including my bedding. Luckily this was not serious, for in a warm climate like South Kanara, one does not need much in this line.

Since I had taken over charge of the district with four months of the official year to run, I could not blame my predecessor for having left a number of forest reserves uninspected. But he certainly was not considering me when he decided which of the obligatory inspections to postpone. I had to get to some pretty inaccessible spots between November and the end of March. Right down in the south of the district there were about three reserves in a very remote locality. I had to go down the coast by train, as there was no road, and then do a two-day trip up a river in a boat, in which I fed and bathed and slept, and was eaten alive by mosquitoes. It was an ordinary dug-out boat, just wide enough to take my camp bed, and was propelled by paddles in deep water, and by poles in the shallows. Along the banks there was jungle for the most part, with a very occasional clearing for a few houses and a grove of coconuts.

The forest reserves did not touch the river, and we had a bit of difficulty in finding them, using maps and compass bearings. Neither the ranger nor the forester who were with me had been there before, as far as I remember, and the forest guard of the beat was to meet us on the spot. When we found the reserves, I made the usual row about the boundary lines being neglected. But I really could not see what possible use these forests were to anybody. The forest department got nothing out of them, and they were much too remote from human habitation for anything to be stolen. They were not even necessary for water and soil conservation, which is the usual reason for maintaining forests which are unproductive.

Another troublesome inspection was the verification of the Mysore frontier. This was very legitimately left for me. One section of the frontier has to be checked every year, and the work can only be done in the hot weather, when the leeches let up a bit.

This section of the boundary is a day's march from the nearest cart road, and the country, in many parts, is impossible for baggage elephants. All kit had therefore to be carried on the heads of coolies. I followed the boundary up hill and down dale, while the coolies and my servants took the easiest line they could, and pitched the tents at pre-arranged places on the frontier, when they reached them. We had three such camps, and got back to a road on the fourth day. The boundary wandered up such steep, high and rugged hills that I was able to inspect only about five miles a day.

Towards the end of the section, the line ran from the top of a high hill, down a steep gully, to a broad river. Unfortunately there were some boundary marks chiselled on bedrock in the gully, and these had to be verified. Most of the way down, walking was impossible. I and my subordinates just jumped from one foothold to another, and slithered down smooth rocks on our behinds, over a descent of about 2,000 feet, until we reached the river, in a state of exhaustion, and with our scanty clothing in shreds. It would have been quite impossible to inspect this section of the boundary the other way round, for one could not climb up many of the rocks which we had slithered down.

There were a lot of wild elephants in this remote part of the country, and we saw herds of them in several places. There were always some of them crashing around in the bamboo jungle near our camps, at night, but fires were always kept going, and they did not try to play any games with our tents.

The camp in the district which I used most is about twenty miles inland, and about forty miles from Mangalore by the circuitous route one is obliged to take, in order to avoid unbridged rivers. It is at the foot of the Ghats, and the forest rest-house is on a hill which stands about 300 feet above a broad, clear river. It is a very beautiful setting, with hill slopes, clothed with tall evergreen forest, rising on both sides of the river valley.

This place was a good centre for inspecting much of the work which was going on in the southern half of the district. Across the river, near the rest-house, there was a most ingenious type of wooden bridge, designed, I think, by the Logging Engineer, and built during the period of development under American methods. It is a fair-weather bridge, being removed before the monsoon and re-erected at the end of the rainy season. The river is about a hundred yards across, so the cost of a bridge with strong masonry piers would have been prohibitive. Instead, firmly bedded rocks in the river were used as foundations. Holes were drilled in these rocks, and round iron bars fixed vertically in the holes. These bars are the only part of the bridge to be left in position during the rains. Cylindrical sections of trees, with holes drilled down their centres, are impaled on the iron spikes, and these, in either pairs or threes - I forget which - form the piers of the bridge. The iron bars and the wooden cylinders are all of different lengths, depending on the height of the rocks to which they are fixed. The tops, of course, are all on the same level. Above the wooden piers come the wooden girders and finally the decking and hand rails. All pieces of the bridge are lettered and numbered, and rebuilding after the monsoon is simplicity itself. The bridge takes a motor car, or a lorry or cart loaded with timber. There were not sufficient bedded rocks in a line to take the bridge straight across, so it has a big bend in the middle, where it follows the line of suitable rocks. The curve adds much to the picturesque appearance of this quaint, but very serviceable bridge.

A flourishing trade in cashew nuts was developing along the Kanara coast when I was there. The nuts were shelled, graded, and exported in sealed four-gallon tins, mostly to America. One European firm in Mangalore had specialised in the business, and had established a big factory for preparation of the nut, and of the by-products obtained from the process of shelling. The local crop, however, was nowhere like sufficient, and for about six months in the year they kept their factory going with nuts which they imported from East Africa.

I had experimented successfully with growing cashew in Nilambur some years before, and now, in a district where there was a big demand for the produce, I turned my attention to it again. I prepared a scheme for planting up a large acreage of land which was growing nothing useful. This work would have given me a real interest in the district, but I was transferred before the scheme was sanctioned. I was convinced that there was much more money in cashew nuts than in timber in South Kanara, and I hope the work prospers.

The climate of South Kanara is enervating. It never gets really hot, but except during the monsoon it is always warm, and the air is saturated with moisture. The slightest exertion - even the use of a pen - brings one out in a muck sweat, and prickly heat is a very common affliction of the skin, overtaxed as it is, by perspiring. It is, however, a great country for coconuts. Wherever there is a habitation, there are coconut palms, and the juice of a tender coconut makes a cold and most refreshing drink when one is hot and bothered.

The ubiquitous coconut is one of the blessings of South Kanara, but the ubiquitous leech is a curse. The forests are almost entirely evergreen, so one is always amongst the leeches. One can keep them at bay fairly well in the dry weather, by wearing tobacco anklets, but it is a nuisance having to be always on one's guard. In the monsoon, forest work comes practically to a standstill.

Christianity is very strong in Mangalore, and all along the coast. Large numbers of the people are of Portuguese extraction, remote in some cases, but they seem very proud of it. The district is full of names such as "de Souza", "Pereira", "Sequiera", "Albuquerque", "de Silva", etc.. There are many social strata amongst these people of mixed blood. Many of my forest guards, for example, were called "de Souza", but wealthy merchants of similar name on the coast would look down their noses at such humble people. And between these extremes there are several gradations.

Our club, with some fifteen members, many of them depressed over coffee and bricks and so on, was either dull, or completely deserted, except on Saturday nights, when everybody turned up and stayed late. This being the case some of my bachelor friends occasionally sought entertainment elsewhere, and I accompanied them several times to parties given by some of these remote Portuguese, who are extremely friendly and hospitable. On being introduced, once, to a snappy little thing, I was amazed to hear that her name, instead of Pereira or de Silva, was O'Brien. Her little bit of the west could not be laid at the door of Vasco da Gama. Not being much of a conversationalist, I made the first fatuous remark that came into my head - "I suppose you are Irish, Miss O'Brien, like myself." "Oh no", replied my dusky beauty, "I am pukka European."

What I liked best about South Kanara was the odd week-end when I left it on a visit to the hills of Coorg, across the eastern border of my district. Coorg is a miniature province under the control of the Government of India. The country is mostly a plateau of 2,000 to 5,000 feet elevation. The climate is cool and pleasant, and there is a large and hospitable European population, mostly engaged in coffee planting. I usually went to my brother-in-law [Ivor Bull. He started the very successful Consolidated Coffee company and retired to Suffolk about 1947] who manages a group of estates in South Coorg, and sometimes looked up the Chief Forest Officer in Mercara, which is the capital. The cool breezes of Coorg, after the sticky heat of South Kanara, were a splendid tonic.

In the spring of 1938 the Congress Government in Madras decided, as a measure of economy, to amalgamate the two forest districts in South Kanara. (If the development envisaged by the Americans had come off, each of these districts was to have been split into two, as being too heavy for a single officer.)

I prepared the ground for the amalgamation, and I was to be put in charge of the combined district, which would give me plenty of work to do. But in early June, just before the north and south districts were combined, I was transferred to Madras as Personal Assistant to the Chief Conservator of Forests.

Chapter XIX

IN THE SHADOW OF OLYMPUS

I viewed my translation to Olympus with very mixed feelings. I was going to the seats of the mighty, not as one of them, but only to sit at their feet.

My previous service had all been in the districts. I had worked in practically all types of forest, and felt that my experience in district work was reasonably matured. I had, in fact, matured in the wood, and here was the opportunity to get a personal insight into the higher administration, and to acquire first-hand knowledge of the working of the forest department "vis-à-vis" the Government.

The time was particularly opportune, since the forest department was well in the limelight. By June, 1938, the Congress Government was settled in its stride, after nearly a year of office. In their election programme they had promised the people a number of reforms and economies in forest administration, and they were now busy implementing their promises. The Chief Conservator's office in Madras was a hive of activity, preparing the schemes demanded by the Government, and answering their very searching questions on matters of policy, and even on details of quite minor importance. There was very hard work ahead, but some of it was obviously of great interest and importance.

The nature of the Personal Assistant's job was, however, against all my inclinations. It is entirely office work, whereas the outdoor work of the department is what has always attracted me. My brain works slowly, and I have always made heavy weather of the office work, for which I have no natural aptitude.

My greatest consolation in undertaking this sedentary job lay in the person of the Chief Conservator then in the saddle. ['Tommy' Whitehead] We were very good friends; I held him in great respect, and as far as ideas were concerned we had a great deal in common. I had been criticised in my earlier service for being too commercially minded. The Chief Conservator was even more so. He expected hard work from his officers, but he himself worked harder than any of them. Finally he was so appreciative of any special effort that I made to assist him in his very arduous duties that it was a real pleasure to work for him. He made me feel more like a partner than the dog's body which the rest of the department considered me to be.

In point of fact the Personal Assistant has a very responsible position. It differs, however, from the other jobs in that if he goes off the rails, it is his chief who gets the blame. This, to my mind, makes his responsibility the greater, for surely it is worse to get someone else into trouble than to take it in the neck oneself.

The volume of work in the head office is so great that it is quite impossible for the Chief Conservator to be "au fait" with it all. Countless letters which go out in his name are never seen by him. He naturally deals with all matters of policy, and important correspondence with Government, but even here he has not the time to delve into files, perhaps six inches thick, to ascertain the facts. These have to be produced by the Personal Assistant in the form of a brief note, with references to the files on all points, so that he can verify the facts where he thinks it necessary.

The assistant has to use his discretion the whole time, to decide how much he can do on his own, how much it is essential for his chief to look into, and how much the latter would wish to see simply to keep his own knowledge of current questions up to date. It is therefore necessary for the assistant to merge his individuality in that of his chief so that he can tell the latter's answers to many of the questions that arise, without even asking them. He has to hold the fort when the Chief Conservator is out on tour, and give the right answers to visitors or telephone enquirers, and, at times, to Government, on matters which are too urgent for reference to the Chief Conservator's camp.

Except for the preparation and revision of budget estimates, the Chief Conservator is, fortunately, not greatly concerned with accounts. The cash accounts of subordinate officers are audited by the Accountant-General, while the timber accounts are supervised by the Conservators. The greater part of the work in Madras consists of correspondence, and the preparation and consideration of reports. Disciplinary matters also take up a great deal of time.

The Personal Assistant opens all incoming letters, and approves the drafts of everything that goes out. Even when the Chief Conservator writes a draft in his own hand, it is not copied until the assistant has read and initialled it. This is just a precaution against the Chief Conservator slipping up, through ignorance of some fact that is known only to his assistant, who, of course, is supposed to be conversant with all matters that go through the office.

Before my time, the assistant also checked and signed every fair copy that left the office. I found that I was spending about three hours every day simply reading quickly through the typed copies, and signing my name. The matter was put up to Government, who agreed that it was sufficient if letters to them were signed by an officer, and that most of the remainder might be signed by the office manager. The latter belongs to the most highly-paid class of ministerial servant, and is perfectly competent to check letters against the approved drafts, all of which he has already read in any case, before distribution to the typists.

I wrote the drafts on all the most important subjects myself. In the case of those prepared in the office, I tried to curb the verbosity in which the Indian clerk seems to delight. I also tried to insert some style and dignity into their correspondence. Most of the letters drafted by the clerks are destined for subordinate officers, and I considered it the duty of the head office to set and maintain as high a standard as possible. Of even more importance did I consider the letters to the public, and I often re-wrote entire drafts in order to prevent correspondence leaving the head office in ungrammatical and slovenly English.

Apart from questions of grammar and style, I aimed at letters which were definite, authoritative, and convincing. The Chief Conservator is the fountain head. He may not know absolutely everything, but he is more likely to know everything than any of his subordinate officers. In any case he has the last word, so let it be absolutely clear and convincing, and open to no misinterpretation, doubt or argument.

Disciplinary cases against officers were unusual, but those which did come up had to be handled with the greatest care and exactitude. As regards the subordinate ranks, there was no end to the disciplinary decisions which had to be made. Rangers can be reduced in grade by the Conservators, but only the Chief Conservator has the power of dismissal, so all the most serious charges against rangers are referred to him for action. In the case of lower ranks the Chief Conservator is usually the final court of appeal against the orders of the Conservators or of the District Forest Officers. Further appeals may be made to Government, but the appellants often realise the futility of going further. Even if they do go further, the Chief Conservator still has to submit to the Government his comments on the appeal.

These disciplinary files were the most distasteful part of my work, and they took up a great deal of time. In ordinary matters one can rely on the office to do much of the ferreting out of facts, but in matters of discipline it is not only unwise to do so, but may also be unfair on the accused person. A clerk may have some axe to grind. He may be the friend or the enemy of the accused, or even, for all one knows, a close relative. If none of these arguments apply, there is always the danger that he may give the benefit of any doubt there may be to a man of his own cast, or make unnecessarily damning points against one of a different faith. The preparation of notes to assist the Chief Conservator in such cases was a job I loathed.

Office hours are from 11 a.m. to 5 p.m. The late start is a relic of the days when all clerks were Brahmins, who require several hours to themselves in the morning, for religious ceremonies. I usually went to the office about 10, and stayed till 6, but even then I generally had to take files home with me, to keep reasonably up to date.

About the only exercise I had time for was sea-bathing before breakfast. This was very pleasant, for the only cool place in Madras is by the sea, in the early morning and in the evening. The Chief Conservator's office is on the sea front, and my room got its share of ozone through the wide open windows. But ozone, when well warmed up in the sun, and churned around by an electric fan, seems much the same as any less beneficial air, and did not reconcile me to the weary hours in my office chair.

In such conditions Sunday assumed a new importance. On tour in a district I often forgot when Sunday came round. Now it was a very welcome respite from labour. I was usually lazy, sometimes spending the whole forenoon in and out of the sea, and sometimes watching a match at the Cricket Club and indulging in the excellent oysters which the club produced, on previous order.

In the alleged "cold weather", I sometimes went snipe-shooting with the Chief Conservator, on Sundays and other occasional holidays. There is really excellent snipe-shooting to be had some 40 miles out of Madras. One aims to be on the ground at dawn. For a couple of hours one walks up the birds in the paddy fields or the grass swamps, but as soon as the sun gets well up they take to the jungle. The jungle in question is the very poorest of scrub, often not more than six feet high. It once belonged to the forest department, but was handed over long ago to the villagers, for communal management. The old boundary lines and interior rides have, however, been maintained. Guns take position on the rides or outside the boundaries, and the jungle is driven by beaters. The snipe come over, very low and very fast. One has to be quick to get them. I usually missed, but I thoroughly enjoyed the fun.

I was not particularly fit during my six months in the Madras office, otherwise I should have missed the active life of the jungle even more than I did. I had acquired a bit of a hob-nailed liver in south Kanara, where the excessive moisture of the air did not suit me. I perspired so profusely that my system did not retain enough liquid to perform its functions adequately. This, at any rate, was my theory. It is possible that I did not help matters when I returned from my camps to the comparative civilisation of Mangalore, by replacing the lost moisture with considerable quantities of iced beer. Anyhow I felt better when I went on to warm beer, and better still when I cut it out altogether, as I did in Madras except on Sundays.

I have mentioned the reforms and economies which the Congress party had promised during their election campaign. Foremost amongst these was the halving of the fee for grazing in reserved forests. The fee in respect of cattle in most districts was only three annas (a penny halfpenny?) per head per annum. For any man who considered he could afford to keep a cow, I always thought this was an absurdly low charge for maintaining it for a year in the state of semi-starvation which is the common lot of the common cattle owned by Hindus in Madras. To reduce the fee by half seemed fantastic, but it was extremely popular with the people, and since it made them more contented, one cannot say it was other than a good measure. But it meant a huge drop in forest revenue, which neither the Congress nor any other Government could afford. We were called on to rack our brains to make good the loss by other means, and did our best to oblige. Actually the deficit amounted to less than half the previous revenue, for more permits were sold at the reduced fee. The latter was now so low that it was cheaper for rogues to pay the fee than to bribe the lower subordinates to wink at their illicit grazing. In this way the country gained in a certain access of honesty.

Actually the Government themselves went a long way towards paying for their generosity to the people in the matter of grazing, by their reductions in the establishment of the forest department. Most of these reductions took place, or were set in motion, during my time in Madras, and they gave us a great deal of extra work. In the first place we were given the opportunity to justify the retention of the posts or establishments which the Government proposed to abolish. A few of the reductions were very appropriate, and no attempt was made to oppose them. But generally a reasoned case was prepared in favour of retention, since it was the view of the forest department that the abolition of the posts would result in loss of efficiency, with ultimate financial loss to Government, despite the temporary saving which would undoubtedly be effected. It is not my wish to criticise the Government in the slightest for the action ultimately taken by them. They considered each case with great care and fairness. The Premier himself went into the most minute detail of each proposal. A number of modifications were made in deference to the professional opinions put before them, and I am quite convinced that they were satisfied that the reductions they ordered were for the greatest good of the greatest number.

As these reductions were ordered, the Chief Conservator had to work out the doubling up of charges so as to carry on the work with the least possible dislocation. This was extremely difficult, for many of the charges were already very heavy. But it had to be done. There was also the matter of selection of the officers to be "axed" - a difficult, as well as painful task.

I have referred, in an earlier chapter, to the abolition of the Madras Forest College. Several districts were also abolished, and their ranges divided up amongst neighbouring districts, or amalgamated with each other. Two posts of Conservator, with their office establishments, were done away with. This involved a most unsettling shuffle of clerks all over the department, and the axing of a number equal to that of the posts which had ceased to exist.

The innovations made by the Congress Government were not by any means restricted to the use of the axe. They inaugurated a number of constructive schemes in all departments, and made searching inquiries into costs, which resulted in many reductions of expenditure that in my opinion were long overdue. They started a sort of economic survey of the resources of the Presidency which may well lead to a considerable increase in prosperity, although I presume that things have been held up by the second world war. Although we of the forest department disagreed with a number of their measures, I think most of us will agree that in their short term of office, the Congress Government gave our own as well as other departments a shaking-up which, generally speaking, was very salutary.

Half-way through my spell in the Madras office, I was shattered to hear that Peter Dawson, the Forest Engineer, had been drowned in the bathing pool at Nedungayam, in Nilambur district. He had dived in, under the eyes of his unfortunate wife, and never re-appeared. His body was not recovered for nearly two days. He was a strong swimmer, so his accident was the more difficult to understand. Heart failure was presumed. Like Hugo Wood five years previously, he was buried on the site of his greatest work, on the river bank within a hundred yards of the big girder bridge which he had designed and built. It was his wife who chose his last resting place, for Peter was the embodiment of life and liveliness, and not the sort of chap to think of dying. Nevertheless he had done a very wise thing less than a year before. He never had any money, owing to his early marriage, his considerable family of three, and the exceeding generosity of both himself and his wife. When he insured his life only some months previously, he had taken out a double accident endowment policy at a small extra premium. He told me at the time that he was damned if he was going to die in his bed should his time come while he was still in service. In consequence of his provision for accident, his estate received double the amount insured, which made a very great difference to his bereaved family.

Peter's death was the greatest loss to the forest department, and a source of great sorrow to his large circle of friends, in fact to everyone who knew him, for I believe he had no enemies. To me the department never seemed the same after his departure, and from that point of view the outbreak of war a year later came as something of a relief, providing me with a complete change of scene and conditions of life. Elsie was as cut up as I was, for she shared my great regard for Peter, and it was amply reciprocated.

The Congress Government's economy measures provided me with my release from the office stool. One of the Conservator's posts which they abolished was that of Working Plans. Although they saved the pay of the Conservator and part of his office staff, the work of supervision of working plans had to go on, and the job was given to me, to my great satisfaction. The work remained essentially the same as when it was done by a Conservator, but it came under closer control by the Chief Conservator in that I was made Working Plans Personal Assistant to him, thereby providing the department with the clumsiest abbreviation from which we suffer, namely that of "W.P.P.A." We have done our best to avoid the awkward title. "Superintendent", "Supervisor", and even "Manager" of Working Plans had been suggested to Government for the new post. But they would have none of these, so we had to put up with their choice.

Elsie arrived out from England, leaving the family at home, just before I assumed my new duties. Her journey out had cost considerable heart-burning both to her and to me. She was due to sail during the Munich crisis of September 1938. War seemed inevitable, so she cancelled her passage and cabled me accordingly. When Mr. Chamberlain had secured what he considered was "peace in our time", she arranged to sail a fortnight later. Though the expression is a common one, I had never before heard of anyone "missing the boat", but this is exactly what Elsie did, and she is never likely to hear the last of it.

She went overland to Marseilles, got in the wrong end of the train in Paris, and before she had time to get out at Marseilles, she was being wafted off towards the Riviera. When she realised that she had really left Marseilles and that the train was not just shunting, she pulled the communication cord, stopped the train, and got into a frightful argument in her rusty French with the train officials. The latter naturally got the best of it, and she was taken on to Toulon. When she got back to Marseilles her ship had sailed. She tried to fly to Egypt so as to overtake it at Port Said, but the airlines were heavily booked. She encountered a companion in distress who had also "missed the boat", and when finally a single passage by air was offered, she resigned her claim, since he was an army officer who was likely to get into trouble if he overstayed his leave.

As if this were not enough, she got involved in the big fire in Marseilles, when the Cannabiere was pretty well burnt down. She got out of her hotel just in time, and went off to Cassis, a small seaside place up the coast, where she remained for a fortnight, until there was another sailing of the line by which she had booked.

The next mishap was my fault. I had arranged to meet her ship at Cochin, but I had to take to my bed with an obscure fever, and send a servant to escort her to Madras.

She swore she would never travel by sea again on her own. But within the year she was to embark alone on a wartime voyage, to take charge of the children in England. The trip lasted seven weeks, and the minor thrills of the voyage culminated in the sinking, by a magnetic mine, of the ship in front of hers, as the convoy was creeping up the estuary of the Thames.

Chapter XX

WORKING PLANS AGAIN

The headquarters of the Working Plans Circle had been Ootacamund, so we went there as soon as I had handed over as Personal Assistant, about the end of November, 1938. We travelled by road, and spent a night in the comfortable rest-house maintained by the Public Works Department at the Mettur Dam, about 250 miles from Madras.

It was good to see the Nilgiris again, even though it was but a brief visit. I took over charge from the Conservator, and spent a few days getting in touch with the work on hand. The records were packed up and sent off to the Chief Conservator's office in Madras, and the office staff was dispersed. About half the clerks were transferred to Madras to maintain the new working plans branch which was now added to the head office. The remainder were either transferred elsewhere, or "axed", according to their seniority.

There were five working plan officers employed at that time, four being Indian and one English. They were scattered pretty widely throughout the Presidency, and I set out to do the rounds of the districts in which they were working.

The Working Plans Circle had made great strides since its infancy in 1925, when I had made my first acquaintance with it. Everything was running on oiled wheels. Each officer had his own subordinate staff, trained in the special work which they had to do. Even before one plan had been completely written, the officer would get his field staff busy in the district which he had to take up next, while he himself was engaged in finishing his plan. In this way there was not a day wasted.

Our first tour, a very brief one, was to Nilambur, where the revision of the working plan I had made in 1928 was practically completed. The district was in excellent shape. There had been no essential changes since I had left for the Nilgiris in 1932, but a number of improvements in method had been effected. One which had given excellent results had been introduced by my successor the year after my departure. I had considered that the alluvial flats were not sufficiently well drained for planting Teak stumps, and while recommending stumps everywhere else, I had retained the old method of planting entire seedlings in making second rotation plantations on alluvium. The change to stumps was, however, successful, and had given better results, generally, than the old method, though I did not see anything that could compare with the one small freak plantation that had been the apple of my eye in my last year.

From Nilambur we went to North Malabar, known as the Wynaad. This is a district which has altered out of all recognition during the period of development which started after the first Great War. From being a very backward district, with timber operations on a small scale, and next to no planting, it is now second only to Nilambur in point of timber output. As regards annual area of Teak planting, it leads Madras.

The timber exploitation has been organised in a most businesslike and economical manner, despite very considerable difficulties due to the peculiar location of the forest. The district lies mainly on the Mysore plateau, far from any timber market. Most of the logs go to our two depots in the Mysore State, between 40 and 60 miles away by road. Not only is the lead a long one, but the timber is subject to a tariff levied by the State authorities. Transport used to be by bullock cart, which greatly restricted the size of log that could be carried. Of recent years carts have been replaced by motor lorries, and some of the big six-wheelers which are used can carry logs of almost any size. A special point has been made of roughly squaring the timber after felling. This saves the cost of carrying timber which would in any case come off as wastage in sawing. It also gives the logs an attractive appearance, which is a big point with the Indian buyer. In spite of the initial disadvantages from which our timber suffers, it competes very successfully with home-grown Mysore timber and brings in a large annual profit.

A small timber depot at Tellicherry on the North Malabar coast has been expanded considerably, and the most recent development has been to open a sale depot in Calicut, some 80 miles away on the coast of South Malabar. This was started about 1935 when a sudden demand came from Europe for rosewood logs of a large size, and Calicut was the port of shipment. The Wynaad in particular, and the Nilgiris, South Coimbatore and Nilambur to a lesser extent, took immediate advantage of this temporary boom, and the forest department made a deal of money. The prices paid at the port for the biggest sizes was fantastic. As far as I remember logs of 8 feet girth and over fetched something like fifteen rupees, that is over £1 per cubic foot, whereas in the ordinary way we are doing pretty well when we get three rupees a cubic foot for this timber. Some of this rosewood went to France and some to Germany. I cannot think why they wanted it at these fancy prices. Perhaps Germany had some "secret weapon" in mind.

On the hill slopes of the Wynaad, between the plateau and the Malabar coast, there are big evergreen forests, traversed by the ghaut road down to

Tellicherry. This road makes the question of extraction much easier than in our other evergreens in remote hill tracts, and a large and profitable business is done in railway sleepers.

The Wynaad Teak plantations, which are being extended at the rate of about 400 acres a year, are doing very well. In quality - as determined by size - the trees are inferior to the plantation Teak at Nilambur, but nevertheless they will be of great and increasing value, as they grow up.

With its large timber and planting operations, the Wynaad is a most interesting forest district. About 40 elephants are employed, and elephant capturing is done most years. The headquarters and most of the forest are on the plateau, which enjoys a very cool and pleasant climate, being at an average altitude of about 3000 feet. Tellicherry is about the only camp in the plains, and this is a beautiful little seaside resort, with a small residential club on the cliff above the sea. Below the club there is a bathing lagoon, surrounded by a reef of rock which keeps the sharks out.

As regards sport, there is big game of nearly all kinds in the Wynaad, and in the cold weather there is excellent snipe-shooting. There is also good duck-shooting to be had in the Mysore State, across the eastern boundary of the district. Altogether it is a district that I always hankered after, but never got.

Field work for the preparation of the Wynaad working plan was in its final stages at the time of my first visit. I made a general inspection of the forests and plantations, and discussed the proposed plan with the Working Plans Officer. Although the field work was nearly finished there were a number of debatable points about new proposals which had to be settled. The Chief Conservator came up from Madras for a conference on the spot. The Conservator of the Circle and the District Forest Officer were also present, and we had two very pleasant camps in the district, and argued out the points at issue, after joint inspection of local conditions. There were three wives in the party, and rest-house accommodation was limited, so most of us used tents, and found the nights pretty cold.

As far as I remember, Elsie and I returned to Madras after these combined camps. We went via Mysore and Bangalore, and spent a few days in the Chittoor district, which lies to the east of the Mysore State, and where another working plan was in its concluding stages. Chittoor is a pleasant district at the lowest level of the Mysore plateau. The forests are of the small, dry deciduous type, of no great value, but being less than 100 miles from Madras, fetches good prices. Bamboo is scarce, as far as I remember, but steps were being taken to introduce it by planting. There is a good deal of firewood-working by the coppice system, and in the west of the district there is sandalwood. The forest grazing is better than in many districts, and was being improved by the adoption of the rotational system of grazing blocks. The annual grazing revenue is large, and altogether the district is very profitable, despite the low rainfall and the unimpressive appearance of the forests.

We spent a couple of weeks in Madras, while I organised the new working plans branch of the Chief Conservator's office. There was little space for this new activity, but I was given a long room for the clerks in a sort of attic under the roof. It contained a lot of skylights, so one was in frequent danger of sunstroke, but the light was excellent, which was a great advantage, since map-making is an important activity in a working plans office. I worked in my old room, which the new Personal Assistant was good enough to share with me.

There was a good deal of office work in my new job, but not so much as in the ordinary district, and most of it was of an interesting nature. Routine correspondence and cash accounts from the working plan officers did not take up much time. The working plans, as they were written, came to me a chapter at a time, for approval, and had often to be sent back for alterations or additions. Reconnaissance reports, which are the preliminary to every working plan, require very careful preparation and scrutiny, before they are sent to the territorial officers of the district concerned, for remarks. The reconnaissance report gives unlimited scope to the working plan officer for airing his views and proposing innovations. To minimise the necessity for alterations in these reports after preparation by the working plan officers, I introduced an innovation by inspecting each new district before the Working Plan Officer went to it, and writing a brief note for his guidance. He could still make as many new proposals of his own as he thought fit, but my method insured that what I considered the most essential points were incorporated in the reconnaissance report.

After correcting and approving the chapters of the working plans as they came in, I passed them to the typists in my office for final typing. Any doubtful point I took to the Chief Conservator, and he gave his instructions then and there. This simplified his task of examining the plan on completion, before according his sanction. After sanction by the Chief Conservator the plans went to the Government Press for printing. There then remained only the infuriating job of correcting the printed proofs.

In my capacity of assistant in working plans, most questions on forest policy and management were held to come within my province, and files of this nature were gleefully passed to me by the Personal Assistant, who, but for the creation of my new job, would have had to worry them out himself. These are the most interesting type of subject in the head office, so I did not mind. What

I did object to was when he would send me a telegram, while I was on tour, to hasten my reply to some burning question whose file was still in transit between Madras and my camp.

Since my outdoor work took me from end to end of the Presidency, I used to go out on tour sometimes for two months or more at a time. I was usually several hundred miles from my headquarters, and the boxes of papers which were sent out daily from Madras often took a long time to reach me. In these circumstances I used to take a steno-typist on tour with me. He kept a sort of camp office going wherever I was, doing all my typing on the spot, and despatching letters direct to all addressees except Madras. This saved much time, and compared with the normal method in a district of sending all drafts back from camp to headquarters for copying and despatch. This tour clerk was also extremely useful in arranging transport and so forth. Despite the long distances covered, I have never had such carefree touring. The clerk kept a copy of my dated tour programme, and saved me all the petty annoyances of arranging moves, reserving accommodation in traveller's bungalows, and so on.

The next tour took me, for the first time in my service, to the northern part of the Presidency. Following the coast road to the north of Madras for about 250 miles our first camp was by the sea, in the Guntur district. Guntur has always been considered, by my generation, to be our Number 1 "punishment station", and it has been a standing joke, when an officer has made a blob, to assure him that he is booked for Guntur. For most of the year the heat is terrific. I have heard the annual rainfall described as "either scanty or absent". The local population has little or no forest conscience, and the main work of the staff is chasing goats, which, as I have mentioned before, are prohibited from grazing in reserved forest. The people, however, are great goat fanciers, and do not stop short of murder when their illicit grazing is opposed. A year seldom passes without the murder of at least one forest subordinate in this district.

What with the heat, the low rainfall, the pilfering of man and the browsing of goat, the forest is mostly of a very inferior type of scrub. From the point of view of height growth a good picture of the so-called "forest" can be had from the story that is told of the young Englishman whose first district was Guntur. Like us all he was very impatient for his first sight of the forest, and went out to camp at the earliest opportunity. The nearest forest reserve was about a mile from his camp, and he set out to inspect it with his ranger. After walking for nearly an hour he asked the ranger how much further they had to go to reach the forest. The ranger said they had been walking by the side of the forest for the last half hour. "Where is it?" said the officer. "I cannot see any forest." "Oh no", replied the ranger, "we cannot see the forest with this field of cholam in between." Cholam is a grain that stands about five feet high, and on the flat Guntur plain the trees could not be seen above it.

The jungle, however, is not all so miserable as this. In some of the worst parts I seem to remember occasional trees ten or twelve feet high. But the picture is not very greatly over-drawn. The wretched trees stand little chance. The climate is against them in the first place. Much of the soil is poor. Small seedlings are browsed by goats, and such trees as survive all these adverse factors often have their tops lopped off for goat feed. What remains is not a tree but a pollard, whose shoots continue to be cut for the goats when the forest guard's back is turned. Finally, if and when these struggling pollards have at last reached a girth of about eighteen inches, they are very liable to be cut and stolen for making into the wooden plough of the country. It is a disheartening district, quite apart from the heat.

As can be imagined, the typical Guntur forest is very open as regards tree growth. This gives herbage a good chance, and even the light rains which the country receives are sufficient to produce good crops of grass. Grazing, of the legitimate variety, is therefore important, and the grazing revenue is one of the principal sources of income.

Our first camp, being in the littoral belt, was in a different type of forest. There is a considerable extent of mangrove swamp, which I inspected by traversing the backwaters and creeks in a motor boat. This is a pleasant, lazy way of making an inspection, but there is not much else one can do about it. At low tide the mangrove swamps are feet deep in mud, and at high tide the mud is under water. The mangrove trees breathe through "pneumatophores" or "aerial roots" which grow up from the root proper, and keep their heads above the mud.

The mangroves are worked for firewood, and bring in a good revenue. They seed themselves naturally, which assures the perpetuation of the forest.

On our way up a long backwater, parallel and close to the sea, we put up clouds of duck, teal and waterfowl of all kinds. I shot a couple of duck more by luck than anything. The noise of the motorboat usually drove them off the water before we had approached within a hundred yards. It was aggravating, with such quantities of birds about, not to be able to get near them.

In sandy soil near the sea, some good plantations of Casuarina have been made in recent years. The plant requires watering in its early years, but this is done cheaply by carrying water from shallow wells dug in the sand at intervals throughout the plantation area. Once it is established the tree grows rapidly and is big enough to cut for firewood in something like twelve years.

The trees are closely planted, and are thinned out about twice, before the plantation is finally felled. The thinnings have a sale value, but the bulk of the profit comes from the final crop, which is very heavy. The fuel fetches a high price locally, and it even pays to send it to Madras, where there is a huge demand for firewood.

Our camp by the sea was very pleasant. The month was early February, and the hot weather had not quite started. Bathing in the surf was good, and we had lots of fresh fish caught by the local fisher folk who live along the shore.

We made two or three camps inland and saw the types of dry scrub forest. I do not remember much about them, except that to one who had served for many years in the moist forests of the west, they were very depressing.

We spent one night in Guntur, where I had to inspect the office of the Working Plan Officer. We were very hospitably entertained by the Indian District Forest Officer and his wife. They had been about three years in the district, and were applying for a transfer. Their description of the hot weather was lurid.

I do not think I was able to add anything worthwhile to the Working Plan Officer's ideas for improving the Guntur forests. We agreed that there should be a considerable extension of Casuarina planting, and that plantations of fruit trees should be made in suitable places. Amongst fruit we included the "soapnuts" that are largely used as soap in Madras. We also discussed the improvement of forest grazing.

From Guntur we went westward through very hot and arid country to the Kurnool district. The Kurnool revenue district at that time was divided into three forest districts, but their number was about to be reduced to two, under the economy scheme of the Government. This entailed a general re-shuffle in Kurnool and the districts to the east and south of it.

Kurnool is on the low Deccan plateau. The soil is mostly stony and poor, and the climate is very hot and dry. It is one of the so-called "famine districts", and when crops fail, as they quite frequently do, Government relief measures are required in order to save men and cattle from starvation.

The feature of the district, so far as the forest department is concerned, is the huge range of hills known as the Nallamallais, which rise above the general level of the plateau to a total height of about 3,000 feet. Except for the occasional small clearings where the hill people known as the "Chenchus" live, the whole of this mass of hills is reserved forest.

The Madras and Southern Mahratta railway runs south and west of the hill range, and in the old days when wood fuel was used in the locomotives, the outer slopes were heavily exploited for firewood. Fuel working is now confined to the lower slopes and the belt of forest at the foot of the hills, within economic distance of Kurnool and a few biggish towns and villages in the south.

There is an undulating plateau on the top, and both here, and in the valleys, the rainfall is sufficient to grow deciduous timber up to about 4 feet in girth. The best of this timber would only be considered as pole size in the forests of the Western Ghats, but no better is available locally, and it can be extracted at a small profit.

There is excellent grass in these forests for some months after the first rains of the year, and thousands of cattle are then brought in from the dry country to the east and south, and penned in the hills for grazing. But nothing like all the grass is utilised.

It is possible that extensive cattle-breeding and dairying could be undertaken in the hills, and the forest department would welcome such development, for the timber is of low value in the first place, and the lead to the markets is long, so that timber production is never likely to be important.

I did not see the completion of either of the two working plans which were being made here in my time, so I do not know what new proposals were made in this matter. We were experimenting with the making of silage. Hay-making has always to be undertaken in years of famine, and the process is familiar. There is little money in either hay or silage, where they have to be carried for long distances. But if cattle were to be kept permanently on the hills, hay and silage could be produced cheaply for hot-weather feed. The great drawback to any enterprise involving the settlement of plainsmen in the Nallamallais is the prevalence of malaria, which is very bad in the hot weather. Even the Chenchus, who have always occupied the hills, are riddled with it. Malaria, however, has been controlled elsewhere, and I have no doubt that a few centres of habitation could be made reasonably free of fever. Water shortage in the dry weather is another difficulty, but nowadays this matter can usually be solved, if one is prepared to spend money on it.

We only camped round the foot of the Nallamallais on this tour, as I had not sufficient time to go up into the hills. I meant to do a long tour later in the year, but the war interfered, and I only managed one more brief camp.

From Kurnool we moved south into the Anantapur forest district, which includes the reserved forests of the Bellary revenue district as well as those of Anantapur. These are also "famine districts" with much stony and inhospitable soil, and a hot, dry climate. There are a very large number of widely scattered reserves in this forest district, and it is a difficult charge to manage, being something like 150 miles from end to end. Here the flat of the Deccan plateau is broken by low, rocky hills, and wherever there is a hill, there is a forest of sorts. The growth is generally poor scrub and thorn. A better type of forest was supported in the distant past, but it was ruined by cutting and lopping, goat-browsing and fire. Almost all the hills have suffered severely from soil erosion, and the drying up of such water sources as they contained long ago.

There has been a slow improvement in the jungle growth after some forty years of protection by the forest department. This can actually be seen by comparison of the growth in places where two hills lie close together, one being a forest reserve, and the other unprotected waste land. But even now it is sometimes difficult to recognise an area as any attempt at a forest until one gets close enough to see the white-washed cairns along the boundary line. The establishment of a better and denser jungle on these hills would do a great deal to improve the lot of the agriculturist and of his cattle, both by preventing the deposit of silt on his fields, and by increasing the supply of water to the small "tanks" or artificial lakes which are dotted all over the country, but which now hold water for only a couple of months in the year.

The process of nature in rehabilitating these very degraded jungles is extremely slow, and I had a great mind to do something to accelerate it. Conditions of soil and climate are very adverse. Many of the hills are almost down to bedrock, with only occasional small pockets of soil here and there. The soil can never come back without assistance, either by mechanical means or by the establishment of vegetation, or, better still, by a combination of both. The mechanical means would consist of contour trenches, or some form of terracing, probably by making low contour wells of the loose stones which cover the hillsides. Such works would retain moisture after rain, and would collect eroded soil and fine rock particles. Some sort of vegetation would then establish itself naturally along the contour lines, and would play its part in soil formation. The establishment of vegetation could be accelerated by sowing or planting.

I made some tentative suggestions on these lines. They were not, in fact, altogether original, for some work in the way of building stone walls had been done long ago in these arid tracts. This work did some good but was not really effective, partly because of lack of continuity, and partly because protection of the reserve was even less effective than it is now, and fires did much to prevent the establishment of a good ground cover.

I hope it will be possible to do something about it when normal conditions are restored, after the war. The provision of funds is an undoubted difficulty. But it is possible that a scheme could be at least partially financed by making remunerative plantations of fruit trees beside perennial water. There is not much perennial water in this parched country, but it does exist in places, and will be increased when a proposed hydro-electric and irrigation project is put through.

Another crying need in these parts is a cheap supply of firewood and of small timber for ploughs and other agricultural implements. The people are too poor to pay anything but the lowest prices, so it is impossible to supply them from distant sources such as the Nallamallais in Kurnool. Fuel series are worked in several places, but the yield per acre is extremely low, and the poor forest which is thus exploited becomes progressively poorer with each cycle of felling. Much of the forest is too poor even to consider felling for fuel and small timber.

Since the forest department is not in a position to supply the needs of the people at a price they can afford to pay, one can hardly be surprised that they help themselves when they can find anything worth stealing, and when nobody is looking. Thus the slow healing process of nature is further delayed.

The main source of forest revenue in Anantapur district is the lease of the right to collect bark for tanning from a shrub called Cassia Auriculata, which is one of the few things that grow reasonably well in the inhospitable soil. Grazing revenue comes next, and the rest nowhere. This is forestry as known in Anantapur. There is no competition for the post of District Forest Officer.

We found it very pleasant touring the district in the latter half of February. The hot weather had not started. The nights were chilly, and the mornings fairly cool up to mid-day. The country was a complete change to anything we had ever seen before, and the twilight appearance of the low, rocky hills had a beauty of its own.

As if to make up for the poor impression given by their forests, the staff seems to go out of their way to make a show of the forest rest-houses. Those we camped in were comfortable, tidy and scrupulously clean. Their compounds were equally well kept, and usually had flower borders or ornamental shrubs to add to the general air of prosperity.

I had some very enjoyable duck-shooting, in a small way, during this tour. I have mentioned that the countryside is dotted with small "tanks", and at this time of year many of them held duck and teal. Being a single gun I seldom got more than a couple, and sometimes none at all, before the birds flew off elsewhere. But on one tank where they were more persistent, I picked up ten or a dozen in half an hour.

We returned to Madras for the first part of March, and then, for some reason that I have forgotten, I had to go again to the Wynaad. The hot weather had started in Madras, so we were not sorry to leave for the cool plateau of North Malabar.

From the Wynaad we went north into Coorg, which lies next door. I left Elsie with her brother and his family, while I did a trip with the Chief Forest Officer to see some special work he was doing in his evergreen forests on the lower slopes facing the coast.

On the return journey to Madras we spent some days on the plateau in the north of the Salem district, where I studied, amongst other things, the artificial regeneration of sandalwood, which they were doing in several ways.

From the middle of April until about the middle of July, we were out on tour continuously. The Government had decided, if possible, to reduce the very large amount of money which leaves Madras every year in payment for imports of South African wattle bark for tanning. They required a scheme for the introduction of wattle in our higher hills, and they wanted it urgently. The Provincial Silviculturist had already written a note dealing with the propagation of the wattle, from such information as he was able to collect, and the preparation of the scheme was a working plans job. No working plan officer was available, so I had to do the job myself. I borrowed a few foresters from the different working plan officers, for the field work, and got busy.

The Palnis, in the Madura district, and the Nilgiris were the hills most likely to provide the cool climate the wattle requires, and I dealt with the Palnis first.

We had a very hot and weary drive from Madras, across the sweltering plains of South Arcot, Trichinopoly and Madura, but the Palni hills when we reached them, were delightful. Kodaikanal is the only place of any size in these hills. Its altitude is about 6,000 feet, and it is a very popular hill station, especially for people living in the south of the Presidency. Fortunately the forest department has a rest-house here, otherwise we should have difficulty in getting accommodation, since the summer season was at its height.

We spent nearly a month in the Palnis, partly at Kodaikanal, and partly at forest rest-houses elsewhere on the plateau. Had we no previous acquaintance with the Nilgiris, we should have thought that the Palnis were the best part of Madras. They are certainly a very good second.

The cool, bracing mountain air is the same as in the Nilgiris, but the winters are milder, and the rainfall lighter. There is nothing resembling the terrific rain to which the more exposed parts of the Nilgiris are subject during the south-west monsoon.

The plateau is something like 30 miles square, and consists mostly of undulating grassland, which is much less interrupted than are the Nilgiris, by prominent peaks and large water courses. The proportion of woodland is, if anything, less than in the Nilgiri grasslands, but the trees are usually better developed, in view of the lower altitude and the milder climate.

The silver wattle, which we proposed to use, is a species of Acacia. Several kinds of Acacia, including this one, have been grown with some success in sheltered parts of the Nilgiris and Palnis. But to all intents and purposes its introduction was experimental, and nobody was in a position to say where it would grow and where it would not. In these circumstances I could only make a rough and ready allotment of land for planting. I excluded a large area round Kodaikanal so as not to interfere with the hill station, or to cause aesthetic offence. I excluded also such land as was required for pasturage, and all existing woodlands. For the rest I ruled out such obviously unsuitable areas as sheet rock, swamp, the most exposed hilltops, and so on.

The mapping on these lines was done by foresters. I got out when I could, but I had to control much of the work from my bed. For some time back I had been suffering from some obscure complaint characterised by stomach pains which were often severe, pain in the back, and an almost constant low fever. Various doctors whom I had consulted had made light of it, though they usually gave me a mixture of some kind. On one occasion, on tour, I felt so rotten that I went into a country hospital. My blood showed traces of a microbe of the typhoid group - possibly from an inoculation I had had some months before. This, together with the fever, led the doctor to believe that I had probably had a mild form of typhus from which I had then practically recovered. Since typhus is carried by lice, and I do not harbour lice in peace time, this tentative diagnosis merely annoyed me, and when the coast was clear, I walked out on them.

I got worse, however, rather than better. I lost about two stone in weight in a very short time, and became as weak as a kitten. The hot and weary journey to Kodaikanal, where I hoped the hill air might effect a cure, was the last straw, and I took to my bed on arrival. I was lucky enough to find the doctor I required in Kodaikanal. The others had not attached any importance to a slight streptococcus infection of my kidneys which had been discovered some time before. This one correctly assumed that it was the root of the whole trouble, and put me on a course of that wonderful discovery of recent years - sulphonamide. I was out and about in a week. I could not walk more than a mile or so at first, but I was improving every day, and eventually managed to do a reasonable amount of inspection in the Palnis. Once the infection was scotched I never looked back, though it took some months to recover my normal strength.

From Kodaikanal we went to the Nilgiris, about the middle of May. Here I was on my home ground, so to speak. I knew what grasslands were available for planting. I knew, from five years of experiment, that the exposed country in the outer Kundahs was not an economic proposition. Government required a large extent to be set aside for wattle planting in the Nilgiris, so I selected the least unfavourable of what remained. Mapping was done on the same lines as in the Palnis, and it had to be done in a great hurry, for the monsoon was approaching, which would make mapping work impossible.

I was not optimistic about large-scale wattle planting in the Nilgiris, in such land as we had available. I shall be very pleased if it succeeds, but I consider it will be a personal triumph for the officer who does the job. The Palnis seemed to me to be much more suitable. They have a milder climate generally than the Nilgiris; the dry weather is of shorter duration, and there is very little frost.

Our time in the Nilgiris was spent between Ootacamund and several forest camps. I was still not fit enough to do much walking, so I spent more of my time in writing up the details of the scheme than in supervising the mapping work.

In the scheme I made provision for planting on the large scale that the Government required, but in view of the experimental nature of the work at the outset, I recommended that only small areas be attempted until expansion was justified by results. Little will be lost if the work is a failure. In the event of success there is big money in it.

From the Nilgiris we went to Coimbatore. The working plan for South Coimbatore was shortly due for revision, and I made a short tour in the district, and prepared a note for the guidance of the Working Plan Officer. We renewed our acquaintance with Mt. Stuart, which was scarcely recognisable in view of the enormous expansion of the Teak plantations during the fourteen years that had elapsed since I had nearly broken my heart over burning my first Teak clearing in the pouring rain.

We completed this lengthy tour with about a week in the Chitteris, a small range of hills to the north-east of Salem. A working plan was about to be made for these forests since they had previously been managed under the rather haphazard method of annual proposals.

Sandalwood is the important crop. There is no road up the hills, but sandalwood can be carried down by manpower. Bamboos are extracted by the same agency.

The lower slopes contain forest which would give a good yield of firewood, but the distance to Salem is too great for economical transport of such a bulky commodity of relatively low value. I therefore arranged for the new Working Plan Officer to start the experiment of making charcoal in these forests. Charcoal is both valuable and light to carry, and it finds a very ready market in Salem.

The hills are about 3,000 feet high, with a plateau on the top. There are a few hill villages on the plateau, with small enclosures for cultivation, but most of the area is under forest. The footpath up is quite well graded so it was a reasonably easy walk, of about ten miles, from the shed at the foot of the hills where we left our car.

We found the plateau delightfully cool, and had a pleasant camp. There is a herd of Bison in the hills. We frequently saw their tracks and once heard them crashing off in the jungle when we had surprised them, but we did not get a view. This small herd is entirely isolated on their small island of luxuriant vegetation, surrounded by the parched plains of Salem. They must be very much in-bred. I have often wondered whether wild animals deteriorate from this cause.

After an absence of three months I found a great deal to be done in the office in Madras. This included a good deal of work on maps, which is one thing that cannot be done on tour. The weather was extremely hot, being July, but I could not complain, since we had been in cool places for most of the long tour which we had just completed.

When we next took the road it was for Salem, which had been my first station in India. We stayed for a day or two with the Collector, and when I wanted a drink, I had to provide my own and drink it in my bedroom! Salem was the first district which the Congress Government made "dry" under their prohibition scheme. Europeans could get permits for liquor, provided they satisfied the authorities that they were what the latter described as "addicts". I forget the rule in respect of Indians. For the bulk of the population alcohol was absolutely prohibited. A few Indians had permits, but they were extremely rare.

The Collector of Salem was not a teetotaller by inclination, but as head of the district, and responsible for the maintenance of the new law, he did not consider it fitting that he should get himself exempted from the prohibition which he enforced on others. He therefore abstained completely from alcohol while he was within his own district, and he worked extremely hard and successfully in introducing and administering a measure which met with the greatest opposition in its early stages.

As a licensed "addict" I was entitled to six units. A unit, as far as I remember, was one quart of spirits such as whisky, brandy, etc., or three quarts of wine, or a dozen quarts of beer, and so on. No minimum period was prescribed for consumption of these six units. If physically capable and so inclined, one could drink the lot in the morning and load up with a further six units in the afternoon, and one could always make partial renewals so as to keep one's stock close to the maximum. So far, therefore, as the individual "addict" was concerned, there was no hardship, unless he were unduly given to mixing his drinks.

South Salem district was due for attention by a working plan party, so I spent about three weeks inspecting the reserved forests which lie in the south of Salem revenue district, and in the north where the forests are of the inferior, dry deciduous type [......]

[...] and in the northern part of Trichinopoly there are a few hill ranges which carry better timber than [... ... ...] the bulk of the forests of the inferior dry, deciduous type, poor but nonetheless important. They cater for a very big demand for firewood, bamboo, sandalwood and forest grazing in a highly populated district and a variety of minor forest products of which tanning bark is the most important.

The district offers considerable scope for improvement of the forests, and enhancement of their value, and I found much of interest in pondering plans for the future. The south-west monsoon was in progress during our tour, and though South Salem does not get much rain out of it, there is a great drop in temperature, and we found the weather conditions very pleasant.

The camp we liked best was in the Kollimalai hills, in the extreme south. Most of these hills are in the revenue district of Trichinopoly, but as we have little reserved forest in the latter district, it is combined with the forests of Salem.

There is no road up these hills. The sides are extremely steep, and both of us made pretty heavy weather of the climb of about six miles, up the rocky, dusty way that goes by the name of a footpath. I was not quite back to my old form, and Elsie has never been enthusiastic about climbing hills, though she clearly loves their summits once she gets there. From the top we had still several miles to go over the plateau to the forest rest-house, but this was easy money.

They get more rain on the plateau than in the plains below. The altitude is about 3,000 feet, and in parts the forest is of a sufficiently evergreen type to harbour leeches. We were not prepared for this, otherwise we should have had a supply of country tobacco. But all was well, for the locals have a protective method of their own. A very sour orange which the hills produce, cut in half and squeezed over the boots or shoes, proved quite as effective as tobacco, or even more so. The local people treat their own bare feet in this manner, and the leeches do not trouble them.

The chief function of the forest in these hills is that of water catchment. For want of a road no forest produce can be exported except by headloads. Jack fruit, from trees growing in and near the few hill villages, finds a ready sale in the plains, and it may pay the forest department to plant jack and possibly other fruit trees in suitable areas.

From the Kollimalais we moved back by stages to Salem, camping in several places for inspection of different types of forest reserve in the plains. I had some days' work in Salem both studying office records regarding past management, and discussing various matters with the District Forest Officer, with whom we stayed. A drink was not a secret ritual in his bungalow, for he also was a licensed "addict".

I also made several inspections with the District Forest Officer of reserves within easy reach. This included a day on the plateau of the Shevaroy hills, which are not of much importance to the forest department, since a great deal of the plateau is under coffee cultivation.

While staying in Salem, Elsie was laid low with an extremely severe attack of malaria, the first she had had in fifteen years in India. She must have picked it up in the Kollimalais ten days before. These hills are well-known for malaria, like many others in South India where the altitude is below 4,000 feet.

She was very ably treated by an Indian doctor, and was nursed with great care by our hostess, but had to keep to her bed for about ten days. It was a miserable time for her from all points of view. It was the latter half of August 1939, and war was boiling up in Europe. Each day's news seemed more hopeless than the last. Our host's wireless was turned on most of the time, always in the hope of hearing something better, but actually fraying everybody's nerves.

I did a short camp with the Working Plan Officer who had just arrived in the district, and was a newcomer to the Working Plans branch. On my return to Salem, Elsie was up, but in no state to continue touring, so I saw her on to a train for Ootacamund where she stayed with friends, while I went on with the tour I had arranged.

I spent several days in a camp on the river Cauvery, just above the lake which had been formed by the construction of the huge Mettur Dam. We had been in this camp earlier in the year on one of our return trips to Madras from the west. The forest is of a peculiar type. Devastated by fierce annual fires prior to reservation under the Forest Act, it became extremely open as regards forest growth. A single species of tree resisted the fires with some success, and now considerable numbers of these trees have reached maturity. The wood is hard and heavy, but the locality is miles from anywhere, so the stuff has no value.

The Chief Conservator had had the idea of converting the wood into charcoal, and transporting the latter by boat to the Mettur Dam, whence it could be railed to Salem. My previous camp had been with the object of organising the necessary experiment, and I had now come to see how the charcoal manufacture was progressing.

There are no local inhabitants, and charcoal burners had to be recruited from a considerable distance. But there was no great difficulty in this, and quite a lot of charcoal was ready for transport when I arrived.

Carriage down the lake was not so easy. No boats were available, and our first efforts were to use the local coracles, which are round wicker frames with a skin of leather. Before the days of the lake, the coracles would have floated downstream, but now they had to be paddled all the way, except for a few miles above the fall at the head of the lake. The fall, incidentally, necessitated carrying both coracle and charcoal past the obstacle.

Some time later I learnt that the charcoal had been sold in Salem at a small profit. This was encouraging, for costs can always be reduced as experience is gained, and the organisation is expanded and improved. The outbreak of war should have assisted this project, by increasing the demand and the price for charcoal which can be converted into gas in motor vehicles, and used instead of petrol.

While I was in this camp, the District Forest Officer in Salem sent me the latest wireless news on the night of the 2nd September, which showed that war was inevitable. His message arrived early in the morning of the 3rd.

Being on the reserve of officers, I expected to be called up immediately, so I packed my kit and set off for Ootacamund to take Elsie back to Madras, and set my affairs in order. It is a drive of about 150 miles, and I stopped at several places on the way to enquire for news, but it was not until I reached the railway station at the foot of the Nilgiris in the afternoon that I learnt that England had declared war on Germany.

Shortly after my arrival the Delhi radio announced that there would be no general mobilisation, but that reserve officers like myself would be called up either individually or by categories as required, and they started off by calling up the category of censors immediately. Time was on our side, and they were in no hurry, apparently for more infantry.

We returned to Madras, and arranged for a passage to England for Elsie by the first ship available. Ships were expected nearly every day, so she was packed up to leave at any moment, but nothing appeared until the middle of October. When finally a ship arrived, she was telephoned to embark the same night, and did so. But when settled in her cabin, she was told that the sailing would be delayed for twenty-four hours, so she came home again. The ship, which was a small and slow passenger-cum-cargo vessel had been delayed for weeks in Calcutta, for painting battle-ship grey and having its little gun mounted. On the voyage from Calcutta they had tried out the gun, but it upset the electric [.....] of the ship, so this had to be set right in Madras.

When the ship finally left, I set off belatedly on a tour which had been postponed from week to week while we awaited the sailing. This time I went to the extreme northern limit of Madras where it adjoins the province of Orissa, and inspected forests of the Vizagapatam district, to which the Working Plan Officer from Guntur had now moved on. The plains forests are mostly of the dry, inferior types, fit only for firewood, for which they are worked wherever there is a demand. There is, however, a large hill tract known as an "Agency" where the forest is of a much better type, though of little financial value owing to its remote situation and shortage of communications [...]

[...] wild and require tactful handling, and this country has accordingly a special type of simplified administration under the "Agent" who performs the functions of the Collector of ordinary districts. They had a little rebellion of their own up here in 1924 and 1925, which gave the Government a good deal of trouble.

My camps in the hills with the Working Plan Officer were very pleasant, and I found the country interesting. We decided on some extension of our timber extraction where this was possible, and increased planting of Teak, which was already being tried in small areas.

Minor produce is, however, of more importance than either timber or firewood in this district, and we discussed plans for getting an increased revenue from this source. There are very large numbers of tamarind trees in the hills, many of them being on abandoned village sites of bygone years. This tamarind fruit is collected in very large quantities, and taken to market in the plains, but all the forest department were getting out of this trade was a small tax levied on the fruit by our checking officers as it came into the markets.

From Vizagapatam I returned to Madras, and shortly afterwards I went out on another tour, which I had to curtail, on being called to army service. I went to see the work in Anantapur where I had been earlier in the year, and then to Kurnool. Here the Chief Conservator joined me, with his wife and daughter, and my final tour was most enjoyable. We went up on the plateau of the Nallamallais, which I had had no time to do during my previous tour. It is delightful country, and in one camp we had some good duck-shooting. The month was November, and the duck had arrived in large numbers.

A tiger killed close to this camp while we were there, and the Chief Conservator made a dual purpose arrangement for sitting over the kill. He fixed up a camera with a trip wire and flashlight device, and he also built a machan. The scheme was excellent. The tiger was to touch off the wire and take his own photograph, and then the Chief Conservator and his daughter were to shoot the tiger. Unfortunately the tiger thought otherwise, and did not return to the kill.

Tigers are numerous in the Nallamallais, and it was here that Wimbush shot one inside a forest rest-house several years before. He was Conservator of Working Plans at the time, and was touring with the territorial Conservator, an elderly Brahmin, who was not, of course, interested in shooting. After dark one night they were both sitting in their respective rooms, when the Brahmin Conservator astounded Wimbush by coming in and saying that there was a tiger in his room, and that he had shut the door on it. And so there was, and so he had.

There was no apparent way of dealing with this dangerous visitor, without opening either a door or a window, and the tiger might get his blow in first. But Wimbush soon thought of a solution. He was hoisted on the roof, with his rifle, and after removing a few of the roofing tiles he shot the tiger through the aperture thus made.

The tiger was found to be in a feeble and half-starved condition, with one or more suppurating gunshot wounds inflicted some time before. It was a cold, wet night, and he had apparently come into the rest-house for shelter.

The Brahmin Conservator took this most unusual invasion with great coolness. He is supposed to have said that tigers do not attack Brahmins. What really upset him was the fact that the precious files on his office table were spoilt by the blood of the tiger in its death struggle. The Conservator was a most industrious officer. When the tiger walked in on him, he had been busy at his correspondence, and to him the files were sacrosanct.

I saw the hole made in the wall by one of the bullets that had passed through the tiger. This hole is preserved, without repair, as evidence in support of a true story, which is so very unusual that strangers could hardly be blamed for disbelieving it.

After the Nallamallais we made several camps in the Anantapur district, where I had to break up the party in the middle of December, and go back to Madras, to pack up, and hand over my job, before proceeding to join an Indian infantry battalion in North India.

I had been expecting to be recalled to the colours any day during the previous three months, and it was very difficult to settle down to serious work. In the end I think I probably precipitated matters. I had got tired of the suspense, so I wrote in and enquired whether I was likely to be wanted in the near future, and if not, whether the military authorities had any objection to my going on leave to England - where I had an idea (which was probably erroneous) that I could get back to the British regiment with which I had served originally. I had no reply to this letter, but I got my mobilisation orders almost by return of post.[In April 1942, the Chief Conservator, W.G. Dyson, issued a notice from

His Excellency the Governor to all gazetted and non-gazetted officers in the Forest Service "on the subject of their duty in case of invasion and effective occupation." This made it clear that they "will be considered free either to stay in their homes or to leave with the officers of the security services." In other words, although most of the British Forest Officers were members of the Indian Army Reserve, there was to be no automatic call up but they were free to volunteer if they wished]

In many respects I enjoyed the year that I had been in charge of working plans better than any in the whole of my previous service of seventeen years. The work was extremely interesting, and took me pretty well all over the Presidency, whereas previously I had served in a fairly restricted area in and near the Western Ghats.

The job was of greater importance than the normal work, in that it dealt with management for ten and sometimes as much as fifteen years ahead, instead of the daily routine, and the executive work of the season. It invited originality, and whether this was forthcoming or not, it at least made one think, and think on a broad basis rather than parochially. There was unlimited opportunity for extending one's knowledge owing to the great variation in the forests visited.

From the purely personal point of view it gave my wife and myself more of each other's company than we had had since 1926 when our family began to arrive. We had next to nothing of what might be called home life in this last year, but we toured everywhere together, and since Elsie is as fond of the jungle as I am, this was just the life we wanted. There was an abnormal amount of touring to be done, chiefly owing to the coincidence that four out of the five Working Plan Officers moved on to a new district during the short period I was in charge. Had I remained for a second year, I expect we should have welcomed rather longer spells in headquarters, and a bit less of the road. But for one year it was the ideal life.

Chapter XXI

THE FUTURE (or Conclusion or Epilogue?)

Not having tried writing a book before, I know neither when nor how to stop. I will not further bore the reader who has skimmed through the early chapters seeking thrills, and, failing to find them, has concluded that it were better if I had never started. He has already left the field.

But I still have a few words which I should like to say about the service to which I am proud to belong, and the forests in which I have spent the best years of my life. I therefore ask a little further patience of the reader who has borne with me when describing work which would appear to him to have been repeated monotony, and where I have overdone the technical detail which, though perhaps of interest to others in my profession, is admittedly not everybody's cup of tea.

The Indian Forest Service has a splendid record of achievement. In two generations it has brought order out of chaos, and has built up for India a most valuable forest property out of a no-man's-land where from time immemorial the population had so robbed and abused their birthright that much of it was fit for nothing when it was first brought under control.

"Meliora speramus" is the official motto of the Indian Forest Service, and I have always thought it sounded rather prim and priggish. But I think it speaks eloquently for the conditions as they must have appeared to the first generation. The particular pioneer who suggested it must have put his whole heart behind the words.

The first generation had nothing but hope for their reward. It was not really until my time that the harvest commenced to come in. There is a far greater harvest yet to come, and the harvest will be perpetual provided the forests are managed in a prudent and systematic manner.

So far as can be seen, the service which has done so much for the forests of India is doomed. There is no place for it under provincial autonomy and already the different provinces have started their own small services, which will gradually take over the reins, on the retirement of the officers of the imperial service who still hold office in the provinces. So far as the provinces are concerned, it appears that in about fifteen years the exodus of the Indian Forest Service will be complete, though it is probable that some sort of central body will be retained, under the Government of India, for the maintenance of the Forest Research Institute, which is world famous and of world-wide value.

The disappearance of the Indian Forest Service is a sad thought, but not by any means a hopeless one. It has laid the foundation and pointed out the way to prosperity, and there is no reason whatever why the forests under the management of the new provincial services, should not go on from strength to strength.

The denial to young Englishmen of a very attractive, outdoor career is a pity, but in normal times the number of appointments rarely exceeded about a dozen in a year, so from that point of view, the passing of the Indian Forest Service will be scarcely felt. And by way of compensation there are the different forest services under the Colonial Office, which have been greatly expanded in the last two decades, particularly in Africa. Basically the forest officer's life is much the same in all parts of the world, and I cannot imagine anything much better than forest life in wonderful country such as is found in Kenya and elsewhere.

I will conclude with a few remarks about the forests of Madras in which all my service has been spent. In this age of invention I will not be so rash as to attempt particularised prophecy as to the extent to which timber and other forest products will be required in the future, and the forms in which these products will be used.

When I commenced forestry training in 1920 there were prophets who said that the day of the hardwoods was over, and that there would be a world shortage of softwoods before anything could be done about it.

As regards hardwoods, I expect our forefathers said the same, when steel ships began to appear upon the seas, but the day of the hardwood was not over then, nor is it now.

The threatened famine in softwoods has been averted, partly by check of wasteful lumbering and of the disastrous fires which used to follow it in the United States and Canada, and partly by large-scale afforestation with softwood species in South Africa, New Zealand, Great Britain and elsewhere.

Madras has never exported timber in any quantity. Its markets are within the Presidency, and in other parts of India, and so far we have been able to sell all we have produced, in the few species which are most popular with the public. Most of these have been hardwoods.

Our softwoods are not the conifers of the west, but fast-growing broadleaved timber of little strength or durability. In the past there has been no demand for such timber, except at very low prices and in small quantities for purposes such as manufacture of matches, low grade packing cases, dug-out boats, etc. The future, however, is unquestionably bright. The local manufacture of three-ply has at last got under way, and the development of this line opens up a big market for almost any wood which is light in weight, and preferably also light in colour.

The demand for timber for its cellulose is almost certain to increase enormously, and should give Madras softwoods the opportunity which so far has been lacking. No great price is ever likely to be paid for timber which is to be broken down after use, so it may be necessary to grow plantations of fast-growing species in the most accessible localities, instead of trying to meet this demand from scattered trees in the remote, mountainous forests where our best softwoods are now to be found.

For the Madras hardwoods I foresee an increasing, rather than a diminishing demand. Industrialisation is proceeding in India, which means that more hardwoods will be required for constructional and other purposes. Hand in hand with industrialisation goes an improvement in the standard of living. Improvement of diet is admittedly of foremost importance, but better housing conditions will soon follow. When the less well-to-do can afford to furnish their houses instead of sitting on the floor, and to replace their temporary roofs of bamboo and thatch with timber and tiles, the demand for hardwoods may well overtax the entire exploitable resources of the forest department, despite the ever increasing area which is being planted with Teak.

As regards minor forest products, the prospects are no less promising. In this field I believe there is enormous scope for expansion of output, both by fuller utilisation of what is already there, and by planting for the future. The trouble about minor produce is its widely scattered distribution and consequent difficulty and high cost of collection. This can be overcome by concentration. We have a great variety, for example, of fruit-bearing trees, chiefly of edible and medicinal value, but there are also those which produce a raw material which can be used industrially, such as the kapok. Oils, resins, gums and so forth are to be had either from the trunks or the fruits of trees. I am not suggesting that planting for minor products should replace or interfere with timber planting. We have however vast areas of forest which must be maintained for the protection of water catchment areas, but where good timber either will not grow, or is impossible to extract owing to the difficulty of the country, I see no reason why suitable areas should not be planted with trees which will yield minor produce, in place of the economically useless trees these areas now carry. The protective functions of the forest need not be impaired. A few crops of fruit should recoup the cost of introduction, after which the proceeds would be largely profit.

In my service there has been an enormous advance in the utilisation of the forest resources of the Madras Presidency, and in the artificial reproduction and improvement of the forests. But I believe that far greater things are still to come.

I wish I were just starting now from scratch, instead of entering my last lap.

(The end)

Query. Is this last chapter, or epilogue, not better omitted altogether? RSB 30/6/44

QUINTUS' LETTER

Letter 1

Thailand Jungle
25 August 1945

My dearest darling,

I have almost forgotten how to write and spell! I cannot describe the joy of the prospect of our early reunion, but I know you are feeling just the same, beloved, and we shall soon be sharing all the happiness we have dreamed of during these dreary years. My one concern since hearing of the end of the war has been to get a message to you, for I know your rejoicing at victory must have some shadow of suspense - despite your stout heart and instinctive conviction of happiness to come - until you are assured of my survival. I don't know when I can send this letter off, for we are still nominally under Nip administration, but I expect allied troops will shortly come into Thailand, and take charge. When this happens I am sure letters and cables will be sent as soon as possible, and I want to have this inadequate letter ready for the earliest post. I fear it will be hard to read, for I want to say so much, and paper is almost impossible to get.

As far as I know I am in quite good health, and a few weeks of real food should see me full of energy. Just as the war was ending we were put to a test that convinces me that I am constitutionally sound. We were made to move to this new jungle camp - a nightmare journey lasting six days, and ending with a continuous march of something over 30 miles carrying all our kit - not that we have much, but bedding weighs heavy, especially when sopping wet, this being the monsoon season. This, after 3½ years on rice, and often not nearly enough of it, seems conclusive proof to me of latent strength.

The real food started today, with pork and soya beans and a large slice of buffalo beef for breakfast. It was marvellous. You will find me very easy to feed, darling, for some time to come. The mere sight of <u>bread</u> would fill me with excitement now. I have a fine, slim, schoolgirl figure, but I don't suppose I shall have it much longer.

That is enough about me. I am sure you will send all the home news when you can, but I might indicate what I know and don't know. The Nips took no interest in our letters from home, losing or destroying lots of them, and holding up others for years. I have had about 24 letters and cards from you, of which I got seven in the last few days, when we took more or less control of our own affairs. Two letters from Kathleen, one from Penelope, four from Eileen, but none at all from Ireland. I would particularly like to hear how father is. I heard about Mother's death about 2½ years late. On the whole it was less of a blow that way.

Your latest card is dated 16 December '44, when Penelope and Tim were just home from their first term away. I know P. is at a P.T. college, but where? Bedford is my only guess. I also guess that Tim is at Sherborne, because you said you were entering him there, but I thought he would not go till he was at least 13. However I am very glad he has broken the ice of leaving home, and is happy about it. I heard that Chloë was trying for School Cert. at the age of 15, which seems very young to me, and I hope she got it. But whether then or later, she must be very bright to attempt it so young. I was delighted to hear of Kathleen's scholarship in the Junior school and her brilliant record at that time, but have heard nothing of her since then. I hope she will go to Oxford when the time comes. In what direction do Chloë's tastes lie, when she leaves school? I want them all to do what they wish - within reason of course! (No engine drivers or female equivalent.) I fancy Cambridge for Tim, and a rugger international cap, for which he should have a double chance, as I fancy he would be eligible for either England or Ireland. If compulsory military training continues, I hope a University O.T.C. will be sufficient. I have a grand idea for hardening Tim up, pleasantly, for a year between school and university, but more of that anon.

I feel Eileen has been a tremendous help and comfort to you these years I have been away, and I am eternally grateful to her. I hope she suffers no permanent ill effects from her operation. Please give her my best love.

I am terribly impatient to get home, darling, but I don't know when it will be. I might be shipped straight home within the next few weeks, though I doubt it. I fancy the Indian army officers will go to India first. If I can't get home from there, either on release from the army, or on short leave before winding things up, I hope it may be possible for you to get a passage out, sweetheart. A few months in the Punjab in the cold weather would be delightful, and I promise not to work too hard! Sialkot is near enough to Kashmir for a honeymoon there, which we once thought of, and we are more than due for a second one, my darling. Unless the passes are closed by snow.

I contemplate a year's leave as soon as I can get it. Most of my prison life I thought of two years' leave, but I have now been away for nearly six years, and I don't think the Madras Government would take any but a poor view if I stayed away for two years more. I have often thought of cutting adrift altogether, and taking up farming, and seeing as much as possible of my family. But in the unsettled conditions which must follow the war I feel, now, that it would be very unwise to give up a certain job, which provides the means of completing the education of the young.

Holidays! You need lots, darling, after all your work, and what must have been terrific anxiety. Some of the young seem to have been away more than others, but wartime holidays are necessarily restricted, and I think they all deserve something extra special next year, though I am sure you are doing them proud this summer, with the European war over, the last few months. My big ideas for holidays "en famille" are (1) a winter sports holiday, either this Christmas in Switzerland, or Easter in Norway, and (2) the summer in either Ireland or Norway, depending on where we spend Easter. I would particularly like to work one trip to Norway this leave - for my own pleasure as well as yours, sweetheart, and I hope it will be feasible. Should Ivor and family be home too, it would be fine if they would join us. Also Svana, though I don't know if it would appeal to Patrick! And if Frida and family were to come too, we might even rent a whole village! Think about this, darling, and find out anything you can. I think I would prefer winter sports in Switzerland, and the summer in Norway, but I may not be home in time for Christmas holidays. In which case Easter would be indicated as the Norway season goes on much later than the Swiss. I have been much bitten by salmon fishing, through talking with enthusiasts while in jug, and hope to get some either in Ireland in the spring, or in Norway (off the expensive beaten track) in the summer. Trout fishing as well, of course - for all of us, since all the young are sufficiently grown-up now to try their luck. Should we winter-sport in Switzerland at Christmas, Eileen can take the family home while you and I warm up a bit, all on our own, darling, in the South of France. What about that? I don't mind a bit, dipping into capital for this leave. We have all been deprived of things for years, and must make up for lost time. Anyhow there is probably not much use hoarding money, with this horrid fellow Beveridge making plans to collar it, or, for the matter of that, of hoarding for our old age, when we shan't have the same capacity to enjoy it, or have our family together, to enjoy it with us. Actually I have very little idea how much money we have! The "monthly salary" about which we boasted in the printed postcards was 20 dollars, and even the Nips' own valuation of the miserable food and accommodation they provide, came to no more than another twenty, though I expect the Income Tax people will whittle it down all they can. In several letters you assured me that you had enough to live on, which relieved me much, dearest. Becoming a prisoner was the one risk of war that never entered my head, hence my failure to arrange for you to get at the monthly residue of my army pay. Incredibly stupid of me. I tried to put this right last

Christmas, in the first card that was not printed, but I doubt if the Nips ever sent off that lot at all.

I am not going to waste precious space discoursing on the Nips - it is not a pleasant subject. But their treatment of prisoners has been, for the most part, shocking, and I hope the allies are not going to be generous or forgiving to Japan, until they have heard and considered what surviving prisoners have to tell. It has been a case of the survival of the fittest. Roughly about 15,000 out of some 40,000 British and Australian prisoners in Thailand and the Burma borders (officers and men) have died. Overcrowding and filthy conditions helped the spread of disease. Our doctors have been magnificent but everything has been against them. Our Red Cross food and drugs were mostly pinched for the Jap armies. Malaria, cholera, dysentery, diphtheria and beri-beri have been the commonest cause of death, coupled with sheer starvation and the brutal driving of sick men to work. Many died of tropical ulcers and other festering sores, and hundreds of legs had to be amputated for lack of the means of healing them. My own Colonel - Jimmy Larkin - died an absolute skeleton. Atom bombs are too good for these bastards. I don't know how Indian troops have fared. We were separated from them at the capitulation, but British officers and men have been together - all working on coolie work - till a few months ago when separate officer's camps were formed.

We expect to go to Bangkok in a couple of days - the first step on the way home, I hope. Getting all the world news on a small radio set which has been smuggled from camp to camp. It has been an absolute Godsend, and we have rarely been long without authentic news of the war during the last three years. The difficulties of concealment have been enormous, and the heroes who ran the show have been in constant danger of death. Three officers were actually beaten to death for having a wireless in one of these Thailand camps in 1943.

We end the war in the most appalling rags. All the Nips ever gave me was a pair of wooden sandals, and I have a felt hat from the Red Cross. But nothing matters now.

Your only letter of 1943 which I received was about Diana Jarman. An awful tragedy, but what a fine girl she was. I cannot say I look forward to meeting the Jarmans - it is too painful. I hope anyhow that their second son survived. I don't know how Fritz was killed, but we had to presume him to be dead when he was not brought in as a prisoner. He and his whole company were missing in the withdrawal to our final position on Singapore Island. We were hopelessly mixed up with hordes of Japanese, and only a very small remnant of us got out of the mess. Gwinethu was missing in the same action, but I have good hopes of him turning up. Unless he was killed on the spot, it would be very easy for him to go to ground and turn into a Tamil civil inhabitant, of whom there were lots on the Island. Of course he should not have been in that show at all. He came up with dinner for the officers, on the ration truck the night before, and got left behind through a windy driver going back without orders when advanced parties of Japs started firing on Battallion H.Q. I could not take Gwinethu under my wing, as I had my own job to do, but I put him in the middle of a bunch of stalwart sepoys, and hoped for the best. Last I saw of him he was carrying a grass-mat hold-all, with thermos flasks of hot coffee and sandwiches "for masters". He did us proud in the last half of the campaign, and was quite fearless under fire. I shall be desolated if he is lost to us.

Early in 1944, when coolie work on the railway finished, and I had most afternoons free, I acted on a remark in one of your letters, about it being a good time for "literary effort", and wrote a book of sorts, on forest life in Madras. I had to bury it early this year when the Nips stripped us of paper of all sorts. I may or may not recover it. It is buried in a grave in a P.O.W. cemetery about 150 miles from here. One or two officers who are still in a camp a few miles from the place know of the location, and may have the "savvy" to dig it up for me, though I left no such instructions, as we were all in process of moving, in instalments, when the war ended. Anyhow, I have a very rough precis in three sheets, sewn into my pillow, in case I should ever find the energy to re-write it.

I have had ample time for introspection as a prisoner, and am more than ever convinced how exceptionally blessed I am in my life partner. You are completely indispensable to my happiness, my own sweetheart, and all my plans and ideas for the future are bound up with you, and your probable reactions to them. It is my dearest wish, now, to ensure that you get as much enjoyment out of life as possible. You have had much more than your share of responsibility and work connected with the family, not only during the war, but earlier. We will make up for that, now, my darling, and also as far as we can for those empty, wasted years that we have been parted.

I know the welcome that awaits me. In the meantime I look forward most eagerly to your first cable or letter assuring me that all is still well with you and the children. Send me a photo if and when you can. I have had none to console me these 3½ years.

ALL my love

Your Quintus

QUINTUS' NOTEBOOK

<u>10 August 45</u> With No. 5pty left Kanburi evening open truck - 36 bodies with kit. Eventually stopped Nongpladok where transferred to closed waggons to sleep. Cramped, chin to knees. Sleep impossible.

<u>11 Aug 45</u> Continued in open trucks all day, stopping and shunting. Big portage over busy bridge 30 km. short of Bangkok. Thais friendly to us and inclined to jeer at Nips. Not allowed speak to Thais or buy food of which masses were offered at stations. Arrived at a marshalling yard outside B'kok towards dark. Place a shambles from bombing. Rested by river till about midnight. Small amount tea supplied here, otherwise haversack rations all the way so far.

<u>12 Aug 45</u> Packed tight in barges about midnight using rifle buts to pack. Some incidents. Much abuse and threatening. Miserable sleepless night, being so cramped on top of stores as well as own kit in stifling covered barges. Sentries very worried about escaping. Continually counting us. Tied up in river shortly after starting, to make guarding easier in the dark. Moved downriver at dawn and landed at a big warehouse about 11 a.m. and eventually got inside about 2 p.m. and had a meal. Next door to O.R.s (other ranks). No contact allowed but succeeded in getting their news, which went to show that the war was over or nearly. Latrines across road by guard. Not allowed outside for any other reason, except when marched for a bathe in a tank each evening. Rain first day through broken roof. Kits very wet but not allowed to dry.

<u>13 and 14 Aug</u>. One half went off 14th. Rest stayed put. Lying on concrete floor. <u>Very</u> comfy after nights in train and barge. More stories about end of war but couldn't be certain.

<u>15 Aug 45</u> Left afternoon in closed iron waggons. Hot as hell. Packed like sardines over stores and own kit. 3 Nip guards and 30 officers each truck. Much bomb damage to railway installations round Bangkok. Further signs of war over. A Thai official whispered "Only a few more days" and an Indian engine driver shunted past with a chalked board "England and America win."

<u>16 Aug 45</u> Lousy night in train, but everybody hearty. No sleep. De-trained about 2 a.m. Herded into small shed in pitch dark and raining. Guards very offensive. Scarcely room to sit. Made to relieve nature within 3 metres of shed. No sleep. Paraded in full kit at first light and marched off without food. Met by a lorry with breakfast (rice and veg. stew) No tea or drinking water - about 10 a.m. Moved off again at noon and marched all through heat of day on bare road through paddy, with occasional halt of about ten minutes till 5 p.m. when the one bright spot of the day - a halt of 2 hours when we had evening

meal and a bathe in a muddy creek. Marched from 7 p.m. till about 3 a.m. with occasional short halt. Very heavy rain after dark. Kit increased in weight 20%. Broken boots gave bad blisters in the mud and gravel. Promised a four hour halt in a school, but when we got there the Nips changed their minds and moved on. Eventually slept for about 3 hours in a semi-swamp in the rain. Wet through, cold and exhausted.

17 Aug 45   Starting at daylight we made the new camp at 1 p.m. with no food since 6 p.m. previous day and only such water as we picked up by the way, untreated. A most brutal march. In a party of 200 some 50 fell out on the way (all Dutch. All the 48 Br. Offcs. kept going.) A few were picked up by passing M.T. Many had kits carried by others, themselves being fully loaded. Some we were made to carry on improvised stretchers by loaded men. Total distance 47 km. and almost non-stop with little food or water. I exploded my heart-trouble theory, as I made the grade carrying about 50 lbs. Bad blisters, strained neck and shoulders, and just about done on arrival.

Shortly after our arrival Naguchi announced the WAR OVER!   No surprise, but what a joy. One thing I want now is to get a message home.

18 Aug 45   Nips disgorging all the Red X stuff, not already used by their troops, and our letters that they have been sitting on. Got one food parcel between 5. Also 1 pair pants and 1 pair socks - the first clothing I have had in captivity bar a pair of clogs! 4 cards from Elsie and Eileen of November and December 45 [sic - must mean 44] Tim and Penelope home for holidays (I don't know Tim's school but presume Sherborne) Nips now saluting us. But they keep away B——-Y Bastards!   They are rapidly trying to improve our miserable rations, and to arrange for anything we ask for, but the new camp is away in the jungle, miles from anywhere. Naguchi was horror-struck to be asked for batteries for wireless which was smuggled in in his own kit! British, U.S. and Dutch flags officially hoisted to-day. Also our own bugle calls etc.

Sunday 19 Aug '45. Races

Small ponies brought here for pack transport took part in 4 races. Lost 1.75. Good fun - especially for the bookie. Accommodation shocking. 3 rows of bodies per hut. Beds on the ground 5 to a bay or about 2½ ft width each. Typhus started in O.R.'s camp next door.

Nips turned out the Koreans without pay, food or anything (Korean Guards), and they took refuge with us. Wireless got going and we heard something about closing phase of the war. Also heard that supplies, clothing, newspapers etc. are being dropped from planes on P.O.W.'s but nothing here yet.

Mon 20 Aug '45   Library building work. Had ½ pt hooch tonight. Gave a glow - awful rot-gut really and $4 a pint.

Tues 21 Aug 45   Naguchi said to be in arrest over Dryer - who now has blackwater (fever) in addition to his other troubles. Planes over today, but high.

Wed 22 Aug 45   Getting lots of news on our own makeshift wireless. Promises about food and immediate release of P.O.W.'s, but so far not the slightest interest taken by outside agency. Fine new Red X books now released also vitamin tablets which earlier would have saved hundreds of lives.

Rations shocking - worse than anything since early '42, and no canteen. Red X milk, margarine, cheese etc. finished quickly.

Thurs 23 Aug 45   Food still awful. Rice and sweet potato stew. .... advance of pay but no chance to change 100 notes or to spend. Lots of hot air on the wireless about prisoners being primary consideration. Hope it cheers at home.

Fri 24 Aug 45. Feels more like peace to-day. Got a box of matches for $1.

Sat 25 Aug 45   Real food at last through Thai official help. Pork and soya beans and buffalo beef for breakfast - wonderful.

Sun 26 Aug 45   Farewell to Anglo-Dutch Forestry meeting with good bootlegged hooch.

Mon 27 Aug 45   Dull day.

Tues 28 Aug 45   Babe's 45th birthday. Got my valuables back - 4 bust watches and Jimmy's (Jimmy Larkin) ring and pencil. Shared enormous fowl with Babe - best meal for over 3½ years. Some hooch later.

Wed 29 Aug '45   Radio says P.O.W.s in Siam will fly to Rangoon.

Thurs 30 Aug 45   Radio promises that we will be taken off as soon as possible. Chaps in Bangkok going by air to Colombo and Bangalore via Rangoon.

Fri Aug 31. Waiting.

Sat 1 Sept 45. To Bangkok airport by road, afternoon, with no warning. About 100 miles. Took 6 hours. Nips lorries. Breaking down. Slept on a table in airport. Eaten by mosquitoes. Robbie with me.

Sun 2 Sept 45. Waiting for planes. In hangar from 06.45. Nothing happened. Stood down afternoon. Had too much lao [?] food in airport very scarce but bazaar outside.

Mon 3 Sept 45. Flew off about 11.15, 25 to a plane. Marvellous! Release at last. Got to Rangoon about 13.30. Great welcome at airport. Fed at once in marquee - sandwiches, fruit salad and cream, stew, (in this order) and more sandwiches and sweet milky tea. Packet of English cigarettes pair of rubber boots and a cape. American girls serving food. First sight of a ham sandwich thrilled me much more than first ditto of a white woman, though some good lookers!

Drove some 30 miles to 51 I.G.H. about 15 miles out of Rangoon. Hot shower - bath, good dinner, bed with <u>sheets</u> etc. and a wonderful sleep. Also bottle beer - my opener in much demand.

<u>Tues 4 Sept '45</u>   Sent off printed card to E. Also cable.

<u>Wed 5 Sept 45</u>   Hungry most of the time, being on ½ rations as a precaution. Saw a news film, operations in Germany in April, and in Okinawa and Burma about same time.

<u>Thurs 6 Sept 45</u>   Got clothing and Rs 70 pay.

Postscript: Changes in forestry practice at Nilambur since 1932
Brian Davis

In 1993, the Kerala Forest Research Institute at Peechi published a *History of Forest Management in Kerala* by Mannen Chundamannil. This gives a good review of the whole period from the early 19th century when Captain Watson of the Police Department was appointed in 1806 as the Conservator of Malabar, in fact the first Conservator of Forests in all India, half a century before the appointment of Dr Brandis as Inspector General of Forests. Chundamannil recognises three broad phases in forestry management: *The Rise of Forestry* covering the period up till 1940; a *Period of Turbulence and Change*, covering the next 30-40 years during the Second World War and after Independence; and *The Ascent of Conservation*. Browne's account falls into the latter part of the first period – when, as Chundamannil puts it, 'forestry had risen to the pinnacle of ascent'. The major achievements had been the reservation of forests to protect them from unplanned exploitation, the development of silviculture, the establishment of teak plantations, and the production of working plans to establish clear guidelines for long term sustainable production.

In Chapter 7, Browne described how he was given the task of preparing a Working Plan for the Nilambur forests in 1925. There had been an earlier Working Plan produced by P.M. Lushington for the period 1896-1905 and R. Bourne had tried to update this in 1921 but it had not been adopted so Browne's Plan was a major reassessment. [R.S.Browne. *Revised Working Plan for the Nilambur Valley, 1928-29 to 1937-38*. Proceedings of the Chief Conservator of Forests No. 293. Madras, 1929] In a formal statement at the back of the Working Plan, the Conservator of Forests for the Working Plans Circle, A. Wimbush Esq., writes to the Chief Conservator of Forests, Madras: '…. whereas in the case of several other Working Plans parts have been written by me, in the case of this Nilambur plan, the finished article is entirely the production of Mr. Browne, apart from the petty modifications referred to in paragraph 2 above. I think that the Working Plan reflects great credit upon Mr. Browne.'

One of the main questions was whether it was practicable to grow teak as a second rotation, that is, to replant teak where it had grown before. Earlier attempts had been unsuccessful but he thought it could be done and so he was given the responsibility of putting his ideas into practice as District Forest Officer from 1928 to 1932. For the previous seven years no one had held charge of this forestry division for more that a few months at a time so he was able to establish a major influence on the management that was subsequently carried on. Five years later, my father, P. W. Davis, inherited the role of D.F.O. Nilambur and I have been back twice, in 1996 and 2000, to re-establish contact with the current generation of foresters and forest researchers. It is now just seventy years since Browne left Nilambur and, since 70 years was deemed then to be the rotation time for teak, it seems appropriate to review briefly the main changes that have taken place there. Details for the management of teak are summarised in the accompanying table but it is perhaps worth sketching out the wider forestry scene to set it in context.

The onset of 'turbulence and change' came twelve years after the publication of Browne's Working Plan when the Second World War required a massive increase in timber extraction throughout India. The war also disrupted food supplies, which encouraged the expansion of cultivation into forested areas. All this required major deviations from prescriptions in Working Plans and was only achieved through the efficient organisation of the forest department. Of this period, my father wrote: [P.W.Davis, *The Record of the Forest Departments during the Second World War of 1939-45*. In: E.P.Stebbings. *The Forests of India*, vol.4, 1962.] 'The story is pre-eminently one of team work. It is perhaps fitting here to record the debt owed to that staunch cadre, the Forest Rangers, upon whom fell the brunt of the day-to-day exigencies of physical control and organisation in the field....Yet, in the outcome, the forest legacy was preserved essentially intact, albeit reduced, in striking contrast to the widespread devastation of forest lands outside the jurisdiction of the [Forest] Department. It is this fact which constitutes the real and enduring achievement of those who framed forest policy in former years.'

The next major change, of course, came in 1947 when India gained full independence, most of the British left and the Madras Presidency was abolished. The Nilambur division, together with the rest of Malabar, Cochin and Travancore, then came under the State administration of Kerala. Within the forest service, the hand-over had long been anticipated and the chain of command remained intact. There was a hiatus before gazetted officers were once more recruited through the Indian Forest Service in the late 1960s, but officers appointed to Kerala still have to pass a language exam in Malayalam if this is not their native tongue (or Tamil or Kannada if posted to Tamil Nadu or Karnataka), just as one had to in Browne's day.

Externally, however, there were many new challenges to face. Although the 1952 Forest Policy statement was essentially the same as that laid down in 1894, rapid population growth in the post independence period exerted enormous pressures on forest lands. In the 1970s and 80s the extensive private forests were taken over by the Government, including the large holdings in the Nilambur Kovilakom. Furthermore, Chundamannil states that 'Changes in the political scenario also saw a lack of commitment to conservation …from the top policy makers to the common farmer [owing to] a belief in the inexhaustibility of forests.' Ten-year forestry Working Plans were replaced by Government Five Year Plans which set targets for supplying industry. The lack of a consistent policy on forest lands led to considerable further clearance of forest for agriculture and the encroachment of settlements, all of which tended to undermine the morale and efficiency of staff. The loss of forests in Kerala between 1965 and 1973 was estimated at about four thousand square kilometres.

National concern over the loss of India's forests led finally to the Wildlife (Protection) Act of 1972 and the Forest Conservation Act of 1980. The former established a separate branch within the Forest Service with equivalent rankings up to Chief Wildlife Warden, equivalent to a Chief Conservator of Forests. The latter Act re-established the primacy of forests as an essential natural resource 'to be protected and enhanced for the well-being of the people and the nation.' These acts ushered in Chundamannil's third phase. Even in teak plantations, selective felling was reduced to 25 percent of mature trees while all clear felling in Wild Life Sanctuaries ceased. In a way, this was only a return to the roots of Conservation since the term Conservator goes back to the very earliest days of forestry, and Browne's account vividly describes how his work embraced responsibilities for water catchment, erosion control and game protection as well as timber production. However, it also marked a landmark shift to the fully modern view of conservation in which direct economic benefit is subordinate to sustaining the ecology of areas such as the rich and unique rainforests of Kerala.

At the local level, a notable administrative change at Nilambur occurred in 1988 when it was subdivided into Nilambur North and Nilambur South Divisions with separate D.F.O.s.. Up until then it had continued to be administered as a single district with tours of duty mostly of two to four years. In 1999 the first woman D.F.O. in Kerala was appointed to Nilambur North division. This has especial resonance, as far as Browne's account is concerned, since his wife Elsie was the first, if not only, woman to take a forestry diploma in Britain. Smt. (Mrs) Prakriti Srivastava I.F.S. may therefore be considered as a fulfilment of Mrs Browne's early initiative.

Another recent event at Nilambur has been the establishment of a Teak Museum in 1995. This comes under the aegis of the Kerala Forest Research Institute (K.F.R.I), rather than the Forest Service itself. Browne claimed that Nilambur had some of the most valuable teak forests in all India so I am sure he would have given his full support to the current efforts to build up a collection of records and exhibits. An Entomology subcentre of the K.F.R.I. at Nilambur is still engaged in research to control the teak defoliator moth, which has been a recurrent pest problem for over a century.

In 1999 the K.F.R.I. published a lavishly illustrated volume entitled *Silent Valley, Whispers of Reason*. [T. M. Manoharan, S. D. Biju, T. S. Nayar & P. S Easa (Editors) 1999. *Silent Valley Whispers of Reason*. Kerala Forest Department in association with Kerala Forest Research Institute.] Silent Valley actually comes into the Palghat Division, but the forests there are contiguous with the Nilambur South Division to the east and were similar to those Browne describes in his Working Plan for the Nilambur Hills, published in 1936. This Plan covered the Amarampalam Reserve Forest in what he called the 'Inaccessible Working Circle'. There were suggestions as long ago as 1921 to flood this valley for a hydroelectric scheme and the project was approved in 1973 by the Kerala government. However, local public and scientific opinion rose against this and swelled to international proportions because it was felt that Silent Valley was perhaps the last substantial tract of undisturbed tropical rain forest in peninsular India and should be preserved for its rich and unique fauna and flora. In the end, Silent Valley was declared a National Park by the Prime Minister, Ranjiv Ghandi, in 1986. It has been included with the Amarampalam forests within the Nilgiri Biosphere Reserve and proposed as a World Natural Heritage Site. The book gives a full and fascinating account of this saga as well as details of the animals and plants there. One of the chapters giving '*A Historical Perspective*' is written by a Principal Chief Conservator of Forests, a Chief Conservator and a Conservator, while another describing '*The Management Perspective*' for Silent Valley is written by another Chief Conservator of Forests and two Conservators. Truly, the term has borne fruit.

As a final postscript, it is worth mentioning that the memorial to Browne's great friend, A.S. ('Peter') Dawson, is still carefully maintained by the Kerala Forest Department at Nedungayam with a notice recounting his tragic death in 1937 beside the bridge he built.

I am indebted to Smt. Prakriti Srivastava I.F.S. and to Dr T.V. Sajeev of the Kerala Forest Research Institute for the following details of forestry practice at Nilambur.

Features of forest policy and practice at Nilambur since 1932

Old practices

1. For the purposes of protection the Ranges were divided into sections and beats.

2. Only Reserve Forest was in the custody of the Forest Department.

3. Selection felling of naturally grown trees was in practice.

4. Teak stumps were used for raising plantations. Espacement of seedlings was 2 metres x 2 metres.

5. The Taungya system was practised in which farmers grew crops in the plantation for 2-3 years and looked after the young trees.

6. The rotation was originally 70 years reduced subsequently to 60 years. Mechanical thinning occurred in years 4 and 8, silvicultural thinning in years 12, 18, 28 and 40.

7. Extraction of timber was done by the department. There were 27 working elephants and 25 buffaloes used for this in 1928.

8. Timber was transported by river (rafting) to sawmills at Beypore.

9. There was no central nursery for raising seedlings.

10. Several dumping depots were used for sale of timber.

New practices

1. A forest station system was introduced for protection. There are now seven stations in Nilambur North and four in Nilambur South Division. A Deputy Range Officer is head of each station.

2. Private forests (of Nilambur Kovilakam) was vested and incorporated with the Government Forest.

3. Selection felling was banned.

4. Root trainer seedlings are used for raising teak plantations. Seedlings are spaced at 3 metres x 3 metres.

5. The Taungya system is abolished.

6. The present rotation age for teak is 50 years. Mechanical thinning occurs in year 5, silvicultural thinning in years 10, 15, 20, 30 and 40.

7. A contractor now extracts the timber. There has been a gradual decline in elephant use but they are still essential for felling operations and to drag large logs from felling site to loading site.

8. Rafting has completely ceased and timber is transported to Chaliyam and Aruvacode by lorry.

9. A Central Nursery has been established at Valluvasherry under the charge of a Range Officer for raising seedlings to supply the entire Forest Circle.

10. Dumping depots have been abolished. Timber is now sold only from a Central Depot.

Officers who have held charge of Nilambur Forest Division

1.	R. BOURNE	4.1918	35.	B.J.SINGH	7.1946
2.	G.C.ROBINSON	12.1918	36.	S.G.VENKATTARAMAN	4.1947
3.	E.A.ARDAGH	1.1921	37.	P.S.RAO	3.1948
4.	M.C.CHANDY	3.1921	38.	C.S.MANNADIAR	7.1948
5.	ABDUL Q. SAHIB	8.1922	39.	K.SANKARANARAYAN RAO	5.1949
6.	G.C.ROBINSON	5.1923	40.	P.K.SANKARA MENON	3.1951
7.	GOVINDA MENON	8.1924	41.	E.S.THANGAM	11.1951
8.	P.W.DAVIS	8.1924	42.	K.DURAIRAJ	6.1953
9.	D.F.STILEMAN	10.1924	43.	M.A.SUZA	10.1953
10.	A.F.MINCHIN	12.1924	44.	K.N.R.NAIR	8.1954
11.	A.C.LITTLEWOOD	5.1925	45.	K.A.DEY	6.1955
12.	C.M.KUSHALAPPA	4.1926	46.	V.GOVINDA MENON	8.1956
13.	A.C.LITTLEWOOD	5.1926	47.	P.N.ADIYODI	7.1957
14.	E.M.CROTHERS	6.1928	48.	G.MONIE	8.1957
15.	C.M.BELLIAPPA	4.1927	49.	A.HASSAN KUTTY	7.1958
16.	E.M.CROTHERS	6.1928	50.	T.K.DIVEKARAN	5.1960
17.	N. THRIMURTI	4.1928	51.	P.GOPALA MENON	6.1963
18.	E.M.CROTHERS	6.1928	52.	P.MOHEMMED MOOSA	5.1967
19.	**R.S.BROWNE**	**12.1928**	53.	P.N.ADIYODI	6.1967
20.	J.M.SWEET	4.1932	54.	M.S.NAIR	8.1969
21.	D.M.CURRIE	4.1935	55.	A.HASSANKUTTY	7.1970
22.	P.W.DAVIS	9.1937	56.	T.K.RAGHAVAN NAIR	8.1971
23.	P.W.F.WALPOLE	3.1940	57.	K.V.SANKARAN NAIR	8.1971
24.	A.S.BRAND	6.1940	58.	V.K.RAMACHANDRAN	5.1973
25.	J.S.ROWLAND	3.1943	59.	JAMES VARGHEESE	6.1977
26.	H.A.H.G.HICKS	4.1943	60.	M.K.DIVAKARAN NAIR	2.1978
27.	J.S.ROWLAND	8.1943	61.	E.MOHEMMED	7.1978
28.	H.A.H.G.HICKS	9.1943	62.	K.NANU NAIR	4.1980
29.	N.S.ASUANNA	2.1944	63.	M.V.BALAKRISHNAN	12.1981
30.	J.S.ROWLAND	2.1944	64.	V.A.SANKAR	7.1982
31.	H.A.H.G.HICKS	12.1944	65.	M.RADHAKRISHNAN	8.1982
32.	J.S.ROWLAND	2.1945	66.	POKKAN	7.1984
33.	E.A.LASRADE	7.1945	67.	M.RADHAKRISHNAN	8.1984
34.	K.K.APPIAH	1.1946	68.	K.P.OUSEPH	7.1985
			69.	AMARNATH SHETTY	7.1987

Nilambur North Division		**Nilambur South Division**
1. AMARNATH SHETTY	9.1988	(unavailable)
2. P.K.KESAVAN	2.1990	
3. C.S.YALAKI	7.1990	
4. P.K.PATHAK	12.1992	
5. G.RENNENSEN	4.1993	
6. BENNICHAN THOMAS	5.1993	
7. NOYAL THOMAS	8.1995	
8. D.JAYA PRASAD	1.1996	
9. M.L.THOMAS	8.1998	
10. GANGA SINGH	4.1999	
11. Smt. PRAKRITI SRIVASTAVA	6.1999	

Adapted, and slightly amended from boards in the North Divisional office.

Appendix C

PROSPECTUS OF THE MADRAS FOREST COLLEGE, COIMBATORE.

1. The College trains students for the Forest Ranger cadre in Madras and Bombay Presidencies, Central India States, Ceylon and Indian States of Southern India including Hyderabad.

2. The course commences on 1st August and is of 23 months' duration, terminating on the 30th June.

3. A candidate must be not less than 18 and not more than 25 years of age (unless he has exceptional qualifications) on the 1st April of the year in which he desires admission to the College.

4. With effect from the 1st August 1937, three categories of students will be admitted to the College, viz.,

(i) " Forest Apprentices " in the service of the Government of Madras, who will be selected by the Chief Conservator of Forests annually about April or May in consultation with the Madras Services Commission, after notification has been published in the *Fort St. George Gazette* ;

(ii) Private students paying the prescribed tuition fees who are under no existing contract with Government ;

(iii) Students deputed by the Governments of other Provinces and Indian States.

Private students admitted for training in the Madras Forest College, Coimbatore, should not be more than 22 years and six months old on the 1st April of the year in which they are admitted.

5. All candidates seeking admission as " Forest Apprentices must possess the Matriculation or the School Final Examination Certificate or its equivalent, with at least 40 per cent of marks in the following subjects :—English, Mathematics and Science. Preference will be shown to candidates who have taken Botany as

one of the subjects for the S.S.L.C., E.S.L.C., or higher qualification possessed by them.

(i) The candidates must be not less than 5 feet 5 inches in height.

(ii) must be not less than 32 inches round the chest on full expiration ; and

(iii) must have a chest expansion of not less than 2 inches on full inspiration.

6. " Forest Apprentices "—Selected apprentices will undergo probation for a period of four years. The first year will be spent in preliminary training in a forest district; the second and third years will be spent at the Madras Forest College, Coimbatore; after passing out from the College, apprentices will be posted for work in a Range. During the period of preliminary district training they will be paid Rs. 28 per month. While they are at the College they will receive no stipend, but will pay tuition fees of Rs. 750 per annum payable in advance or Rs. 1,500 for the whole course. After leaving the College they will draw Rs. 28 per month in the fourth year of their probation but will be eligible to draw the pay of the lowest Ranger whenever they officiate as Rangers in leave vacancies.

7. *Scholarships.*—The Government of Madras will award two scholarships annually to selected candidates of the backward and scheduled classes in order as under :—

1st year	...	One Muhammadan and one Anglo Indian, Indian Christian or Non-Asiatic.
2nd year	...	One Muhammadan and one member of the Scheduled classes.
3rd year	...	One Muhammadan and one Anglo-Indian, Indian Christian or Non-Asiatic.
4th year	...	One Anglo-Indian, Indian Christian, or Non-Asiatic and one member of the Scheduled classes.

The fees at the College will be remitted in the case of scholarship-holders, who will in addition receive a grant of Rs. 35 per mensem while at the College. In other respects, scholarship-holders will be treated as '' Forest Apprentices.''

8. Application from private students should be presented in person to the District Forest Officer of the district in which the applicant resides or in the case of Indian States to the Conservator of that State in time for the application to reach the Principal of the Madras Forest College, Coimbatore, not later than the 1st September in each year. No application will be received before the 1st July in each year. Application should be in the form to be obtained from the Principal.

Every application for admission to the College should be accompanied by the following certificates :—

(a) A certificate that the candidate is a " Native of India."

(b) Certificate of age.

(c) A health certificate from an officer not lower in rank than a Civil Surgeon.

(d) Certificate of respectability and good moral character.

(e) The requisite educational certificates.

Certificates (a) and (d) must bear date not earlier than the 1st April of the year in which the candidate applies for admission to the College. All certificates including the educational certificates must be submitted in original.

Private students from Madras Presidency must in addition submit with their applications a certificate from a Revenue Officer not lower in rank than a Deputy Tahsildar that they are natives of the Madras Presidency.

Private students from the Madras Presidency are charged a tuition fee of Rs. 1,000 per year. Other private students have to pay at the rate of Rs. 1,500 per annum or Rs. 3,000 for the whole course.

Prior to admission of a private student at the College, his parent or guardians must satisfy the Principal that they are willing and able to pay the tuition fees and defray the general expenses of the student at the College. These expenses are estimated at Rs. 2,000 approximately for the two years in addition to tuition fees.

Private candidates who have been accepted by the Principal for admission to the College will be required to undergo a course of practical training in the forests of the Madras Presidency or in other selected forest charges for at least six months. Such candidates will not be allowed to join the College unless they can produce a certificate signed by the District Forest Officer under whom they have served, and countersigned by the Conservator of the Circle, that they have undergone the course of practical training in a satisfactory manner and are likely to become useful forest officers.

No assured prospect of Government appointment can be held out to private students even if they complete the two years' course satisfactorily. Intending private students are advised to approach their local Governments first to ascertain what prospects there may be of subsequent employment after successfully completing their College course.

9. *Students deputed by the Governments of other Provinces and Indian States.*—Subject to the general terms of admission contained in paragraphs 1 to 5 of this prospectus, students deputed by local Governments other than Madras Government are accepted, and arrangements can be made to disburse stipends, salaries and allowances in accordance with the conditions of their agreements with the deputing authorities. Applications for the reservation of seats should be despatched to reach the Principal not later than the 1st September for admission in the following August. Candidates for admission are required to have undergone preliminary training under an approved Forest Officer for at least six months before coming to the College; a longer time is advisable. The fee payable for each student is Rs. 1,500 per annum, or Rs. 3,000 for the whole course.

10. The College Calendar is under revision. A Syllabus of studies is available on application (price, three annas).

MADRAS FOREST COLLEGE, }
COIMBATORE. }

J. H. LONGRIGG,.
Principal.

MADRAS : PRINTED BY THE SUPERINTENDENT, GOVERNMENT PRESS.

MADRAS FOREST COLLEGE, COIMBATORE

CALENDAR, PART II

(SYLLABUS FOR 24 MONTHS' RANGERS' COURSE)

Published under the authority of the Chief Conservator of
Forests, Madras, and with the general approval
of the Government of Madras

MADRAS
PRINTED BY THE SUPERINTENDENT, GOVERNMENT PRESS

PRICE, 2 *annas*]　　　　　1935

DIVISION OF THE SYLLABUS.

The following subjects in the Syllabus are taught in the Junior and Senior years :—

Subject.	Junior.	Senior.	Remarks.
Survey and drawing.	I. Free hand drawing. III. Map drawing. IV. Surveying. II. Geometrical drawing.	II. Geometrical drawing. 2. Solid Geometry.	General revision of the whole syllabus should also be done in senior year.
Forest Engineering.	I. Building materials. II. Building. III. Road-making. IV. Working drawing relating to I, II and III. V. Estimating II and III with plates.	IV. Bridges. V. Transport. VI. Wells. VII. Water and Rive Bank works. VIII. Demarcation including Boundary description. IX. Working drawings relating to IV and VI. X. Estimates relating to IV and VI.	A few lectures during first year on parts of the second year work may be necessary for explanation of work done on tour.
Botany.	A. Introduction. B. Morphology.	C. Anatomy. D. Physiology. E. Classification.	The junior year will in addition deal briefly with E. classification in an elementary manner—studying in detail a few common natural orders. The junior division should do practical germination and demonstration.
Physical Science.	Whole syllabus.	Nil.	. . . .
Silviculture.	Part I. „ IV. „ V. „ VI–5.	Part II. „ III. „; VI (except 5).	The junior year will also do Part II 1 (iii) in so far as it concerns important species met with on their tours ; and will also touch briefly on the senior year part of their syllabus where necessary for explaining what they see on tour.
Forest Management. (Working Plans.)	Instruments used in Forest Mensuration. Measurement of felled trees.	Whole Syllabus except the portion mentioned in column 2.	The junior division will touch briefly on Forest Mensuration in Silviculture lectures so far as is necessary for explaining what they do on tour.
Utilization.	I. (1) (b) Firewood. I (3). Felling and conversion of wood. I (5). Wood depots. III. Organization of labour, etc. IV. Forest Industries.	Remainder of Syllabus.	..
Range Administration.	A. Forest Law Part I only, but including the whole of the Forest Act. B. Forest accounts and Procedure—the whole.	A. Forest Law, Parts II and III. C. General principles.	The senior year should do a careful revision of section B—Accounts and Procedure.

MADRAS FOREST COLLEGE, COIMBATORE.

FINAL EXAMINATION—JUNE 1939.

1937–1939 Division.

FOREST MANAGEMENT.

(Maximum marks 100.)

Time—Three hours.

Marks.

I. Prior to the preparation of a working plan for the *natural* forests which **20** you have seen in Kargudi camp, you are required to make a preliminary stock map. State what types of forest you would differentiate in the stock map, giving reasons for your division of the forest into the types you name.

II. (*a*) What, in your opinion, are the reasons which have led to the **20** adoption of the system of simple coppice in those fuel forests you have visited where this system is in vogue?

(*b*) What silvicultural defect has become apparent in the continued application of this system, and what means are now being adopted with a view to overcome this defect

      (i) in the Bluegum coppice forests of the Nilgiris, and

      (ii) in any other coppice forest you have visited—naming the forest?

III. In converting irregular deciduous forests to Teak · plantations, it is **20** usual, in Madras, to base the conversion period on the expected rotation of the future Teak plantations. Suggest the chief reasons why this practice is adopted, instead of undertaking the conversion in a much shorter period—say 15 years.

IV. Describe how you would estimate the stemwood volume of a sub- **20** compartment in the Nilambur Teak plantations, of II quality, age 50 years, area 5 acres

    (*a*) using Bourne's yield tables, and

    (*b*) by the sample plot method.

V. Calculate the following, showing your working in each case :— **20**

    (*a*) Volume, by quarter-girth method, of a round log, 25 feet long and 60 inches middle girth.

    (*b*) The *true* volume of the above log.

    (*c*) Solid volume of fuel billets in a stack 12 yards long, one yard wide, and 4 feet high. Reducing factor 0·65.

    (*d*) Number of plants required to plant 12½ acres in square espacement, 5 feet × 5 feet.

The question on teak was probably set by Browne, and the question on mensuration could have been set by P.W. Davis, Principal of the College in 1934-37 and lecturer in mensuration at Aberdeen University 1951-64.

Extract taken from *The Forest Ranger and his Training* by Sir Harry Champion, C.I.E

The District Forest Officer has to decide what has to be done to carry out the prescriptions of the Working Plan and other directions from the higher administration, but it is the Range Officer who has to do it or get it done. No D.F.O. can run his division well unless he has competent and reliable Rangers.

To carry out the technical work of the range, the Ranger must receive the appropriate technical training; and for the non-technical work he also needs to acquire other qualifications which may be expressed as leadership with a sense of responsibility and duty, and an *esprit de corps*.

What then are the essentials of the Ranger College training? Firstly, a good deal of factual knowledge has to be acquired. The Ranger must learn to recognise the trees of the forests he will be working in, and their timbers. He must be able to read and to make a map, and to survey in forest boundaries, coupe and compartment lines and so on. He must learn how to align, build and maintain a road with the necessary bridges, culverts etc.; he must also learn the essentials of simple building construction and maintenance. He must know something about sawing and the use of many other forestry tools.

It should be a rule that a supervisor should himself be able, and ready if need be, to undertake any task that he is supervising, not necessarily as a practised hand but as one who really knows the best way – be it to wield an axe, or sharpen a saw, or cope with ordinary running repairs of his transport vehicles. A Ranger should use his head even more than his hands, and holding a largely independent responsibility as he does, he should be able to deal with the unexpected when he meets it, as he is bound to do from time to time. He should be able to deal intelligently with the emergency, not leaving it to someone else, or sitting back till he receives instructions from higher authority. The D.F.O. does not expect to receive a message describing what has happened and asking what should be done. What he expects is the description followed by a report on the action already taken with a request for approval and any further instructions.

The Range Officer is usually the head of the more or less isolated little community he lives and works with; even if his headquarters are in a larger place he is still likely to be looked to as a leader when one is needed on many matters outside forestry. He has the reputation of the Forest Department in his hands, and should feel like the leader of a team.

The efficiency of a Forest Department depends to a large extent on the efficiency of its Rangers. India has long had good Ranger Colleges and the Ranger staff has been of exceptionally high quality. The Coimbatore College is a most vital part of the whole forestry organisation.